Oranges & Peanuts for Sale

ORANGES & PEANUTS FOR SALE

ELIOT WEINBERGER

 A NEW DIRECTIONS BOOK

Manufactured in the United States of America
New Directions Books are printed on acid-free paper
First published as a New Directions Paperbook Original (NDP1148) in 2009
Published simultaneously in Canada by Penguin Books Canada Limited

Library of Congress Cataloging-in-Publication Data

Weinberger, Eliot.
 Oranges & peanuts for sale / Eliot Weinberger.
  p. cm.
 A collection of essays.
 ISBN 978-0-8112-1834-4 (pbk.: acid-free paper)
 I. Title.
 PS3573.E3928O73 2009
 814'.54—dc22   2009003390

New Directions Books are published for James Laughlin
by New Directions Publishing Corporation
80 Eighth Avenue, New York, NY 10011

www.ndpublishing.com

for N. S., A. D. & S.

CONTENTS

II.

III.

IV.

V.

Acknowledgments

Nearly all of the essays included here were, in one way or another, commissioned: oranges and peanuts for sale. Part I is on literary works; Part II is a miscellany of travel, anthropology, and the visual arts; Part III is spoken words—a "talk" and two statements for panels; Part IV is on politics and is a continuation of the book *What Happened Here: Bush Chronicles*; Part V continues the serial essay *An Elemental Thing*. The essays are in chronological order within each section.

I.
OPPEN THEN: Preface to George Oppen, *New Collected Poems*, edited by Michael Davidson (New Directions, 2002); also published in *American Poet*.

WHERE WAS NEW YORK?: Afterword to the first German translation of E. B. White's *Here Is New York* in *Lettre International* (Gemany); previously unpublished in English.

INVENTING CHINA: Expanded from the introduction and notes to *The New Directions Anthology of Classical Chinese Poetry* (New Directions, 2003).

VICENTE HUIDOBRO'S *ALTAZOR*: Introduction to the book, in my translation (Wesleyan University Press, 2003).

HANS FAVEREY'S *AGAINST THE FORGETTING*: Introduction to the book, edited and translated by Francis R. Jones (New Directions, 2004).

NIEDECKER/REZNIKOFF: First published on the web in *Jacket* (Australia); reprinted in *Radical Vernacular: Lorine Niedecker and the Politics of Place*, edited by Elizabeth Willis (University of Iowa Press, 2008).

GU CHENG: Written as the introduction to *Sea of Dreams: The Collected Writings of Gu Cheng*, edited and translated by Joseph R. Allen (New Directions, 2005), but unpublished as such, due to objections from the Gu Cheng estate. It appeared in the *London Review of Books* and in translation in *Granta en Español* (Spain), *Lettre*

International (Germany), *Lettre Internationale* (Denmark), and *Mayaan* (Israel). The Gu Cheng translations cited are all by Joseph R. Allen.

KENNETH COX: Written for a section on Cox, following his death, in the web magazine *Jacket* (Australia), edited by Jenny Penberthey.

THE CRITIC NATKIRA: Written as a short response to a long questionnaire on poetry and criticism for *Fulcrum*; also appeared in *A Public Space*.

BECKETT/PAZ: Originally written as the introduction to a limited edition of selections from the Paz/Beckett anthology, *The Bread of Days*, with artwork by Enrique Chagoya (Yolla Bolly Press, 1994); revised and expanded for a special issue of *Fulcrum* dedicated to Beckett's poetry.

SUSAN HOWE'S *MY EMILY DICKINSON*: Introduction to a new edition of the book (New Directions, 2007); reprinted in translation in *Parmentier* (Holland).

JAMES LAUGHLIN: Review of James Laughlin, *The Way It Wasn't*, edited by Barbara Epler and Daniel Javitch (New Directions, 2006) for *The New York Review of Books*.

SUSAN SONTAG: Review of Susan Sontag, *At the Same Time: Essays & Speeches*, edited by Paolo Dilonardo and Anne Jump (Farrar, Straus & Giroux, 2007) for *The New York Review of Books*; reprinted in *The Australian Financial Review*, and expanded here.

ALTER AND THE PSALMS: Review of Robert Alter, *The Book of Psalms: A Translation with Commentary* (W. W. Norton, 2007) for the *London Review of Books*.

THE T'ANG: Review of A. C. Graham, *Poems from the Late T'ang* (New York Review of Books, 2008) and *China: At the Court of the Emperors*, the catalog for an exhibition at the Palazzo Strozzi, Florence, edited by Sabrina Rastelli (Skira, 2008) for *The New York Review of Books*.

II.

POSTCARD FROM CHINA: Written for the *London Review of Books*; reprinted in translation in *Lettre International* (Germany), *Letras Libres* (Spain), *Lettre Internationale* (Romania), and *El Malpensante* (Colombia).

ORANGES & PEANUTS FOR SALE: Written for a project in Mexico: a hundred writers were each assigned one photograph from a collection assembled by Manuel Álvarez Bravo. I was given the 1934 photograph of a Mexico City street vendor by Anton

Bruehl that is reproduced on the cover. Photos and texts were published as a book, *Fotografía*, by Fundación Televisa in 2005. First published in English in *The Southern Review*.

EPSTEIN: EXOTE: Afterword to Mitch Epstein, *Works* (Steidl, 2006).

IN BLUE: A text interleaving nine blue and white engravings by Terry Winters, published as a portfolio under the same title by The Grenfell Press in 2008.

PHOTOGRAPHY & ANTHROPOLOGY: Introduction to a book of photographs, *Human Documents*, edited by Robert Gardner, and published by the Peabody Museum, Harvard University, in 2009.

QUESTIONS OF DEATH: Written for a special issue of *Conjunctions* devoted to death, edited by David Shields.

III.
"POETRY IS NEWS": Statement for a conference with this title, organized by Anne Waldman and Ammiel Alcalay, St Mark's Poetry Project, New York City, February 2003. Published on the web in *91st Meridian* and *Possum Pouch*; reprinted in translation in *Fantom Slobode* (Croatia).

ANONYMOUS SOURCES: A talk on translation, revised and updated here. Published in various earlier versions in *Translation of Poetry and Poetic Prose: Proceedings of Nobel Symposium 110*, edited by Sture Allén (World Scientific, 1999); in pamphlets in English and Spanish as part of the "Encuentros" series published by the IDB Cultural Center in Washington, D. C.; in *Voice-Overs: Translation and Latin American Literature*, edited by Daniel Balderston and Marion Schwartz (SUNY Press, 2002); in Flemish translation in *Obscuur* (Belgium); and on the web in *91st Meridian* and *Fascicle*.

"THE POST-NATIONAL WRITER": Revised and expanded from a statement for a panel with this title at the PEN World Voices Festival, New York City, April 2005. An earlier version published in *Tin House*; reprinted in translation in *Respiro* (Romania).

IV.
WHAT I HEARD ABOUT IRAQ IN 2005: First published in the *London Review of Books* and reprinted in the UK edition of *What Happened Here* (Verso). Reprinted in translation in books published by Era (Mexico), Turner (Spain), Lom (Chile), Agra (Greece), Ambar (Portugal), and Record (Brazil), and in the magazines *Lettre International* (Germany), *Alligatorzine* (Belgium), *Ordfront* (Sweden), *As-Saffir* (Lebanon), *Yang* (Holland), *La Nación* (Chile), and *Al-Iraq News* (Iraq).

"The Arts and the War in Iraq": Response to a questionnaire from *October* magazine, circulated to artists, academics, curators, and workers in cultural institutions—a group in which I was inexplicably included.

The United States of Obama: Written for the *London Review of Books*; reprinted in translation on the web in French and Flemish in *Alligatorzine* (Belgium).

V.

A Journey on the Yangtze River: First published in *TriQuarterly*. The place names are translated by James M. Hargett; some of these places have now been submerged by the Three Gorges Dam. The lines from Su Tung-p'o, Lu Yu, and Chuang Tzu are translated by Burton Watson; those from Meng Chiao by David Hinton.

Special thanks to the translators: Aurelio Major, Marcelo Uribe, Monica de la Torre, Andrés Hoyo, and Anonymous (Spanish), Anonymous (Arabic), Kurt Devrese (Flemish), Aharon Shabtai (Hebrew), Benjamin Schwarz, Eike Schönfeld, and Peter Torberg (German), Alina Savin and Carmen Sandelescu (Romanian), Claus Bech (Danish), Jean-Paul Auxméry (French), Maja Dragnić-Krivošić (Bosnian-Croatian-Serbian), Miguel Serra Pereira and Alexandre Kappann (Portuguese), Johann Berggren (Swedish), Spiros Vergos (Greek), and Han van der Vegt (Dutch).

ORANGES & PEANUTS
FOR SALE

OPPEN THEN

NEITHER PEDAGOGICAL nor oracular, more preoccupied with questions than answers, George Oppen was nonetheless surrounded by young writers in the 1960s and 1970s as a model—an impossibly inimitable model—of how to be a poet in shifting, disastrous, and what seemed to be apocalyptic times. He had an aura about him, that of the honorable man trying to speak in the roar of history, much like the aura that has now gathered posthumously around Paul Celan.

There were, first of all, the facts of his life, which had particular resonance in the era of the Vietnam War and of hectically mutating events and values. A product of the 1930s, Oppen had spent the first years of that decade attempting to rally a second generation of American modernism, relocated from Europe to the American city, that would continue and modify the poetic principles of its immediate predecessors while rejecting their political principles: A poetry that might not be for the masses, but one that did not loathe them. He had published a tiny book of enigmatic poems in 1934, then had joined the Communist Party and stopped writing. He was perhaps the only Party writer, anywhere, who had never written stirring doggerel or prose propaganda; who both had doubted the efficacy of poetry in hungry times and had resisted the Party's manipulation of the arts; who had believed that the proper role of a Party member was no different for a writer or a factory worker, that the work to be done was agitation and organization, in which poetry could have no place without compromising itself. Oppen's silence was political and not personal, ideological and not "writer's block," and not, as Hugh Kenner famously suggested, a mere glitch in time until the next poem. It had lasted twenty-five years, and it hung over us—young writers adrift in trying to respond, wondering if it was possible to respond adequately and usefully to the present in which we found ourselves—like the extreme act of a saint. We too had the faith, but would we be willing to stand silently for twenty-five years to prove it?

Moreover, in a time of war, and our pragmatic attempts to avoid it individually and utopian attempts to end it collectively, there was George Oppen, who had fought and had been seriously wounded as an infantryman in World War II, perhaps the only enduring American poet to participate in ground combat since the Civil War, the only one who knew first-hand: "Wars that are just? A simpler question: In the event, will you or will you not want to kill a German." (A question, it should be noted, without a question mark.) Then, in the 1950s, in the Cold War that warped our childhoods, he had been the only hero, of sorts, among American poets: Forced out of the country by McCarthyism and the House Un-American Activities Committee, he was in exile for nine years, avoiding the inevitable summons to "name names." Oppen's martyrdom, though less severe, was the left-wing counterpart to Ezra Pound's simultaneous, more disputable right-wing martyrdom in St. Elizabeths. Both, strangely, were allowed to return home in the same summer of 1958.

Added to this political romance was a personal one that seemed equally radical and unattainable as we ourselves fell in and out of love: his apparently blissful relationship with Mary, from whom he had been inseparable since age eighteen, fighting the good fight for art and justice. They always spoke in the first-person plural. They were their own little collective: "old" people who lived as we did, with random and shabby furniture, and moreover believed, as we did, that youth was on the verge of saving the world. They had even attended the notorious Altamont rock festival, when hippie love & peace turned into Hell's Angels violence—an event that seemed emblematic at the time—and shared the general disillusionment: Oppen's poem about it (in "Some San Francisco Poems") ends with the word "mourning."

Oppen's return to writing and publishing in the 1960s coincided with the miraculous emergence of an entire lost generation—Charles Reznikoff, Lorine Niedecker, Louis Zukofsky, Carl Rakosi and, in England, Basil Bunting—who for varying reasons had been invisible since the 1930s, and who suddenly appeared among us, now transformed into Venerable Sages. [George always seemed ancient, and I am shocked as I now calculate that he was only in his late fifties when I met him. That this was not merely an adolescent perspective is confirmed by photographs: in them, his gaunt and

geological face makes him look twenty years older than his contemporaries.]
All of these elders enlarged the possibilities of poetry—in a moment when
there was an exhilarating racket of new ideas—but only Oppen, among
them, spoke directly to the political consciousness and the political crisis of
the time. In 1968, amidst the powerful (and still powerful) overtly political
poems being written by Robert Duncan, Denise Levertov, Amiri Baraka,
Allen Ginsberg, and so many others, it was Oppen's *Of Being Numerous*
that, from its opening words, struck me, still a teenager, as the poetry that
had captured the interior essence of where we are, who we are, right now:

> There are things
> We live among 'and to see them
> Is to know ourselves'.

These lines are now philosophical, but they were once political, for then
the things we lived among included the first televised scenes of war and the
photographs of napalmed children: was seeing them knowing ourselves?
Over and over Oppen emphasized that the function of poetry was a test of
truth; he may have been the last writer in the West to use the word "truth"
without irony. For him, "So much depends upon a red wheelbarrow" was
a moral statement, with "wheelbarrow" both a thing and a word. The poet's task was to restore meaning to words—particularly in a time of official
lies—and this was only possible through direct experience of the words
themselves. Speaking of H. D., he once asked, in amazement, "How can
you write a word like 'angel'?" Words, he said, had to be "earned"; words
were "frightening."

Oppen's standard, his obsession, was "honesty" in the poem, Pound's
ideogram of a man standing by his word. He insisted on writing only about
what he himself had seen, and the act of seeing them: the angels he had
mentioned in a poem were the ones in the windows of Chartres. [This insistence also created an obstinate blindness to all forms of surrealism, which
he saw as an escape from, and not a way into, current realities.] Uniquely
among American poets, there are almost no mythological references and no
myth-making, no exotica, no personae, only one or two passing historical
references, and almost no similes in his work: in Oppen's world, things are
not "like," they are there, right in front of you, and there with an exclama-
tion point. His metaphor for "seeing" in a poem is apocalyptic: the man in

the ditch, staring at the spinning wheels of his overturned car—as he himself, in his youth, had been the driver in a fatal crash. Until very late, and unusually for an avant-gardist, he capitalized the first letter of every line: poetry was too powerful to trivialize with lower-case.

Curiously, Oppen's struggle for "clarity"—another favorite word—did not result in the kind of small perfection of unadorned speech achieved by Reznikoff and Niedecker, poems that reached what Zukofsky called "rested totality." Oppen's poems represent the struggle itself, and he continually rewrote them, cutting out and pasting words on top of other words, as though he were a mason building a brick wall. But they are not brick walls. They are often abstract, as mysterious as koans, a sea-surge of contradictory forces: assertions and their negations, declarations couched in double negatives, questions without answers, straightforward observations placed next to gnomic statements whose beauty lingers forever because they are never fully understood. It takes work—especially with the later poems—to read them aloud, for their arrangement on the page seems to function at cross purposes to their sound: pauses in the middle of lines, syntactical endings and beginnings in the same line, enjambments across stanza breaks, inexplicable starts and stops, multiple possibilities of emphasis, phrases hanging. A late Oppen poem is like one of those Taoist rocks, full of holes, through which the breath, the force of the poem, circulates.

He wrote short poems and series of short poems, and what is remarkable is that nearly any of the short poems could have been placed in one of the series, any of the series poems could have been a separate short poem, and almost none of them can stand alone as self-contained "anthology pieces." Much like Celan, all of Oppen's work—though this was not his intention, though he was not writing a long and life-long poem like Pound or Olson—seems to belong to a single continuing poem. It is a poem that returns again and again to the same things: the Middle English western wind, Blake's Tyger, the boats of Maine, people in cars, his foxhole in the war, Mary's beauty, Robinson Crusoe, city walls, city streets, crowds, the young, tools, ditches, glass, and the words "little" and "small." His universe was an "immense heap of little things" (Coleridge) and in his quest for truth, he believed that the little things and the little words—pronouns, articles, prepositions, short declarative sentences—were the truest, yet even they had to be taken apart and sometimes left unreassembled.

He may never be the subject of a biography, for his life beyond its outline remains a mystery, and for decades left no paper trail. George and Mary had carefully edited the story, and always told the same anecdotes, all of which are in Mary's autobiography, *Meaning A Life*, the only sustained work of Objectivist prose, and all of which had a quality of wonder like the children's books they loved: the young couple in 1928, sailing in a small boat across the Great Lakes, down the Erie Canal and into the Hudson River to New York City (a dreamlike voyage that always reminded me of the trolley ride into the city in Murnau's exactly contemporary film, *Sunrise*); their anachronistic travels by horse and buggy through France; the rent strike in Queens where they flushed plaster of Paris down the toilets and turned the plumbing into a tree of stone . . . But among the untold stories is the enigma that hangs over Oppen, more impenetrable than his long silence: his relation, in mind perhaps more than deed, to Communism as it evolved. Unlike Neruda or Hikmet or MacDiarmid, it is impossible to imagine George—this man of questions, unsentimentally devoted to honesty, truth, and honor—as a Stalinist. He was always evasive on this subject; no one even knows when he left the Party.

He had lived as a boy next door to D. W. Griffith. He spoke softly and had a certain accent, most notable in its r's, common to cultivated New York Jews of his generation, that has now almost completely vanished. Though his poems rarely have any humor, he himself was very funny, and he would punctuate his wisecracks with a bobbing of his prominent eyebrows that was identical to Groucho Marx. He and Mary were nomadic for most of their lives, living on boats or in hotels or trailers or cheap apartments communally with other couples and families; his whole life was in resolute flight from a wealthy childhood. He tried, and it is not easy, to live "honorably"—his word—as an American poet: he never taught writing or served on any literary panels or juries or committees; he wrote only one extended book review; and he largely refused to give readings after he won, to everyone's surprise, a Pulitzer. In his last years, there was a piece of paper pinned over his desk that read "Only one mistake, Ezra! You should have talked to women." The last public line he wrote was: "My happiness is the knowledge of all we do not know."

A lifelong sailor, builder of his own small boats, when he appeared among us in the 1960s he seemed a shipwreck survivor, a returned Crusoe, who had lived through disaster and now saw the world more intently, who no longer had any answers, and struggled with the precise articula-

WHERE WAS NEW YORK?

E. B. WHITE'S long 1948 magazine article "Here Is New York" was republished in the US a few years ago, after having been unavailable for decades, in a handsome little edition as a bit of nostalgia. On the dust jacket, Russell Baker, the avuncular, retired humorist for the *New York Times*, writes: "New York was the most exciting, most civilized, most congenial city in the world when this book was written. It's the finest portrait ever painted of the city at the height of its glory." Roger Angell, White's stepson and beloved writer on baseball for *The New Yorker*, provides an introduction where he imagines how "appalled" White would be by the city's "sharp diminishment in charm and tone," as though *arrivistes* had taken over the club.

Angell's introduction ends imperially: "Like the rest of us, he wanted it back again, back the way it was." But it's somewhat difficult to determine exactly when "was" was: the reader in 2002, nostalgic for the city in 1948, at the presumed height of its glory, discovers that White in 1948 was nostalgic for the 1920s. He had been living far to the north, in a small town in Maine, for more than a decade when Angell persuaded him to come down to the city for a few weeks to write something for *Holiday* magazine. White, like any returned exile, revisited a few of his favorite haunts and, unsurprisingly, found them not the same as they had been. Returning exiles rarely take into account their own aging: if a place seems less marvelous than it was when they were young, obviously it is because things are much worse and not that they themselves are no longer full of wonder.

Certainly it is easy to read White and check off all the items that have vanished since: New York with the densest population in the world, New York as a major seaport, the ice-coal-wood cellars, the elevated railway on Third Avenue, the shoeshine shacks, even his tiny sweltering hotel room, which would now be air-conditioned (although—at the Algonquin—just as small). But perhaps the most obsolete item about New York in the essay is—his publishers notwithstanding—nostalgia itself.

New York is a city of perpetual change largely within existing structures. Unlike European cities, shops and restaurants do not remain the same or in the same location for decades: five years is normal, and it is not unusual for a commercial space to change every six months. But unlike many Asian cities, New York has generally not, until quite recently, erased its past by tearing down the old. As George Oppen once observed, in New York the youngest people inhabit the oldest buildings. It is in a state of continual renovation, both physically (architecturally) and culturally. And, unlike the cities of the Third World, its population has remained—again until quite recently—exactly the same since about 1930. New York is both the lowest and highest rung of the ladder of success. Immigrants arrive poor and inhabit the boroughs of Queens or Brooklyn or the Bronx. If they rise to the middle class, they tend to move out to the suburbs, and new immigrants take their place. If they become wealthy, they now move to Manhattan.

In Paris, say, one can be nostalgic for the days when Paris was alive with artistic innovation. In Mexico City, one can long for the time when it was a beautiful colonial city of two million people under the twin volcanoes, and not the endlessly anonymous sprawl and impenetrable smog of twenty million. In Hong Kong or Shanghai, it is almost impossible to remember what the city once looked like. But in New York, nostalgia—that is not a nostalgia for one's own youth—seems inimical.

In the years since White's essay—coincidentally my entire life—New York has lost very little. It has torn down some wonderful buildings (Pennsylvania Station, the old Metropolitan Opera House) and built some hideous ones (the new Metropolitan Opera House and—it must be admitted—what was the World Trade Center). Like everywhere else, it is much more expensive, and a bohemian life of voluntary poverty and devotion to art is extremely difficult for the young. Like everywhere in the US since the Reagan era, the polarities of rich and poor are even more exaggerated, but New York has always had vast numbers of the devastatingly poor, in a Calvinist nation that blames poverty on laziness and lack of intelligence, and has denied or only half-heartedly believed in the merits of education or social welfare.

What New York has gained is enormous. Once a city of European immigrants, it has become a vortex for the entire world. Of its eight million people, more than a million arrived from abroad in the 1990s alone. Almost half of the inhabitants were born in another country and much of the other half is their children. At a single public school in Queens, letters must be sent home to the parents in 62 languages. Any major event anywhere in the world—whether a change of government or a natural disaster—has its ramifications in New York. (As, conversely, the attack on the Trade Center had a personal meaning for so much of the world.) With this influx of new people has come an immeasurable flood of things and foods, customs and ideas. New York is perennially the city where more different kinds of people are immersed in more different kinds of activities than anywhere else on the planet.

New York is a city of outsiders where no one is a foreigner because everyone is a foreigner. In the density of the city, the countless cultures are pressed up against one other, as they are not in more sprawling cities with more demarcated ethnic neighborhoods, and they must negotiate with one another in what is, for many, a second language. Consequently—though I've often been accused of obstinate chauvinism for saying so—New Yorkers may well be the most polite people of any major city in the world. New Yorkers have a shipwreck mentality: Things are hard, but it was worse where we came from, and we're all here trying to survive, and possibly make life a little better. It was notable, after September 11, that, unlike the rest of the country, there was no violence against the many tens of thousands of Muslims living here (or against dark-skinned others mistaken for Muslims), nor did New York thirst for military vengeance. Its patriotic fervor—if one could call it that—was directed in support of the firemen, policemen, and emergency workers. They were "our" uniformed heroes, not the one who were creating more innocent September 11 victims among the shepherds of Afghanistan.

Even if New York represented less of the globe in 1948 than it does now, it is precisely White's obliviousness to New York as a world bazaar that makes his essay seem so restricted. He was a New Englander who came to New York in the 1920s, stayed for fifteen years or so, mainly working at *The New Yorker*, and then moved to Maine. The New York of his "New York" is geographically minute. He stays at the Algonquin Hotel, across the street from *The New Yorker* office. He walks five minutes to a play on Broadway, ten minutes to an Italian restaurant on East 53rd Street, fifteen minutes to the bandshell in Central Park. On what seems to be his one excursion, he goes down to Greenwich Village, and walks ten minutes over to the Bowery, whose blocks of cheap boarding houses, once a predictable stop on any visiting writer's New York itinerary, were far more populous in, and associated with, the Depression than the postwar period of the essay. From there he strolls a few blocks to the Lower East Side, for a brief look at some "cheerful" and "folksy" poor people of unnamed ethnic origin—with the exception of one Italian—among the "fly-bitten filth."

The rest of New York is completely ignored. The other boroughs are not mentioned, nor, even in Manhattan, do we hear of Chinatown, Little Italy, the Puerto Ricans in Spanish Harlem, or—then, but no longer—the Irish in Washington Heights, the Germans in Yorkville, the Portuguese in Greenwich Village, to name only a few. Harlem is reduced to two words that will make readers today cringe: "voodoo charms."

White's New York is very much *The New Yorker*'s New York. For some eighty years the magazine has represented the zeitgeist of the upwardly mobile educated white Manhattanite. It is politically liberal (in the American sense of the word) but not leftist; it is occasionally alarmed by injustices elsewhere, but generally oblivious to injustice at home. (Its cinematic avatar is, of course, Woody Allen, who has made some thirty movies about New York where the only black or Hispanic people are prostitutes or servants.) It is permanently fixed in an air of bemused detachment, which it expresses in a style whose sentences are pathologically rewritten by its editors, "polished" (as they call it) until every article, whether a report from Rwanda or a portrait of a professional dog-walker, sounds exactly alike, driven by domestic similes and clever turns of phrases that mix colloquial speech with unexpected synonyms. E. B. White was a master of the style, and it is a sign of the magazine's petrification—if it was ever not petrified—that his sentences from fifty years ago might have been published in last week's issue.

A telling passage is where White writes of his thrill as a young man living in the same city as so many literary "personal giants":

> I burned with a low steady fever just because I was on the same island with Don Marquis, Heywood Broun, Christopher Morley, Franklin P. Adams, Robert C. Benchley, Frank Sullivan, Dorothy Parker, Alexander Woolcott, Ring Lardner and Stephen Vincent Benét.

White's (and *The New Yorker*'s) New York circa 1925 was a landscape of humorists and light verse poets. It evidently did not include John Dos Passos, F. Scott Fitzgerald, Eugene O'Neill, E. E. Cummings, William Carlos Williams, Langston Hughes, Nathanael West, Henry Miller, Djuna Barnes, W. E. B. DuBois, Dashiell Hammett, Charles Reznikoff, Theodore Dreiser, Hart Crane, Marianne Moore, Zora Neale Hurston—all the varieties of American modernism that were not being produced at that moment in Paris. White's insularity was, and remains, typical of his milieu: Discounting late publications of the inescapably famous, it is safe to say that *The New Yorker*, in its hundreds of thousands of pages over the last eighty years, has managed to miss almost the entirety of world literature.

This was because *The New Yorker* always viewed the world through the screen of its cleverness, and never could bear those chunks of life that could not be refracted into its witty prose. White may find the city "tense," but his examples of that tension are the lines for lunch at Schrafft's (the quintessential bourgeois restaurant chain of the time) and the difficulty of finding a taxi. Until a hint in the last paragraphs, one would never know that 1948 was the year that W. H. Auden published a book whose title seemed to epitomize the era: *The Age of Anxiety*. New York was full of men who had witnessed the monstrosities of war, and of people who had lost their loved ones to it or just escaped from the ruins of Europe. The first novels of that war, beginning with Norman Mailer's *The Naked and the Dead*, were just appearing. Freud and existentialism were the intellectual obsessions, and the nation's anti-Communist hysteria had already taken hold with the formation of the House Un-American Activities Committee.

Above all, the spirit of the times found its popular expression in film noir, with its alienated heroes walking the rainy streets of the city at night, trapped in the machinations of some maleficent plot they couldn't control. To recall the famous first line of Jules Dassin's *The Naked City* from that same year—"There are eight million stories in the naked city, and this is one of them"—is to remind us that White tells no stories, except his own; there are no individuals in the crowds he walks among. And, at least for me, any frame from the great films of that year—Abraham Polonsky's *Force of Evil* or John Farrow's *The Big Clock* or Orson Welles' *The Lady from Shanghai* or Billy Wilder's *Double Indemnity*, among them—are more evocative of how the city looked or how Americans felt, than any sentence in White's essay.

The titles of the movies New Yorkers went to in 1948 are a prose poem of their mood: *Cry of the City, The Street With No Name, Ruthless, The Dark Past, Behind Locked Doors, Secret Beyond the Door, I Walk Alone, He Walked By Night, Night Has a Thousand Eyes, A Double Life, For You I Die, Raw Deal, Hollow Triumph, Shed No Tears, I Wouldn't Be in Your Shoes . . .*

It is only toward the end of "Here Is New York" that that mood finally interrupts the nostalgic reveries and minor complaints, and White at last invokes the primary factor in that Age of Anxiety: the atomic bomb. In the months since September 11, his two paragraphs have been quoted often, as eerie prophecies of apocalypse coming from the sky:

> The subtlest change in New York is something people don't speak much about but that is in everyone's mind. The city, for the first time in its long history, is destructible. A single flight of planes no bigger than a wedge of geese can quickly end this island fantasy, burn the towers, crumble the bridges, turn the underground passages into lethal chambers, cremate the millions. The intimation of mortality is part of New York now: in the sound of the jets overhead, in the black headlines of the latest edition.
>
> All dwellers in cities must live with the stubborn fact of annihilation; in New York the fact is somewhat more concentrated because of the concentration of the city itself, and because, of all targets, New York has a certain clear priority. In the mind of whatever perverted dreamer might loose the lightning, New York must hold a steady, irresistible charm.

It is indeed precisely in those lines where the essay seems about to enter into a portrait of the city that is both more profound and more real. But he quickly switches to something hopeful—the construction of the United Nations—and he rather tellingly avoids what would have been, in 1948, the obvious comparisons with London, Dresden, Berlin, Tokyo, Hiroshima: that New York has now become as vulnerable as the other cities of the world, that what we have done to them can now be done to us. In fact, throughout, the war is never mentioned at all.

Even when confronting mass destruction, White remains a prisoner of his style. The apocalyptic planes are "no bigger than a wedge of geese." The bathos of that comparison is astonishing: aerial bombardment not only reduced to the flight formations of suburban birds, but to a clever turn on a cocktail party phrase, "wedge of cheese." It is typical of *New Yorker* writing, then or now, the root of both the endurance of its style and the ephemerality of its individual practitioners, that a sentence that ends with the words "cremate the millions" must also contain a friendly and bourgeois-domestic metaphor.

New York is a city addicted to novelty, but unlike the country it inhabits, it never suffers from collective amnesia. To the contrary, the New Yorker prides himself on his expertise, whatever that expertise may be, and the most typical New York conversation is didactic to the point of pedantry. In the city of the newly-arrived, there is always someone who arrived the day before and knows a little more. Wisdom—more practical or encyclopedic than philosophical—is accumulated and stacked like skyscrapers. The city lives in a perpetual present tense, but it is one that never erases the past, for the past is merely the bottom floors of a skyscraper under permanent construction. To be nostalgic in New York means that one has stopped living as a New Yorker, that one is no longer thrilled by the new, that one's expert knowledge has become out of date. This was the case of E .B. White in the summer of 1948, who on his brief journey back to the city of his youth did not discover anything he didn't already know, and was more concerned with a few disappearances than with the thousands of appearances that had occurred since he left. This famous essay about New York is strangely not very New York at all.

[2002]

INVENTING CHINA

L IKE THE flapping kookaburra in Australia that sets off a tornado in
Kansas, poetry operates under its own version of chaos theory: the
unpredictable effects of remote, sometimes forgotten causes. A 4th century
poet from Gupta India, Kalidasa, becomes a founding father of German Ro-
manticism; Buddhist Jataka tales turn up in Chaucer; a Finnish pseudo-folk
epic sets the beat for the pseudo-folk epic called "Hiawatha"; an 11th century Persian, Omar the Tentmaker (Khayyam) transfixes the Victorians . . .
and, in the 20th century, American poetry is inextricable from classical Chinese poetry and the Chinese language itself.

In 1909, there had been only about a dozen English translations of
Chinese poetry in 150 years, mainly obscure books done by diplomats and
missionaries, and a poet like Li Po sounded like this (the translator is L.
Cranmer-Byng):

> And now Spring beckons with verdant hand,
> And Nature's wealth of eloquence doth win
> Forth to the fragrant-bowered nectarine,
> Where my dear friends abide, a careless band.

The received wisdom, as articulated by Lytton Strachey the year before,
was that Chinese poems

> are like odours, for all their intangibility, the strange compel-
> ling powers of suggested reminiscence and romance. Whatever
> their subject, they remain ethereal . . . perhaps the Western
> writer whose manner they suggest most constantly is Verlaine.

This was no surprise; in 1909, America's most innovative poet, Ezra Pound, was writing like this:

> Autumnal breaks the flame upon the sun-set herds.
> The sheep on Gilead as tawn hair gleam
> Neath Mithra's dower and his slow departing,
> While in the sky a thousand fleece of gold
> Bear, each his tribute, to the waning god.

Six years later, in 1915, here was Pound:

> For a moment she rested against me
> Like a swallow half blown to the wall

And here was Li Po, as translated by Pound:

> Desolate castle, the sky, the wide desert.
> There is no wall left to this village.
> Bones white with a thousand frosts,
> High heaps, covered with trees and grass;
> Who brought this to pass?

What had happened in the interval was Pound's invention of Imagism, formally launched in the March 1913 issue of *Poetry* as an assault on the reigning abstractions and rhetorical excesses couched in predictable meters and rhymes. Its program was "direct treatment of the 'thing,' " without moralizing or commentary, a poetry where every word was essential and lines were organized according to musical phrases. After his revelation, in 1910, that "all ages are contemporaneous," Pound searched through the world's poetries for examples of Imagist principles, finding them in the Troubadours and in Dante, and even more concretely in the unreconstructed surviving lyrics of the *Palatine Anthology* and, in 1913, classical Chinese.

That year, Pound enthusiastically read the manuscript of *Scented Leaves—from a Chinese Jar*, invented "Chinese" prose poems by Allen Upward (1863-1926), a diplomat, politician, colonial judge in Nigeria, spy, erudite occultist, Irish nationalist, gossip columnist, pulp fiction writer, author of a 300-page letter to the Swedish Academy on the meaning of the word "idealist," and ultimate suicide. Pound declared that Upward was also an Imagist (Upward: "I had no idea what he meant.") and sent his poems on to *Poetry*.

Upward's leaves had been inspired by a reading of Herbert A. Giles' 1901 *History of Chinese Literature* (Upward: "I perceived that we in the West were indeed barbarians and foreign devils, and that we knew scarcely anything about poetry.") and he urged Pound to get the book. It was the first such history in English, a work of excellent scholarship, though of dreadful translations. Pound, remarkably—given what was known about Chinese poetry at the time—extracted four short poems from Giles' verbiage. Along with two other poems, they became his own contribution to the *Des Imagistes* anthology, which he edited, publishing it the following year.

Giles' version of a famous poem by the First Century BCE poet Pan Chieh-yü (Lady Pan):

> O fair white silk, fresh from the weaver's loom,
> Clear as the frost, bright as the winter snow—
> See! friendship fashions out of thee a fan,
> Round as the round moon shines in heaven above,
> At home, abroad, a close companion thou,
> Stirring at every move the grateful gale.
> And yet I fear, ah me! that autumn chills,
> Cooling the dying summer's torrid rage,
> Will see thee laid neglected on the shelf,
> All thoughts of bygone days, like them bygone.

became a haiku:

> FAN-PIECE FOR HER IMPERIAL LORD
> O fan of white silk,
>   clear as frost on the grass-blade,
> You also are laid aside.

The ten-line, half-Chinese, half-Dionysian poem "After Ch'u Yuan" ("I will get me to the wood / Where the gods walk garlanded with wistaria") was somehow found in a prolix five-paragraph prose translation, of which the first reads:

Methinks there is a Genius of the hills, clad in wistaria, girdled with ivy, with smiling lips, of witching mien, riding on the red pard, wild cats galloping in the rear, reclining in a chariot, with banners of cassia, cloaked with the orchid, girt with azalea, culling the perfume of sweet flowers to leave behind a memory in the heart. But dark is the grove wherein I dwell. No light of day reaches it ever. The path thither is dangerous and difficult to climb. Alone I stand on the hill-top, while the clouds float beneath my feet, and all around is wrapped in gloom.

And one of the best-known Imagist poems, "Liu Ch'e":

The rustling of the silk is discontinued,
Dust drifts over the court-yard,
There is no sound of foot-fall, and the leaves
Scurry into heaps and lie still,
And she the rejoicer of the heart is beneath them:

A wet leaf that clings to the threshold.

was "translated" from Giles' English:

The sound of rustling is stilled,
With dust the marble courtyard filled;
No footfalls echo on the floor,
Fallen leaves in heaps block up the door . . .
For she, my pride, my lovely one, is lost,
And I am left, in hopeless anger tossed.

The last word of the first line in Pound's translation was originally "delicate," but Richard Aldington had been parodying his overuse of the word. Pound changed it to "elaborate," which his future wife Dorothy Shakespear found "rococco & heavy." She suggested "discontinued," producing one of his most famous lines. The last line was Pound's Imagist invention, or intervention.

[Pound, ever on the lookout for enlightened rulers, declared in 1914, on the basis of a few poems in Giles, that Liu Ch'e—the Emperor Wu of

Han—and the Greek poet Ibycus were the quintessential Imagists, and, in 1915, that the poems of Liu Ch'e and a few others would be as great a stimulus to the 21st century as the Greeks were to the Renaissance.]

Classical Chinese was thus already on the Imagist agenda when, in November of 1913, Pound received the Rosetta Stone of American modernism: the Fenollosa manuscripts. Ernest Fenollosa (1853-1908) had gone from Harvard to the University of Tokyo, as Japan was opening to the West, to teach philosophy and economics. There he amassed a vast art collection, sold it to the Boston Museum, and became its Curator of Oriental Art. He knew little Japanese and no Chinese. A keeper of notebooks rather than a writer of books, his two-volume study, *Epochs of Chinese and Japanese Art*, was assembled by his wife Mary after his death; though more impressionistic than scholarly, it remained a standard text for decades.

From 1896 to 1901, Fenollosa undertook a study of Japanese Noh plays and Chinese poetry under the guidance of a series of Japanese professors, accompanied by interpreters. They worked through 150 Chinese poems, character by character, with Fenollosa meticulously writing down the Japanese pronunciation and literal translation of each, followed by a translation of the line and occasional commentary. The first line of what was to become Pound's "The River-Merchant's Wife: A Letter" ("While my hair was still cut straight across my forehead") looked like this in the notebooks:

Sho	*hatsu*	*sho*	*fuku*	*gaku*
mistress	hair	first	cover	brow

Chinese lady's I or my beginning
My hair was at first covering my brows
        (Chinese method of wearing hair)

In her husband's belief that the "purpose of poetical translation is the poetry, not the verbal definitions in dictionaries," Mary Fenollosa almost psychically selected Pound, whom she barely knew, to do something with the notebooks, and gave him £40 for his time. A few weeks later, Pound left for Stone Cottage in Sussex, the first of three winter retreats with W. B. Yeats—Pound ostensibly serving as Yeats' secretary—working under the very trees that would be immortalized in *Winnie-the-Pooh*.

Pound turned first to the Noh plays, and his enthusiasm led Yeats to invent a kind of Irish Noh (most notably, *At the Hawk's Well*) which he would later describe in detail in his introduction to Pound's 1917 *'Noh,' or Accomplishment: A Study of the Classical Stage of Japan*. Sometime in 1914, Pound began work on the Chinese poems. (There are drafts, in various stages of completion, for many of the poems, but these have never been collected.) In 1915, he selected fourteen (later expanded to eighteen) of them, mainly from the T'ang Dynasty, added his translation of the contemporaneous Anglo-Saxon poem "The Seafarer"—partially to demonstrate that when English poetry was first forming, Chinese poetry was at its height—and published them as a pamphlet, *Cathay*.

The *Cathay* poems have become so acclimatized, seem so "normal"—if just slightly old-fashioned—in American poetic practice, that it is difficult to recuperate their impact. Pound had indeed become, in T. S. Eliot's often-repeated line, "the inventor of Chinese poetry for our time," but this wasn't saying a great deal. (For "Chinese," substitute the word "Hungarian" or "Swahili.") More to the point was Ford Maddox Ford's comment about the poems: "What poetry should be, that they are":

> The poetry of great quality is that without comment as without effort it presents you with images that stir your emotions; so you are made a better man; you are softened, rendered more supple of mind, more open to the vicissitudes and necessities of your fellow men. When you have read 'The River-Merchant's Wife' you are added to. You are a better man or woman than you were before.

Cathay was the first great book in English of the new, plain-speaking, laconic, image-driven free verse:

THE JEWEL STAIRS' GRIEVANCE
The jewelled steps are already quite white with dew,
It is so late that the dew soaks my gauze stockings,
And I let down the crystal curtain
And watch the moon through the clear autumn.

This was so novel that Pound needed to explain:

I have never found any occidental who could "make much" of that poem at one reading. Yet upon careful examination we find that everything is there, not merely by "suggestion" but by a sort of mathematical process of reduction. Let us consider what circumstances would be needed to produce just the words of this poem. You can play Conan Doyle if you like.

First, "jewel-stairs," therefore the scene is in a palace.

Second, "gauze stockings," therefore a court lady is speaking, not a servant or common person who is in the palace by chance.

Third, "dew soaks," therefore the lady has been waiting, she has not just come.

Fourth, "clear autumn with moon showing," therefore the man who has not come cannot excuse himself on the grounds that the evening was unfit for the rendezvous.

Fifth, you ask how we know she was waiting for a man? Well, the title calls the poem "grievance," and for that matter, how do we know what she was waiting for?

More startlingly, what was most modern was derived from poems more than a thousand years old. The new poetry was revealed as an eternal verity. Conversely, and proving Pound's point about the contemporaneity of all ages, that which was ancient was the most immediate: In the midst of the Great War, *Cathay* was a book of soldiers, border guards, ruined cities, abandoned wives, and friends saying goodbye. Pound's friend, the sculptor Henri Gaudier-Brzeska, writing from the trenches shortly before his death, said he read it aloud to the other soldiers to give them courage.

Yet *Cathay* is a book the Sinologists still love to hate. It was, after all, written by an American who knew no Chinese, working from the notes of an American who knew no Chinese, who was taking dictation from Japanese simultaneous interpreters who were translating the comments of Japanese professors. Fenollosa (or his interlocutors) made mistakes; Pound made mistakes reading Fenollosa's handwriting and was sometimes confused by the arrangement of the poems (notoriously, in one case, running two poems together as one). In the book, proper names weirdly appear in their Japanese pronunciations: among the poets, for example, Li Po is Rihaku, Wang Wei is Omakitsu, T'ao Ch'ien is To-Em Mei. (Pound knew the Chinese names, but kept the Japanese versions perhaps to pay homage to Fenollosa's informants, perhaps to emphasize the idea of transmission from language to language and century to century.) And yet, scholars such as Wai-lim Yip have shown how Pound intuitively corrected errors in the notebooks.

Unexpectedly, it was not only Chinese poetry that spoke directly to the new age, but the perceived nature of the Chinese language itself. In 1914, early in the Fenollosa work, Pound was still thinking of poetry as a succession of clear and solid images. In an essay, he quotes a haiku (by, oddly, a Japanese naval officer):

> The foot-steps of the cat upon the snow:
> (are like) plum-blossoms.

commenting that he has added the words "are like" for clarity. (This is surprising, as he had already written "In a Station of the Metro," where "like" is replaced by a colon.) Sometime later, Pound read Fenollosa's draft of an essay, "The Chinese Written Character as a Medium for Poetry," and that copula, literally and metaphorically, would vanish from American modernism, and the image sequence would become a complex.

Fenollosa described how Chinese characters were "ideograms" composed of pictographic elements that combined to form a new word or concept. Thus the sun rising in the branches of a tree became "east." (In fact, this is true of only a small fraction of Chinese characters, which are largely phonetic, but the mistake was fruitful.) More than a still life of elements placed side by side, a word and its meaning were generated by the dynamic relations among the elements. Moreover, Chinese made no distinction between noun, verb, and adjective (again, only partially true), which meant that every ideogram was a node of energy—thing and action and its description—a configuration of elements that, in turn, became an element, without Western rhetorical glue, in the succession of characters in a line of poetry. Fenollosa saw this as a "moving picture" (as did, completely independently, Sergei Eisenstein, whose studies of Chinese led to his theory of montage and his 1929 essay, "The Cinematographic Principle and the Ideograph"). Pound saw it as a simultaneity. Here was modernism—Cubism, collage and assemblage, Apollinaire's "Zone"—recapitulated in every word of an ancient language. And here was something deeper: According to Fenollosa's Emersonian transcendentalist outlook, Chinese was "a vivid shorthand picture of the operations of nature" itself, which knows no pure verbs or nouns, things or actions in isolation, where everything is in active relation. (Henri Michaux would write: "Like nature, the Chinese language does not draw any conclusions of its own, but lets itself be read.") Chinese was the most natural language and therefore the most perfect for poetry.

For Pound, this ideogrammic way of both perceiving the world and creating art would ultimately radiate from the Chinese character itself (and his lifelong preoccupation with Chinese etymology, spurred on by the Rev. Robert Morrison's early 19th century dictionary) to the making of the *Cantos*—individual ideograms composed of "radiant gists" of disparate elements, which in turn formed one, huge, unfinished ideogram—to Pound's whole life and work, a universe or metropolis of countless interacting, harmonious and contradictory things, writings, people, and ideas.

American poetry ever since can be divided into the linear (Frost, Stevens, later Eliot, Bishop, Lowell . . .) and the ideogrammic (early Eliot, Zukofsky, Oppen, Olson, Duncan . . .), but there is one more story to tell from those years. In 1913, a young Chinese student at Cornell, Hu Shih, read Pound's "A Few Don'ts by an Imagiste," applied it to the state of Chinese poetry (then still written in an attenuated literary language), and in 1917 published a manifesto, "Tentative Proposals for the Improvement of Literature," which later became known as the "Eight Don't-isms." ("Write with substance . . . Don't imitate the ancients . . . Emphasize grammar . . . Reject melancholy . . . Eliminate old cliches . . . Don't use allusions . . . Don't use couplets and parallelisms . . . Don't avoid popular expressions or popular forms . . .") The following year he waved the banner of the new in a series of even more Poundian formulations. ("Speak only if you have something to say . . . Say what you have to say, and say it as it is said . . . Speak your own language, not the language of others . . . Speak the language of your own time.") Its clarion call for a new writing in the vernacular and a new literature for a new China flowed into the larger currents of the nationalistic, anti-imperial, and iconoclastic May Fourth Movement of 1919. Hu Shih found in America what Ezra Pound had found in China.

For a few years after *Cathay*, Pound translated more of the Fenollosa poems, but published no more Chinese poetry translations until the 1954 *Classic*

Anthology Defined by Confucius, better known as *The Confucian Odes*. In the 1930s, he spent four or five hours a day studying the language, but the Chinese corner of the Pound ideogram was preoccupied with translations of Confucius—the *Ta Hio* in 1928, the *Analects* in 1937, two Italian versions in 1944 and 1945, *The Unwobbling Pivot & The Great Digest* in 1947—and *Cantos LII-LXXI* in 1940, a drastic condensation of the entirety of Père de Moyriac de Mailla's twelve-volume 18th century *Histoire Générale de la Chine*, which he placed alongside the history of John Adams' America.

But *Cathay* had set off a small landslide of Chinese poetry translation. It was the fifteenth book in English since the era of Adams and de Mailla; in the next forty years there were at least another fifty—in a time of not many poetry books, and even fewer poetry translations—though most were unmemorable. Notable among them were, above all, the books of Arthur Waley, the first Sinologist capable of writing poetry, but one whose translations were often sunk by his fondness for Gerard Manley Hopkins and a theory that the number of stresses in the English line must match the number of characters in the Chinese. (In the end, Waley's greatest work may well be in prose and from Japanese: *The Tale of Genji*.) Among the others, there was Amy Lowell, whose hostile takeover of Imagism—Pound quickly moved on to Vorticism—included a drippy 1921 collaboration with Florence Ayscough called *Fir-Flower Tablets* ("When the hair of your Unworthy One first began to cover her forehead"); and Witter Bynner and Kiang Kang-hu's *The Jade Mountain* (1929), important as the first English translation of the complete *300 Poems from the T'ang* anthology, and an inspiration for Kenneth Rexroth and Burton Watson, but written in ethereal Chinoiserie mode, with many lines beginning or ending in ellipses:

A SIGH FROM A STAIRCASE OF JADE
Her jade-white staircase is cold with dew;
Her silk soles are wet, she lingered there so long . . .
Behind her closed casement, why is she still waiting,
Watching through its crystal pane the glow of the autumn
    moon?

The postwar period brought a second flowering of Chinese translation, and it began, again, with Pound, in 1946. Awaiting trial and possible ex-

ecution for treason for his wartime radio broadcasts, he was locked in the
ward (he called it the "hell-hole") for the criminally insane in St. Elizabeths Hospital in Washington, D.C., with few privileges and infrequent
visitors. He preoccupied himself with a translation of the *Shih Ching*, the
earliest Chinese anthology, for, as he would translate, "Only antient wisdom is / solace to man's miseries." As Confucius said, in Achilles Fang's
translation:

> Why don't you study the Odes? The Odes will arouse you, give
> you food for thought, teach you how to make friends, show you
> the way of resentment, bring you near to being useful to your
> parents and sovereign, and help you remember the names of
> many birds, animals, plants and trees.

A first draft was written, based only on James Legge's 1876 bilingual
edition, *The She King,* and Matthews' dictionary of modern usage. (Achilles Fang: "Would you use Webster's Collegiate Dictionary to translate
Chaucer?") Later, when he was moved to a more benign section of the hospital, he had some Chinese visitors, a correspondence with Fang and, most
important, access to the work of the Swedish Sinologist Bernard Karlgren,
whose 1950 translation, *The Book of Odes,* had the Chinese text, transliterations (including reconstructions of the archaic pronunciations for the
rhyme-words) and a prose version. Pound's translation went through three
completely different drafts before it was published in 1954.

The Confucian Odes was a very different book from *Cathay*. It was a complete text—all 305 poems of the original anthology—rather than a selection,
which meant that Pound had to work through some dull stretches. It was
an "ideogrammic" translation, in that Pound attempted to incorporate into
the poems, along with the literal meanings, the etymological, pictographic
elements of certain characters. Also ideogrammically, he inserted the poems
into the simultaneity of all ages by frequently giving them wacky, culturally
and historically specific titles like "Polonius on Ostentation," "Evviva la
Torre di Pisa!," "Strip-Tease?," and "Ole Man River."

We can follow Pound's method of translating the Odes by looking at
Legge and Karlgren and—though Pound never mentioned it—Arthur Waley's 1937 version, *The Book of Songs.*

Pound:

> Pine boat a-shift
> on drift of tide,
> for flame in the ear, sleep riven,
> driven; rift of the heart in dark
> no wine will clear,
> nor have I will to playe.

Legge:

> It floats about, that boat of cypress wood,
>> Now here, now there, as by the current borne.
> Nor rest nor sleep comes in my troubled mood;
>> I suffer as when painful wound has torn
>> The shrinking body. Thus I dwell forlorn,
> And aimless muse, my thoughts of sorrow full.
>> I might with wine refresh my spirit worn;
> I might go forth, and sauntering try to cool
> The fever of my heart; but grief holds sullen rule.

Karlgren:

> Drifting is that cypress-wood boat, drifting is its floating [So
> I am drifting helplessly along, without means of steering my
> way]; I am [bright =] wide awake and do not sleep, as if I had
> a painful grief; but it is not that I have no wine, to amuse and
> divert myself.

For the third line, Pound takes the components of the character *keng* (bright/awake), "ear" and "fire," sees in Matthews' dictionary that *keng* also means "disquieted," and produces "flame in the ear, sleep riven." For the fourth line (literally, "like having hidden sorrow") he sees the "heart" radical in the last two characters, and writes: "driven; rift of the heart in dark." And for the sixth line, he may have found "playe"—spelled archaically to suggest antiquity without altering the sound—in Waley:

Tossed is that cypress boat,
Wave-tossed it floats.
My heart is in turmoil, I cannot sleep.
But secret is my grief.
Wine I have, all things needful
For play, for sport.

Most of all, Pound had become interested in the music of Chinese poetry. By the time *The Chinese Written Character* was first published in book
form in 1936, Pound was already moving away from Fenollosa's purely visual
reading. In some new notes to the text, he emphasized the "verbal sonor-
ity" of Chinese ("I now doubt if it was inferior to the Greek.") and, moreover, that the poems must be sung. In the insane asylum, Pound carefully
transcribed the sounds of each line of the *Odes*, mixing modern usage with
Karlgren's reconstructions of the archaic pronunciations, and he practiced
chanting them. (The original edition was supposed to include the Chinese
text and these transliterations, but the publisher, Harvard University Press,
objected to the expense.) The entire book was conceived as a songbook, with
Pound's oceanic eclecticism finding models from the Troubadours to the
Elizabethans, hillbilly folk songs to some syncopated boogie-woogie. Rarely
discussed by Pound scholars (other than Richard Sieburth, who thinks it
Pound's greatest translation) and largely dismissed by Sinologists, *The Confucian Odes* remains—alongside Samuel Beckett's anthology of Mexican
poetry and Louis Zukofsky's Catullus—one of the masterpieces of idiosyncratic translation: a radical invocation of the spirits, if not always an
accurate transmission of the words.

In 1947, Robert Payne had a poetry bestseller with *The White Pony*, the first
anthology to survey the entirety of Chinese poetry, from the *Shih Ching*
to the still renegade Mao Zedong. In 1956, Kenneth Rexroth had another
bestseller with his *One Hundred Poems from the Chinese*. Thirty-five of the
hundred poems were by Tu Fu ("without question the major influence on
my own poetry"), who at the time was still eclipsed in English by Pound's
Li Po and Waley's Po Chü-i; the rest were the first important translations of
various Sung Dynasty poets, who had generally been neglected in the prevailing T'angophilia. Rexroth, in his unreliable *An Autobiographical Novel*,
claimed that he first began learning Chinese as a boy; in 1924, at nineteen,

he met Witter Bynner in Taos, who spurred his interest in Tu Fu. According to his introduction to *One Hundred Poems*, the poems were derived from the Chinese texts, as well as French, German, and academic English translations, but the sources hardly matter. Rexroth had reimagined the poems as the work of someone on the other side of the Pacific Rim, speaking in a plain, natural-breathing, neutral American idiom. Ignoring the Chinese line, which is almost always a complete syntactical unit, Rexroth enjambed his, often with end-stops in the middle, to give them the illusion of effortless speech, as in this Tu Fu poem:

NIGHT THOUGHTS WHILE TRAVELING
A light breeze rustles the reeds
Along the river banks. The
Mast of my lonely boat soars
Into the night. Stars blossom
Over the vast desert of
Waters. Moonlight flows on the
Surging river. My poems have
Made me famous but I grow
Old, ill and tired, blown hither
And yon; I am like a gull
Lost between heaven and earth.

One Hundred Poems was followed in 1970 by *Love and the Turning Year: One Hundred More Poems from the Chinese*, possibly his best translation, a selection of favorite poems from two thousand years of poetry.

More than any other translator of Chinese, it is almost impossible to separate Rexroth's translations from his own poetry; they tend to speak as one. And in the 1970s, his Chinese (and Japanese) translations became part of a strange project in old age to reinvent himself as a woman poet. Along with his creation of a young Japanese poet, Marichiko, and her erotic lyrics, and an anthology of Japanese women poets, Rexroth collaborated with the scholar Ling Chung on *The Orchid Boat: Women Poets of China* (1972) and, two years later, an edition of the complete poems of the great Sung poet, Li Ch'ing Chao. Like Whitman, Rexroth was containing multitudes, but they were all East Asian women.

In 1957, William Carlos Williams—who, though a few years older, always seemed to play the competitive kid brother to Ezra Pound—at age 74 began to translate Chinese poetry, even taking on the Li Po poem Pound had called "The River-Merchant's Wife: A Letter." (David Hinton, by the way, has pointed out that "there is no reason to think that the husband is a river merchant.") Williams' scholarly collaborator was the exceedingly bizarre David Rafael Wang (1931-1977). Wang, also known as David Happell Hsin-fu Wand, was born in China—a direct descendent, he claimed, of Wang Wei—escaped to the US after the revolution, and became surely the only Chinese-American who was both a neo-Nazi white supremacist (and a member of the seedier circles around Pound in St. Elizabeths) and a Black Panther (in Oakland in the 1960s). Among other things, he was also a stodgy professor, active in the academic bureaucracy; a bisexual boxing and martial arts fanatic who had long talks about poetry with Muhammad Ali; a poet ("in the Greco-Sino-Samurai-African tradition") and friend of many of the Beat and Black Mountain poets; a translator of Hawaiian and Samoan oral poetries, included in the Rothenberg *Technicians of the Sacred* anthology; and a possible suicide (at a MLA convention) who some people believe was murdered. Williams, however, apparently kept the conversation to Chinese poetry, and their four-year collaboration resulted in "The Cassia Tree," a group of 37 poems, published in 1966, after Williams' death.

Cathay had led Williams to Giles' *History*, and references to China and Chinese poetry appear as early as *Kora in Hell* (1918). In his library were most of the major translations of poetry and prose, and it is quite possible that the progressively thinner poems he began writing in 1917 were inspired by a book he owned called *Chinese Made Easy* (1904), which included the text and a translation of the pedagological *Three Character Classic* running down the page. That the strict formal qualities of Chinese poetry would also have their effect on American poetry is unexpected but true: Louis Zukofsky, for one, explicitly following the Chinese, wrote passages of *"A"* using the number of words, not syllables or stresses, as the unit of measure.

Among the things in Chinese poetry that directly appealed to Rexroth and Gary Snyder (and later to such translators as David Hinton, Sam Hamill, and Red Pine) was its celebration of wilderness—something that had been neglected by Pound and Waley, Lowell and Bynner. Many Chinese poets, whether in exile or in Taoist or Buddhist retreat, had inhabited landscapes as dramatic and wild as those of the American West, and the poems they wrote had no equivalent in world literature, where nature tended to be domesticated or fearsome. Both Snyder and Rexroth, because of their extensive wilderness experience—and a Buddhist training to place it in context—were able to see the natural specifics of Chinese poetry in a way that more deskbound translators were not. Snyder writes:

> In getting into the Han-shan poems . . . I found something that
> I had not suspected . . . Something happened to me that I had
> not experienced before in the effort of translation, and that
> was that I found myself forgetting the Chinese and going into
> a deep interior visualization of what the poem was about. . . .
> I had just been a four month's season in the high country of
> the Sierra Nevada . . . So when I came back, I was still full
> of that; and when I went into the Han-shan poems, when he
> talked about a cobbly stream, or he talked about the pine-wind,
> I wasn't just thinking about "pine-wind" in Chinese and then
> "pine-wind" in English, but I was hearing it, hearing the wind.
> And when a phrase like "cloudy mist" or "misty mountain" or
> "cloudy mountain" or "mountain in the cloud" comes up . . .
> the strategy ultimately is this: You know the words . . . in the
> original text, so drop them and now remember what it looks
> like to look at cloudy mountains and see what they look like,
> in your mind—go deep into your mind and see what's hap-
> pening: an interior visualization of the poem, which means of
> course that you have to draw on your senses, your recollection
> of your senses.

Snyder's Han-shan, "Cold Mountain Poems," first published in *Evergreen Review* in 1958, a colloquial classic and immediate hit, managed to transform a semi-legendary Buddhist itinerant monk into an American Beat:

> When men see Han-shan
> They all say he's crazy
> And not much to look at—
> Dressed in rags and hides.
> They don't get what I say

& I don't talk their language.
All I can say to those I meet:
"Try and make it to Cold Mountain."

Along with the poets, the postwar period was also a time of excellent translations by Sinologists: among them, A. C. Graham and David Hawkes in the
UK, and J. P. Seaton and Jonathan Chaves in the US. Rare among foreign-
language experts, they were readers of contemporary English-language poetry, and they not only knew where the poems were coming from, but where
they were going. Unquestionably the greatest of all has been Burton Watson.
His long shelf of poetry translations (along with classics of philosophy, history, and Buddhism, and his own critical studies) are written in a modest,
plain-speaking English almost as concise as the Chinese, with rarely a super-
fluous word, as in this short poem by the Sung Dynasty poet Su Tung-p'o:

> VIEWING PEONIES AT THE TEMPLE OF GOOD FORTUNE
> I'm not ashamed at my age to stick a flower in my hair.
> The flower is the embarrassed one, topping an old man's
>   head.
> People laugh as I go home drunk, leaning on friends—
> ten miles of elegant blinds raised halfway for watching.

David Hinton represents a new generation in this tradition. A prolific
scholar-translator-poet, heir to Watson, his poetry versions are a new chapter
in the history of Chinese translation. Against the reigning style—forged by
Rexroth, Snyder, and Watson, and continued most notably by Sam Hamill,
Red Pine, and Arthur Sze—which assumes that the Chinese direct appre-
hension of the real world must be presented in direct, conversational speech,
Hinton has attempted to recreate some of the density of classical Chinese by
charging the language, and not resorting, as some others have done, to a pid-
gin English. He is the only one besides Rexroth to regularly enjamb the unen-
jambed Chinese lines, but to opposite effect: complexity, rather than ease, as
in this section from the T'ang poet Meng Chiao's sequence, "Cold Creek":

> Men pole boats, banking jade stars aside,
> trailing out scattered fireflies. And cold

north plunging icy lament deep, starved
hunters chant invocations to hidden fish.

Frozen teeth gnaw and grind at themselves.
Windchimes clatter in sour wind. All this

immaculate grief—it's inescapable. It
rinses hearing clean of the least sound.

The current of rippling emerald is gone,
and colorful floss fallen, flight-tattered.

Ground glare ice, branches splintered,
things can't walk, can't roost. Wounded,

they squawk and shriek, yelp and howl,
accusing heaven: *will things ever rest?*

How classical Chinese entered into American poetry is a simple story, but its effect may never be fully unraveled, for it is often impossible to determine whether the Americans found in it a revelation or merely a confirmation of what they had already discovered.

In the Imagist aesthetic, which has dominated American poetry for the last ninety years, Chinese was perhaps the greatest example of direct presentation without generalizing comment, of "no ideas except in things." Poets as dissimilar as Charles Reznikoff and Stanley Kunitz, to take one example, each publicly cited the Sung Dynasty critic, Wei T'ai (from the epigraph to A. C. Graham's *Poems of the Late T'ang*): "Poetry presents the thing in order to convey the feeling. It should be precise about the thing and reticent about the feeling."

In the modernist project of a poetry that would be about everything, that was open to anything, even (or especially) the most ordinary experiences, Chinese was a poetry where Tu Fu could begin a poem with the crumbling of the state and end complaining that he's gone bald. It was a poetry that made no distinctions about what was suitable for poetry, and one where it was already assumed that so much depended upon a red wheelbarrow.

As the postwar poets moved into the American wilderness, they found that Chinese poetry, created in a similarly vast landscape, slaked (in Gary Snyder's words) "the modern thirst for natural, secular clarity" for it

> seems to have found, at its finest, a center within the poles of man, spirit & nature. With strategies of apparent simplicity and understatement it moves us from awe before history, to a deep breath before nature, to a laugh before spirit.

For those who believed, like Pound, that a wise government consults its poets, Chinese was a poetry largely written by civil servants with varying degrees of political power, and sometimes by the emperors themselves. For those like Snyder and Rexroth in Cold War America, who believed in poetry as opposition to the State, the Chinese poet's role as the exiled or self-exiled recluse-sage in the wilderness was a model—and one, as Snyder has pointed out, not dependent, as is usual among Western oppositional figures, on an alternate theology or political ideology.

In the daily assault of mendacious or empty language, Chinese poetry promoted the Confucian "rectification of names"—that words should mean what they say, that it is the poet's task to restore meaning, that the poet, like the enlightened ruler, was a person who stood by his word. In the new morality, the eroticism of Chinese lyrics was unabashed, polymorphous, and just plain sexy. In the age of cinematic montage, Chinese poetry leapt from word to word, line to line, and let the reader supply the transitions. Particularly for those who could not read the original, it seemed to be a kind of concrete poetry, just at the moment when American poets were preoccupied with the look of the poem on the page. Most of all, it was a poetry where one found the whole panorama of enduring human emotions and experiences, lofty and mundane: war and the weather, loneliness and politics, drunkenness and minor aches and pains, friendship, gardening, bird-watching, failure, river journeys, religious and sexual ecstasy, aging, poverty and riches, courtesans and generals, princes and children, street vendors and monks. Chinese poetry as a whole was a Balzacian human comedy from a distant place and time that ultimately didn't seem so remote at all.

[2003]

VICENTE HUIDOBRO'S *Altazor*

"Yes, the imagination, drunk with prohibitions, has destroyed
and recreated everything afresh in the likeness of that which it
was. Now indeed men look about in amazement at each other
with a full realization of the meaning of 'art.'"
                                —William Carlos Williams, 1923

*A*LTO, high; *azor*, hawk. *Altazor*, a poem in seven cantos, written by
a Chilean living in Paris. Begun in 1919 and published in 1931, the
poem spans those extraordinarily optimistic years between global disasters.
An age that thought itself post-apocalyptic: the war to end all wars was
fought and over, and now there was a new world to create. A time when
the West was, literally and figuratively, electrified; when the mass production of telephones, automobiles, movies, record players, toasters, radios,
skyscrapers, airplanes, bridges, cameras, blimps, and subways, matched an
aesthetic production obsessed with celebrating the new, an aesthetics that
(in Margaret Bourke-White's famous remark) found dynamos more beautiful than pearls. Painters, sculptors, and photographers saw their task as
making the new out of the new, dismantling and reassembling everything
from egg-beaters to spark plugs to the Hoover Dam. Poets, the citizens of
international progress, wrote in other languages or invented their own. Cinematic jumpcuts, verbal and visual Cubism, simultaneity and collage: on the
page and on the canvas, all time collapsed into the single moment of now.
"Speed," said Norman Bel Geddes, who redesigned the world, "is the cry
of our era," and *Altazor* is, among other things, surely the fastest-reading
long poem ever written. What other poem keeps reminding us to hurry up,
that there's no time to lose?

Vicente Huidobro was born the Marquis of Casa Real in 1893, and grew up in a house in Santiago, Chile, with 84 servants. He arrived in Paris in November 1916, at age twenty-three already the author of seven books, and for thirty years remained in the thick of it:

He wrote, in Spanish, French, and English, poems, novels, plays, screenplays, film criticism, manifestos, political articles and pamphlets, collaborative poems with Max Jacob and collaborative novels with Hans Arp—sometimes publishing four or five books a year. He edited an anthology with the young, still Vanguardist, Borges. He wrote the libretto for an unrealized opera, *Football*, to be staged by Diaghilev with music by Stravinsky and sets by Robert Delaunay. Sonia Delaunay turned his poems into dresses; Edgar Varèse set them to music; Pound wanted to translate them, but never did.

He edited countless short-lived magazines with Reverdy, Apollinaire, Tristan Tzara, Le Corbusier, César Vallejo. His portrait was painted by Gris, Picasso, and Torres-García; Arp photographed him shooting a pistol; Robert Delaunay designed covers for his books; an exhibit of his own "painted poems" caused a riot in Berlin. Other friends and public enemies—one often turning into the other—were Breton, Marinetti, Cocteau, Cendrars, Éluard, Satie, Schoenberg, Braque, Picabia, Diego Rivera, Lipchitz, Léger.

He took up the cause of Irish nationalism, published a pamphlet against British imperialism, and claimed to have been kidnapped by British agents. He joined the Masons; he campaigned against Surrealism ("nothing but the violin of psychoanalysis"); he joined the Communist Party, named one of his sons Vladimir, after Lenin, and left in disgust at the Munich Pact.

In Chile, he founded a newspaper that was shut down by the government; survived an assassination attempt; founded another newspaper; ran for President as the "Candidate of Youth"; survived another assassination attempt, and lost. He had a lifelong feud with Pablo Neruda that isolated him in Latin America.

In New York, he wrote for *Vanity Fair*, was friends with Charlie Chaplin, Douglas Fairbanks, Gloria Swanson, and innumerable now-forgotten starlets. A screenplay of his won a $10,000 prize from the League for Better Pictures, and he announced he'd use the money to erect a monument to Charles Lindbergh, which was never built, so he wrote a long poem in English to the aviator, which remains unpublished.

In Spain he argued with García Lorca and Buñuel, wrote propaganda for the Republicans in the Civil War, and traveled to the front to give rallying speeches to the troops.

Scandalous love affairs; bitter polemics in the press. In the Canary Islands, he worked on a scheme to introduce nightingales into Chile. In Chile, he proposed the creation of a new nation, Andesia, composed of Chile, Bolivia, Peru, and Paraguay, to withstand US control of Latin America. In 1930, he planned an artists' colony in Angola as a refuge from the "next World War."

In World War II, he was a correspondent in France, was wounded twice, and entered Berlin with the Allies. He died on January 2, 1948, a few days before his 55th birthday, from complications from his war wounds. His biography has never been adequately written. His tombstone reads:

> Here lies the poet Vicente Huidobro
> Open the tomb
> In the depths of this tomb you will see the sea

"Contemporary poetry," he claimed, "begins with me," and, at least for his own language, it was no exaggeration: his Cubist poems of 1917 and 1918, exploding over the page, effectively pulled Spanish poetry out of its symbolist *modernismo* and into international modernism. Huidobro's banner, in the proliferation of isms, was Creationism, a movement of which he was essentially the only member. It declared that poetry, the gloss on, or simulacrum of, reality, was dead. In the new world, the poets, "little gods," would invent their own worlds: "Why sing of roses, oh Poets? Make them bloom in the poem." It was a movement that was simultaneously modern, in its belief that in the new era human imagination would be able to do anything, and archaic, reflecting the contemporary preoccupation with the "primitive," particularly the spells and charms of sympathetic magic. Whether or not he succeeded in making the roses bloom—and who's to say?—Huidobro did make them speak, and in their own language.

His masterpiece was *Altazor*, a poem that begins in the ruins of the war—the date 1919 appears on the title page to locate the poem, not its composition—and rushes headlong into the future, as its hero, Altazor, the "antipoet," hurtles through space. It is undoubtedly the greatest poetic expression of the European aeromania that had begun with Wilbur Wright's arrival in 1908 (hired by the French after the US Army had decided his flying machine had no military uses) and Louis Blériot's sensational crossing of the English Channel the following year. Within a year, Gabriele D'Annunzio was proclaiming "A new civilization, a new life, new skies!" and already was asking "Where is the poet who will be capable of singing this epic?" as writers and artists flocked to the air shows.

The new age required a new language: Marinetti, after his first ride in an aeroplane, "felt the ridiculous absurdity of the old syntax inherited from Homer. A furious need to liberate words, liberating them from the prison of the Latin sentence!" And flight was a new vision: Malevich, for one, demonstrated how academic painters were inspired by peasants and farm animals, Futurists by bridges and trains, and his own Suprematists by aerial photographs and the sight from the ground of specks of aeroplanes in the sky.

During the composition of *Altazor*, the new age became incarnated in Lindbergh. He is the poem's unnamed icon, the high-hawk aeronaut who is the new Christ, the liberator, and the airplane is his Cross: not as an agent of suffering, but as a vehicle for ascension. Apollinaire, in "Zone," had first made the connection, and the American expatriate poet and sun-worshiper Harry Crosby described watching Lindbergh's landing in his diaries in precisely these terms:

> Then sharp swift in the gold glare of the searchlights a small white hawk of a plane swoops hawk-like down and across the field—C'est lui Lindbergh, LINDBERGH! and there is pandemonium wild animals let loose and a stampede toward the plane . . . and it seems as if all the hands in the world are touching or trying to touch the new Christ and that the new Cross is the Plane . . . Ce n'est pas un homme, c'est un Oiseau!

The aeronaut was a Nietzschean superman, a man turned into a god, but this new Christ was taking us further than the moon and stars of the ballads. He was traveling into Einstein space, a place where speed is capable of telescoping time, but where the obstacle to total simultaneity is mass. *Altazor* is a poem of falling, not back to earth—though certain critics have insisted on reading it as a version of the Icarus myth—but out into space. The faster Altazor falls, the faster the poem reads. As his body burns up like a meteor, mass transforming into energy, all ages become contemporaneous,

the tombs open—the poem is also a product of the contemporary Tutmania—
and all places become one. Above all, the old language of poetry is consumed
with the body of the poet, and a new language, progressively more radical, is
created out of puns, neologisms, animal and plant dialects, and pages of identical rhymes. (His 250 variations on "windmill" is simultaneously an homage
to Rabelais' "balls" and to Cervantes, a shamanic chant, a mimesis of mo-
notonous machinery, and a "trance music" decades before Glass and Reich.)
By the last canto, the poet has become pure energy, a language of pure sound:
opposite to the Pentecost, the poet has risen into, has become, the tongues of
flame. Altazor is both an archaic shaman, leaving his body to travel to other
worlds, and the new aeronaut who, like the polar explorers—and Huidobro
was crazy about polar explorers—travels into the realms of nothingness, the
"infiniternity," regardless of the small hope of coming back:

> Ahee ah ee aheee ah ee ee ee ee oh eeah

Alto, high, *azor*, hawk. Or is it an anagram for *Alastor*, Shelley's long
poem of "a youth of uncorrupted feelings and adventurous genius led forth
by an imagination inflamed and purified through familiarity with all that is
excellent and majestic, to the contemplation of the universe?" Shelley's Ro-
mantic poet-hero, first at peace with the "infinite and unmeasured," grows
dissatisfied with eternity, and in the end is literally consumed, killed, by
desire for the Other he has invented in his total solitude. In contrast, Huidobro's Nietzschean anti-poet/hero abandons his Other (the beloved of Canto
II) to reach satori in the pure energy of pure language.

"All the languages are dead," he wrote, and so was "poetical poetry poetry." In the future poems would be written in bird-language, star-language,
aeroplane-language, and we would all inhabit a "beautiful madness in the
zone of language." For decades it was thought that *Altazor* was a noble
disaster that admitted its own failure by its descent into gibberish. More
recently, the post-moderns have used it as a prophesy of their revelation of
the fundamental meaninglessness of language. This wasn't what he meant
at all: Once upon a time, the new was sacred, space became the unexplored
territory, and the future was the only mythical era.

[2003]

HANS FAVEREY'S
Against the Forgetting

A RISTOTLE: "[Thales] declared the first-principle to be water . . . heat itself is generated out of moisture . . . the seeds of everything have a moist nature."

Aristotle: "Thales conceived of the soul as somehow a motive power, since he said the magnetic stone has soul in it because it sets a piece of iron in motion."

Faverey: "All is born of moisture, / even life's heat. Lifeless / nature is animate too. / Proof: lodestone, / / amber. Hence seed, / too, is always / moist in temperament."

Alcmaeon of Crotona: "Men perish because they cannot join the beginning with the end."

Outside of Holland almost no one has heard of Hans Faverey, for fate and his own predilections kept his work a secret abroad.

Heraclitus: "Nature loves to hide."

He wrote in a language not many speak and few foreigners now know. Boswell: "In the latter part of his life, in order to satisfy himself whether his mental faculties were impaired, [Johnson] resolved that he would try to learn a new language, and fixed upon the Low Dutch . . ."

He died in 1990 at age 56, at the moment when his national reputation might have propelled him onto the international circuit, which he probably would have avoided.

Faverey: "What hides beneath the / wordline, hides all but / in vain."

In Holland, despite prizes and acclaim, he tended to elude the gaze of the public eye. In his rare interviews, the answers were evasive.

Faverey: "Facts / consist of nothing."

He was born in Dutch Guiana, now Suriname, and moved to Amsterdam as a boy. His tropical childhood almost never enters the poems.

He worked as a clinical psychologist. Psychological insights, experiences, language, almost never enter the poems.

Democritus: "Man must learn that he is divorced from reality."

He met his wife on an island without vowels: Krk.

Friends have described their happy marriage, but in the poems the beloved is absent, remembered, the subject of a dream or a day-dream.

Faverey: "Memory is perception."

He played the harpsichord and wished he had composed more than a few occasional pieces.

He wrote series of short poems, and he wrote listening to Baroque fugues and variations.

Faverey: "in the repetition / shows the futility."

He called his poems "exercises in absence: detachment-exercises."

Faverey: "The utter emptiness / in every thing which actually / is . . ."

Melissus: "What is empty is nothing, and what is nothing cannot be."

He loved the moment when a bouncing ping-pong ball stops bouncing, but one doesn't know if it has finally come to rest.

Zeno: "If anything is moving, it must be moving either in the place in which it is or in the place in which it is not. However it cannot move in the place in which it is and it cannot move in the place in which it is not. Therefore movement is impossible."

He loved Zeno's arrow. His "Tortoise" is the one that outruns Achilles.

Melissus: "If Being were divided it would be in motion, and if it were in motion it would not be."

He titled a series "Sur Place," a psychological tactic from velodrome racing: the cyclist remains on the side, motionless, feet on the pedals, and lets the opponents pass.

Faverey: "it works: the world stands still."

He shared the national obsession with still lifes, a term coined by the Dutch. Guy Davenport: ". . . *leven*, 'alive,' or drawings made from a model. A *vrou-wenleven* was a female model, and one who, from time to time, while posing, needed to move; a *stilleven*—fruit, flowers, or fish—remained still."

Xenophanes: "God always abides in the selfsame place, not moving at all."

For Faverey, a still life is not only time arrested, but decay arrested. A still life is the opposite of a *nature morte.*

Still life: The subject of the individual painting is unchanging; the subjects of the genre are unchanging; the genre is unchanging. Absolute stillness. Davenport: "All the genres of painting except still life are discontinuous, and only the lyric poem, or song, can claim so ancient a part of our culture among the expressive arts."

Faverey: "I do not wish to know time."

His first book was called *Poems*; his second, *Poems II*. When asked how his work had changed over the years, he replied that the poems had gotten a little longer.

Faverey: "When there is nothing left / to do it for, / to do it with, / / it stops of its own accord."

When asked if his later poems were more accessible, he replied: "I am better at it now."

Faverey: "Of course it's the principle that counts, / / if there's a principle that counts."

Many of the poems have "it" for a subject, but it is difficult to know what "it" is.

All of his "homages" seem pitched to an opposite pole: the melancholic, melodramatic landscapes of Seghers; the perfect ricercars of Cavazzoni; the *Epic of Gilgamesh*; the delicate ornamentations of Couperin, composer of *The Bees, The Butterflies, The Voluptuous Lady, The Nightingale in Love.*

Heraclitus: "The hidden harmony is better than the obvious."

In all of his "homages," a glimpse of the coattails of his ostensible subject before it vanishes.

Faverey: "I have grown to love Sappho / since destruction / abridged her texts."

Among American poets, his company would have been George Oppen, William Bronk, Gustaf Sobin.

Like Oppen, free-floating, enigmatic, unforgettable lines. Like Oppen, *Poems* is his *Discrete Series*: contrary to most writers, the earliest work is the least loquacious, has the least connectives.

Oppen: "Closed car—closed in glass— / At the curb, / Unapplied and empty:" Faverey: "Standstill / / under construction, demolition / Under construction. 'Emptiness, / / So stately on her stem':"

Faverey: "As far as the eye can see, / / the discrete has been seen."

Like Bronk, paradoxes in plain language, and lines that erase the preceding line.

Bronk: "We aren't even here but in a real here / elsewhere—a long way off." Faverey: "It is not yet now; / / yet now has not just been."

Empedocles: "What is right may properly be uttered even twice."

Like Sobin, Mediterranean efflorescence—in Faverey, the Dalmatian coast—bursting through the seeming aridity of few words.

Sobin: "that the flowers aren't ours, aren't / flowering for our voices . . ." Faverey: "What the vine wants / / happens."

When asked what happens in his poems, he replied: "Things happen and at a certain moment they don't happen anymore. Finished, basta, the end."

Faverey: "He who cannot wait for the unhoped-for / will never hold out / until he cries: enough."

Against the Forgetting: "Oblivion knows no time."

[2004]

NIEDECKER / REZNIKOFF

MUCH, perhaps too much, has been written about Lorine Niedecker's relations with Louis Zukofsky—her friend, colleague, lover, commiserater, and 40-year obsession—but the curious thing is that if one knew no biographical details, it would be difficult to put them together as poets. Only rarely in their writings do they resemble each other, usually in those moments when they resemble William Carlos Williams. In contrast, almost nothing has been said about Niedecker's true kindred spirit in poetry, Charles Reznikoff.

Take a blindfold test on two short poems from around 1950:

(1)
One of my sentinels, a tree
sent spinning after me
this brief
secret on a leaf:
the summer is over—
forever.

(2)
Two old men—
one proposed they live together
take turns cooking, washing dishes
they were both alone.
His friend: "Our way of living
is so different:

    you spit
    I don't spit."

The first is quintessential Niedecker—a tiny moment of nature com-municating to a first-person narrator and at least three unexpected musical changes in six lines and twenty-one words—but the poem is by Reznikoff. The second is quintessential Reznikoff—the flat narration pared to the min-imum necessity, the lives of ordinary people captured with a gentle humor by a bit of real speech—but the poem is by Niedecker. Flipping through their respective collected works, this game can be played endlessly.

What we know about the relationship between the two is very little, and there may well be little to know. They met in the 1930s when Niedecker was living off and on with Zukofsky in New York. Reznikoff sent Niedecker his books for thirty years. She does not appear in the very badly edited selec-tion of his letters, but Niedecker, writing to Zukofsky in 1946, quotes his reaction to *New Goose*: "I picked it up when I was tired and dispirited and put it down quite refreshed by the words and music." (Niedecker notes with amusement that "good, quiet, cautious Rez" had added the word "quite" as a correction.) After her death, Reznikoff, unlike the bilious Zukofsky, con-tributed a short poem to Jonathan Williams' *Epitaphs for Lorine*. And that is as far as the Reznikoff paper trail goes.

On the Niedecker side, there is a little more. In the 1951 poem "If I were a bird," which pays homage to her poetic contemporaries, Reznikoff appears with H. D., Williams, Moore, Stevens, Zukofsky, and Cummings. In a 1959 letter to Zukofsky, she wonders who could help Reznikoff. She writes: "You get the idea he leads a lonelier life than I do but freer of trash?" And: "I have always felt he was writing my poems for me only better." In a letter to Reznikoff at the same time—she sent a copy to Zukofsky—she says, "I often find a kinship between us in the short poem. And if you are my brother-in-poetry then we have Chinese and Japanese brothers." Also from the same letter: "Hard to write and then get it printed. I try to, along with scrubbing floors in a hospital. Every now and again, tho, there's a chink where a poem comes thru. Altogether life is not really too hard—I gather this is what you say too."

Niedecker tended to route all things poetical through Zukofsky, and whenever she mentions Reznikoff in passing it is always with reference to Zukofsky's essay from the 1931 "Objectivists" issue of *Poetry*—an issue she largely copied out by hand—"Sincerity and Objectification: With Special Reference to the Work of Charles Reznikoff." (Zukofsky, characteristically, cut out all mention of Reznikoff when he reprinted the essay for the first time in the 1967 *Prepositions*.) That essay, the Magna Carta of Objectivism, while sharp in certain particulars, is generally vague to the point of meaninglessness, was interpreted in contradictory ways by its supposed fellow travelers, and has been largely misremembered, blurred with the Imagistic ideal of emotion expressed through concrete details. [I, for one, will never understand why Reznikoff's one-line poem "The ceaseless weaving of the uneven water" is sincerity, not objectification, but his three-line poem on the death of Gaudier-Brzeska, "How shall we mourn you who are killed and wasted, / Sure that you would not die with your work unended— / As if the iron scythe in the grass stops for a flower" is objectification but not sincerity.]

Niedecker always associates Reznikoff with the word "sincerity," and it's a safe guess that she was thinking of that aspect of the word defined by Zukofsky as writing "which is the detail, not mirage, of seeing, of thinking with the things as they exist, and of directing them along a line of melody." But there was something else in that essay, and in Reznikoff's poetry, which Niedecker never acknowledges (at least, in the published letters) and the critics never mention, but which surely came as a revelation to her.

Niedecker and Reznikoff are kindred spirits in their difficult lives of isolation; their dedication to condensation and the excision of superfluity as the prevailing aesthetic; their preoccupation with the local—a local they almost never left; their perfect lyrics that often turn on a rhyme or a musical phrase; their sweet ironic humor; their personification of the natural world; their first- and third-person anecdotal narratives of ordinary people (the former, direct descendants of Edgar Lee Masters' *Spoon River Anthology*— which, like it or not, is, with *The Waste Land*, the century's most influential book of American poetry); and in their pathological self-effacement. These are matters of sensibility and personality and aesthetic comradeship. But there was also an idea that Niedecker got from Reznikoff—as important as anything she learned from Zukofsky—and that was the way to incorporate history into the poem.

Pound, in the early poems and in the *Cantos* (that "poem with history") and Williams in *In the American Grain* had used two techniques: first-person invented monologues by historical characters in the manner of Robert Browning, and the verbatim importation of historical documents. Reznikoff invented a third technique: the severe condensation of actual documents into first-person monologues or third-person narratives. It was a new way of performing poetry's traditional and largely lost function as a re-teller of tales.

He had begun—in the 1927 *Five Groups of Verse* and the 1929 "Editing and Glosses" series (which Zukofsky mentions)—by condensing passages from the Old Testament. In 1930, he first applied the technique to American history, using the diaries of Captain John Smith to write "The English in Virginia, April 1607," a poem that was included in *An 'Objectivists' Anthology*. Further poems were written soon after out of Spinoza, Marx, the *Mishnah*, more passages from the Bible, Jewish historical documents, and a book called *American History Told by Contemporaries*. He also began work on a series of prose poems based on a range of American documents, from ships' records to court cases. Originally called *My Country 'Tis of Thee* (parts of which are also in *An 'Objectivists' Anthology*) it was published in 1934 as *Testimony*—a wonderful book that has never been reprinted). In the 1960s and 1970s, he returned to condensing court cases, this time into poems, for his American anti-epic, also called *Testimony*, and for the devastating *Holocaust*, based on the Nuremberg trials.

In "Sincerity and Objectification," Zukofsky writes that "Interested in craft, Reznikoff has not found it derogatory to his production to infuse his care for significant detail and precision into the excellent verbalisms of others." Describing the Biblical versions, and anticipating the charges of 'impersonalness' or 'anyone could do it,' that later dogged Reznikoff, he notes: "The narrative has been rendered concisely in emphasized cadence and given the condition of Reznikoff's mental bearings and literal art." And, surprisingly, in a passage that is rarely cited, he says, "It is more important for the communal good that individual authors should spend their time recording and objectifying good writing wherever it is found . . . than that a plenum of authors should found their fame on all sorts of personal vagueness."

Niedecker first experimented with the method in 1945, with "Crèvecoeur," a condensation of *Letters from an American Farmer* into 45 long lines in the first person. The poem was unpublished, and she later condensed it further into two short, third-person poems in the "For Paul" sequence. These were followed by very short first-person poems taken out of the writings or letters of Kepler, the naturalist Aimé Bonpland, Linnaeus, John Adams, T. E. Lawrence, and Santayana, and third-person tiny capsule biographies of Margaret Fuller, Mary Shelley, and Swedenborg. Finally, in the

1960s, in her last years, more than half of her work was devoted to historical condensation: the great long sequences, "North Central" (out of Radisson, Joliet, Schoolcraft, and other explorers), "Thomas Jefferson," "His Carpets Flowered" (out of William Morris), and "Darwin," as well as short poems from or on Jefferson (again), John and Abigail Adams, Gerard Manley Hopkins, Michelangelo, and Wallace Stevens.

This was a return to one of poetry's primary traditional roles, as the repository for what a culture has known about itself. A role explored by only a handful of the American modernists: Pound, Williams (in *American Grain* and *Paterson*), Eliot (in *The Waste Land*), Reznikoff, Rexroth, Rukeyser, Olson, Duncan and, these days, perhaps only Susan Howe and Ed Sanders. Niedecker, among them, was the most extreme and the most crystalline. In her history poems, she was an intense lyric poet with epic content, and she has neither peers nor followers for her "holy / slowly / mulled over / matter."

[2004]

Gu Cheng

IN 1987, Gu Cheng wrote: "The poet is just like the fabled hunter who naps beside a tree, waiting for hares to break their skulls by running headlong into the tree trunk. After waiting for a long time, the poet discovers that he is the hare." These words turned out to be prophetic; six years later, his terrible and sordid crash against the tree would nearly obliterate what had come before. He had been a major cultural figure in contemporary China; now his poems were being read as flashbacks from his death.

He was born in 1956 in Beijing, the son of a well-known poet and army officer, Gu Gong. At 12, he wrote a two-line poem, "One Generation," that was to become an emblem of the new unofficial poetry:

Even with these dark eyes, a gift of the dark night
I go to seek the shining light

In 1969, the Cultural Revolution sent his family into the salt desert of Shandong Province to herd pigs. The locals spoke a dialect Gu Cheng could not understand, and in his isolation he became absorbed in the natural world: "Nature's voice became language in my heart. That was happiness." His favorite book was Jean-Henri Fabre's 19th century entomological notes and drawings; he collected insects and watched birds; he wrote poems in the sand with a twig, poems with titles like "The Nameless Little Flower" or "The Dream of the White Cloud." Like John Clare, he found his poems in the fields and wrote them down. He later said: "I heard a mysterious sound in nature. That sound became poetry in my life." He wrote that his "earliest experience of the nature of poetry" was a raindrop. His childhood was a vision of paradise from which he never recuperated.

He returned to Beijing in 1974, and worked in a factory. He wrote furiously, even—like Charles Olson—on the walls of his room. He hated the city, "those small light-filled boxes, the crucibles in which age-old humanity is melted down." He thought of himself as a live insect, "pinned to a board with its legs dancing." But he fell in with a group of poets—Bei Dao, Duo Duo, Yang Lian, Mang Ke, Shu Ting, and others—most of them seven or ten years older, who were producing China's first *samizdat* magazine, *Jintian* (*Today*). The literary expression of the new Democracy Wall movement—indeed, their first "issue" was a series of broadsides surreptitiously plastered on walls in Beijing—the group had rejected socialist realism, with its epics of revolutionary heroes and glorious harvests, to write first-person, introspective and imagistic lyrics.

One of Gu Cheng's earliest poems:

> Gray sky
> gray road
> gray buildings
> in the gray rain
>
> Through this wide dead grayness
> walk two children
> one bright red
> one pale green

was attacked by an official critic as *menglong,* and the word became attached to the group as a whole. *Menglong* literally means "misty," but without the sentimental and ephemeral associations the word has in English—"obscure" would be a less literal and more accurate translation. Bei Dao has suggested that they should simply be known as the *Today* Group, but unfortunately the "Misty Poets" has stuck in English. As Gu Cheng said at the time: "It's not misty at all. In fact, some things are becoming clearer."

They became the conscience of the generation and its pop stars. Bei Dao was their cerebral John Lennon and Gu Cheng their Bob Dylan, the lyrical *poète maudit.* They read their poems in stadiums packed with young people, and had slapstick adventures, straight out of *A Hard's Day Night,* escaping the throngs of adoring fans.

Officialdom didn't know what to with them. Their works were banned, and they were condemned in the Anti-Spiritual Pollution and Anti-Bourgeois Liberalism campaigns. In an act perhaps unprecedented in literature, Gu Cheng's father, Gu Gong, wrote an essay that begins: "I am growing more and more incapable of understanding my son's poetry. I am getting more and more annoyed." Full of phrases such as "the more I read, the more angry I get," "I became furious," "I became disappointed, miserable," the article finally, in the end, attempts a half-hearted reconciliation: Well, we must try to understand this new generation . . .

Gu Cheng's work took a crazy leap from introspective lyricism in 1981 with "Bulin's File," the first of his poem-sequences. Centered on a trickster figure, Bulin, much like the Monkey King of the classic Chinese novel, *The Journey to the West*—and Gu Cheng himself was born in the Year of the Monkey—it is a set of goofy fairy tales and deranged nursery rhymes that seem to have been written by a child who accidentally ate some hallucinogenic mushrooms:

> Everyone with long golden fingernails
> should have them cut
> because Bulin is out of work
> the newly sprouted moon is thin and curved
> because bars of gold and blocks of ice
> are about to be wed
> every home needs a combination lock
> every purse, a zipper
> because danger is born
> the crab and round brown cupcake crawl
> out of the film studio
> down to the beach

Although "Bulin" was unlike anything that had ever been written in Chinese—or probably any other language—Gu Cheng didn't consider it a poetic breakthrough. That was to come a few years later.

In 1983, he married a pretty student poet he had met on a train, Xie Ye. On their wedding day, he told her: "Let's commit suicide together." She was vivacious and practical; he was lost in a dream and often melancholic. He persuaded her to drop out of school so that they would remain inseparable.

In 1985, he had a revelation. Before, he had "tried to be a human being," but now he realized that the world was an illusion, and he learned to leave his self behind and inhabit a kind of shadow existence. Before, he had written "mainly lyrical poetry." Now he "discovered a strange and unique phenomenon: that words themselves acted like drops of liquid mercury splashing about, moving in any direction." He titled one of his long sequences "Liquid Mercury." He wrote: "Any word may be as beautiful as water so long as it is free of restraints."

In an interview with the translator Simon Patton, he said: "I thought the important thing about language at that time was not to change its form, not a question of how you used it—it wasn't a matter of taking this piece of wood and making a plank out of it . . . The important thing was to rap it—it turns into glass; rap it again and it turns to brass; again and to water. Changes in the texture of language." Patton writes: "Many of the characteristics of Gu Cheng's previous work (predictable rhyme, organization into stanzas, recoverable metaphor, recognizable themes) were jettisoned in an effort to forge new principles of organization. These principles—which include homophony, homography, graphic association (exploitation of various features of written Chinese characters), parataxis, deviant syntax and nonsense strings—were all inspired by an intensely anti-lyrical desire."

One of the "Liquid Mercury" poems reads:

> The overturned pail is seen from afar
>   dee dee da
>   delicate fish
>   dancing in the air
>
>   dee dee da dee da
>
> fish bring trees into the air
>   Dee dee da
>
> Fish bring trees into the
>   air
>   rust colored legs sticking up in the
>   air

What is extraordinary is that Gu Cheng, largely ignorant of Western modernism—the few poets he knew and admired in translation were Lorca, Tagore, Elytis, and Paz—had independently recreated much of the literary history of the 20th century. From the Imagism and Symbolism of the early lyrics, he had moved on to Dadaism or one of the Futurisms. (Two previous translators, Sean Golden and Chu Chiyu, said they were continually reminded of Gertrude Stein, whom Gu Cheng had never read.) He ultimately landed in some completely idiosyncratic corner of Surrealism. It is probably safe to say that Gu Cheng was the most radical poet in all of China's 2,500 years of written poetry.

In 1988, Gu Cheng and Xie Ye moved to New Zealand. At first, he had a job at the University of Auckland, teaching conversational Chinese. He would sit silently staring at his students, waiting for them to begin the conversation, and they would sit waiting for him to speak. Soon the students all stopped coming to class, and when eventually this was discovered, he was fired.

The couple moved into a dilapidated house without electricity or running water on Waiheke, an island in the Hauraki Gulf. It was Gu Cheng's attempt to regain the paradise of his childhood. They gathered shellfish and roots and berries—he wouldn't allow Xie Ye to cook—and got ill from eating the wrong things; they made spring rolls and crude pottery that they attempted to sell in a local market; they had a son whom they named Mu'er (Wood-Ear), after a fungus that grows on rotten wood, common in Chinese cuisine. Xie Ye typed and edited all his manuscripts, and he paid her in gold and silver play money that he painted. He refused to learn English, or any other language, for, he explained, "if a Chinese person learns another language, he will then lose his feeling of the existence of the Self, his being." He ruined their kitchen pots making lead casts of their footprints. He was always seen wearing a tall cylindrical hat that had been made from the leg of a pair of blue jeans.

This was more or less what I knew about Gu Cheng, and what was generally known, when I met him in 1992. That year, he was living in Berlin on a DAAD fellowship, and was visiting New York with four other poets from the *Today* group, in connection with an anthology of their earliest poems, *A Splintered Mirror*, edited by Donald Finkel and Carolyn Kizer (who referred to them as the "Misties.")

The first night, Gu Cheng, Xie Ye, and I went to a restaurant in Chinatown. As we sat down, my first question, predictably, was about his hat. He told me that he always wore it so that none of his thoughts would escape his head. Xie Ye said that he also slept in it, in order not to lose his dreams.

Gu Cheng picked up the menu and selected a dish. Xie Ye was amazed. He had never before ordered anything in a restaurant, preferring to eat whatever he was served. She then put a tape recorder on the table to record our conversation. She told me that everything Gu Cheng said should be preserved.

We talked for hours, but I understood little of it. Every topic immediately led to a disquisition on cosmic forces: the Cultural Revolution was like the chaos before creation in Chinese mythology, before things separated into yin and yang, and Tiananmen Square represented their continuing imbalance; Mao Zedong, in a way I couldn't follow, was somehow the embodiment of *wuwuwei*, Taoist non-non-action. Xie Ye gazed at him adoringly the whole time, and both of them radiated an innocent sweetness. With Gu Cheng, I felt I was in the presence of one of those crazy mountain sages of Chinese tradition.

Somewhere in the evening, Gu Cheng left for the bathroom, and as soon as he was out of sight, Xie Ye turned to me smiling and said, "I hope he dies." She explained that, in New Zealand, he had forced them to give their son to a Maori couple to raise, as Gu Cheng demanded her undivided attention and wanted to be the only male in the house. She said: "I can't get my baby back unless he is dead." I had just met them for the first time a few hours before.

Their private travails would soon become public knowledge. Before leaving for New Zealand, Gu Cheng had fallen in love—but had not yet had an affair—with a student, Li Ying, known as Ying'er. They continued to correspond, and Xie Ye came up with the scheme that by inviting Ying'er to Waiheke Island, she would be able to replace herself as wife, leave Gu Cheng, and be reunited with her son. She paid for Ying'er's ticket. Gu Cheng, however, wanted to live the life of the hero of *The Dream of the Red Chamber* (*The Story of the Stone*), as the prince of the "Kingdom of Daughters," surrounded by women improvising poetry in a pleasure garden far from the world. (Women, he said, were only beautiful when they did nothing.) Ying'er, in turn, though she did become Gu Cheng's lover, was appalled by their living conditions. After a year of a complicated arrangement, Gu

Cheng and Xie Ye left for Berlin to earn some money to fix up the house. Ying'er was supposed to wait for them, but disappeared, supposedly with a much older English martial arts instructor.

In Berlin, he wrote one of the strangest books ever written: *Ying'er*, which he called his "dream of the Gu Cheng chamber," a barely fictionalized account, with long passages of physical detail, of the love affair and its breakup. It is obsessive and hallucinated, narcissistic and self-pitying, precise and incoherent, kitschy and terrifying—in the end perhaps more of a document than a piece of literature, and now impossible to read at a purely aesthetic distance. Gu Cheng dictated the book on tape, and Xie Ye transcribed it, adding some paragraphs and chapters of her own to the story. Between typing the manuscript, Xie Ye began seeing another man. She told a friend: "My way is the way of death."

At the same time, he was writing some of his best poetry, particularly his last sequence, "City" (*Cheng*), a panoramic and simultaneist evocation of the Beijing he had hated and lost. (Under the chestnut trees in a park that summer, Gu Cheng was heard muttering to himself over and over, "I wonder what China looks like now.") The poem was autobiographical in ways that were not apparent. The title was the *Cheng* of his name, and at a public reading he introduced the poem by talking about his "horror of bus trips across Beijing, when the conductor yelled out, 'Next stop, Forbidden City (*Gugong*),' for it sounded like 'Next stop, Gu Gong,' my father." ("Family," he had written, "is the place where destruction begins.") Its occasional moments of violence are now read as auguries:

> They watched you
> they were not wearing clothes
> you did not feel it lasted long
> you were not wearing anything either
> I said there would be other programs that night
>
> I put my hand under my shirt
> one of my knives was gone
>
> I didn't believe leaving would be like this
> the knife was too short
> I let you walk ahead as swiftly as the wind

The most annoying thing about committing murder is finding
   the opportunity
she caught up with us
                what the hell was she doing
I stared at her in the hallway
girls cannot be killed

But yesterday they killed four
two in the bedroom   two at her door
you showed her the knife
saying   you were going to die
she smiled   asking how many kids you had

But, most of all, its collage of vignettes—as though written by a hallucinated William Carlos Williams—were meant to be self-erasing illusions in
an illusory world. "In my poetry," he had written, "the city disappears and
what appears instead is a piece of grazing land." In its way, it is the Taoist
version of the slogan the Situationists had written on the Democracy Walls
of Paris in 1968: "Under the sidewalk, the beach."

By all accounts, Gu Cheng had grown increasingly megalomaniacal and
violent. He had taken the parables of Chuang Tzu too literally and turned
them into a kind of "all things are permitted" to the Nietzschean superman.
In a speech in Frankfurt, he said: "He who follows the Tao is entitled to kill,
to kill himself, and in fact to do anything, as he is actually engaged in doing
nothing." Asked about Buddhism in an interview, he replied: "Buddhism
is for those who don't know. If you already know, then it no longer exists."
"But," he characteristically added, "everything is yours." He announced
that he had stopped writing, spent a great deal of his time sleeping, and
said that was his real work: "I only realize how cold the human heart is
when I wake up." He claimed that his favorite book, after Fabre, was now
Othello. He talked about buying a gun, tried to strangle Xie Ye, ended up
in a mental hospital, and was released a few days later when she refused to
press charges and assumed responsibility for him. He said that his greatest
happiness would be if Xie Ye killed him.

    They returned to New Zealand via Tahiti, where they visited the grave
of Paul Gauguin, and arrived back on Waiheke Island on September 24,

1993, his 37th birthday. On October 8, Gu Cheng murdered Xie Ye with an ax, and then hanged himself.

Ying'er was published in China a few weeks later, and the story became a sensation for highbrows and lowbrows. In New Zealand, it was treated as an extreme example of spousal abuse, but in China it was seen as symbolic of the spiritual desolation of the generation that had come of age in the Cultural Revolution, or the tortured life of the exile, or the tortured life of the artist, or the oppressiveness of the Chinese male, or the tragic life of the muse. It seemed that everyone who had ever known them weighed in with a book or article, some calling Gu Cheng a monster, some saying Xie Ye had turned him into one. Gu Cheng's mother said that the troubles had begun when he had fallen out of a window as a child and suffered brain damage. Ying'er herself wrote a book called *Heartbroken on Waiheke*, which had a preface by an ex-boyfriend to show that Gu Cheng was not the only man in her life. There was even a drippy movie, "The Poet," with a beautiful un-clothed Japanese starlet as Ying'er. Gu Cheng and Xie Ye had become the Chinese Ted and Sylvia.

It is a Taoist paradox: When you forget about Gu Cheng, you can begin to read him.

In one of his last letters, Gu Cheng wrote: "If you read my book, you'll know that I'm completely mad. Only my hands are normal."

He wrote: "When I walk the road of my imagination, between heaven and earth there is only myself and a type of light-green grass."

He wrote: "The deepest of me has never been more than eight years old."

[2005]

KENNETH COX

T HERE ARE CERTAIN writers who live long and write little, whose every line reflects long rumination and endless revision, and who achieve an almost mineral hard perfection. Kenneth Cox was one of those, but, perhaps uniquely, he was neither a poet nor a writer of short fictions, but a literary critic.

He published his first, and only, book of essays at age 85. Its title carried understatement to austerity: *Collected studies in the use of English.* (Cox always insisted on the Romance language lower-case style for titles.) With equal allure, an earlier version of the manuscript was called *Preliminary expositions of the work of some 20th century writers. Collected studies* consisted of essays, many of them previously unpublished, on seventeen writers: nine modern masters (Pound, Joyce, Wyndham Lewis, Yeats, Conrad, Zukofsky, Niedecker, MacDiarmid, Bunting); three contemporary poets (Creeley, Turnbull, Alan Jenkins); the 19th century novelist George Gissing; an obscure novelist named R. C. Hutchinson; the modernist polymath Allen Upward; and a close look at a stanza by Chaucer. It is unclear how much else he wrote. His other published book is a translation of a novel, *Eyes Shut,* by the early Italian modernist Federigo Tozzi. There are some scattered short book reviews, and in his letters to me he mentions a translation of a long poem by Leopardi, an essay on Céline, and a poem of his own, "The manor." I don't know if these were ever published, or if there are other writings.

I never met him, and knew nothing about his life. I heard he held some midlevel position in the BBC. He corresponded with some of the writers he wrote about, most notably Niedecker, but said he had no literary friends.

In the early 1980s he wrote me that I was his only active supporter; in the 1960s he had appeared in *Agenda* and later would be a semi-regular in the Australian magazine *Scripsi*. I assumed he lived alone—his letters had the cranky obsession with detail of the isolated—and I imagined him as a kind of George Smiley, an anonymous bureaucrat in a somewhat rundown small flat, smoking, drinking, reading.

In the 1970s, I published whatever he sent me in a magazine I edited called *Montemora*, and for years I would periodically try to find a publisher for a book of his essays. Our correspondence was friendly enough, but somewhere around the twentieth letter, I made the mistake of addressing him "Dear Kenneth." I was sharply rebuked, and he remained "Mr. Cox" until the letters petered out in the mid-1980s. I regret now that I didn't stay in touch, but our letters were exclusively about publishing his work, and there was nothing to say. I still tried to find a publisher, and hoped some-day I could send him good news. After his death in 2005 at age 89, I was surprised to find that he had a family, was brawny and robust, an excellent cook and, unexpectedly, a lifelong Marxist. More exactly to my image, I also learned that he spoke twelve languages, hated England, but after serving in World War II almost never left it.

What Cox wrote were incredibly precise descriptions. I once wrote him that he reminded me of a 19th century British naturalist whose flora and fauna were writers, but he corrected me, saying his style pertained to the 18th; he didn't explain further. As a critic, he advanced no theories or ideology, and (despite his own) was uninterested in the ideologies of his subjects: MacDiarmid's Marxism or Pound's fascism. He was an advocate only inso-far as he chose certain writers to study. His erudition was immense, but only occasionally visible in a modest aside; he was never dazzling like Kenner or Davenport. He may be the only critic with whom one never disagrees; his descriptions and analyses of technique had a kind of scientific accuracy. And he may be the only critic to describe, with equal precision, what it is like to read a given writer.

In his writing, he clearly belonged to the Bunting and Niedecker school of condensation. (In 1969, Niedecker asks Cid Corman if he would be inter-ested in Cox's 30-page poem, "The manor" for *Origin*; in 1978, Cox writes me that the poem is 100 lines long.) The manuscript I have of *Preliminary investigations* looks like an FBI file obtained under the Freedom of Information Act, with many words and sentences blacked out and almost nothing added. He had no time for transitional phrases, and notoriously disliked commas, particularly serial commas. Eliminating the pauses, curiously, had the opposite effect of slowing down, rather than speeding up, the reading. Allen Upward, not an obvious choice, was a prose ideal:

> Hardly a page of Upward passes without some such observation immediately acceptable yet in context so illuminating, the reader is brought up short. The constant recurrence of the feature in passages dealing with matter of great difficulty creates an almost continuous sense of intellectual elation hard to match in modern English. It is further enhanced by a device cultivated in ancient China and found in a few European writers of superior intelligence like Machiavelli Montesquieu and Lichtenberg. These, having made some remark briefly clearly and distinctly formulated, do not stay to amplify but leave the reader to draw from it what conclusions he can at his own peril.

He wrote by far the best essays on Bunting, MacDiarmid, Niedecker, Upward, and Zukofsky, and the best short overview of the *Cantos*. Lorine Niedecker said her poem "Paean to Place" was "set going" by a letter from Cox. She wrote to Cid Corman that "Kenneth Cox says he is not a critic—rather an essayist. I saw the LN essay but nothing else he's written. I think the English are silent, hiding-away people—they've been to the silence of the moon already, I guess. Maybe because of the money situation." (In another letter, she mentions that Cox is learning Dutch.) Jenny Penberthy's great edition of Niedecker's *Collected Works* is dedicated to him. A few years ago, Jenny asked for a blurb in an unsuccessful attempt to drum up some interest in *Collected studies*. I wrote: "Kenneth Cox is the model for how criticism would be written if there were anyone other than Cox who could write it."

[2005]

THE CRITIC NATKIRA

ACCORDING TO THE 16th century Indian poet, Dhurjati, there was a king of Madurai who offered a thousand gold coins to anyone who could compose a poem that would be praised by the critics in his court.

Fierce winds destroyed the crops that year, and a poor but devout farmer prayed to Shiva for his mercy. Shiva appeared, and gave the farmer an erotic poem to present to the king.

After the farmer read the poem to the royal assembly, one of the critics, Natkira, objected to the poem's claim that women by their nature have fragrant hair. This had not been stated in the *Alankara Shastra*, the treatise on aesthetics which delineated how humans or gods could be described. The poem was rejected, and the farmer, who knew nothing about poetry, implored Shiva to appear again and, with great embarrassment, gave him back the poem.

Shiva decided to go to the palace to defend his poem. He asked the assembly what was wrong with it, whether there was anything lacking in the three qualities of verse: its features, its embellishment, or its sentiment. These were irreproachable, said the critic Natkira, but one cannot say that women's hair is naturally fragrant.

Shiva replied that Parvati's hair, perfumed or not, always smelled sweet. Natkira countered that she was a god and not a human, and moreover, personal experiences were irrelevant. Naturally fragrant hair was not permitted by the *Alankara Shastra*.

At this, the god became enraged and revealed his terrifying third eye of flame. The critic said: "I don't care if you have eyes all over your head. Your poem is no good." So Shiva cursed him and turned him into a leper.

[2005]

BECKETT / PAZ

On the flowers the angel of the mist
scattered pearly moisture from his wings,
and Aurora floated on the air,
enveloped in her gauzy topaz robe.

It was the nuptial hour. The earth lay sleeping,
virginal, beneath the bashful veil,
and to surprise her with his amorous kisses
the royal sun inflamed the firmament.

WHO WOULD SUSPECT that the officiants at this pastelled marriage of heaven and earth were none other than two of the primary architects of postwar international modernism? If part of the Surrealist project depended on the fortuitous conjunction of disparate elements in an unlikely place, then surely one of its oddest late productions was an unassuming book called *An Anthology of Mexican Poetry*. For far beyond its ostensible subject matter, the book was the result of an improbable encounter between Octavio Paz and Samuel Beckett on the field of classical Mexican literature.

In 1949, Beckett was forty-three and Paz thirty-five. Both were living in Paris, and both were generally broke. Beckett was trying to find a producer for his play, *Waiting for Godot*, and a publisher for *Molloy*, the first of his trilogy of novels. (His earlier novel, *Murphy*, had sold exactly six copies in its first year of publication.) Paz, though known in Mexico as a young poet, was just finishing the books that would propel his international reputation,

The Labyrinth of Solitude and *The Bow and the Lyre*. His first major long poem, *Sunstone*, was still some years away.

Paz had a low-level position at the Mexican embassy. Beckett was surviving on literary hackwork, some of it for UNESCO, which was then sponsoring a series of representative works of world literature in translation. Beckett called it "that inexhaustible cheese," though his own life at the time, according to his biographer Deirdre Bair, was more rat than mouse: sleeping all day and roaming the streets of Paris all night.

The UNESCO cheese lured Paz into a project for which he had little enthusiasm: an anthology of Mexican poetry to be translated into French and English. Paz, an anti-nationalist, would have preferred to consider Spanish American poetry as a whole. And worse, in Mexico, between the twin volcanoes of the 17th and 20th century poetries lay a gloomy valley of some two hundred years of largely feeble European imitations.

The book was further encumbered when a well-known Mexican poet, Jaime Torres Bodet, became the director of UNESCO. Torres Bodet, with the once-prevalent inferiority complex of the Third World intellectual in the halls of European culture, insisted that each edition should be validated with introductory remarks by a local poohbah. For the French edition, Torres Bodet chose Paul Claudel, then eighty-one, decades past his best poetry, and largely preoccupied with theological questions. For the English, he asked Sir Cecil Maurice Bowra, the Hellenist and warden of Wadham College, Oxford. Neither had the least interest in Mexico. Bowra's introduction, called "Poetry and Tradition," cheerfully rambles for pages through world poetry—not excluding that of the Ainu, the Asiatic Tartars, and "branches of the Southern Slavonic"—until it finally settles, in the third-to-last sentence, on the subject at hand. That sentence—Bowra's only comment on the matter—informs us that Mexico has a "vivid and varied culture." Claudel—identified on the book's cover as "de L'Académie Française"—seems, from the first sentence ("La poésie est un art.") to be dictating in his sleep. With some rhetorical flourishes about the Muses and epic poetry—though there are no epics in the anthology—he surveys his version of world literature (Verlaine, Baudelaire, Rimbaud, Valéry, Boileau, Racine, Bergson . . .), and explicates in detail two lines of Virgil. Mexico is not mentioned at all.

Paz was, as he recalls, furious, and further disappointed when Torres Bodet decided that Alfonso Reyes, the Grand Old Man of Mexican letters, would be the only living poet admitted in the book. This meant eliminating the work of poets such as Xavier Villaurrutia and José Gorostiza, members of the *Contemporáneos* (Contemporaries), the vibrant and internationalist Mexican poetry group that had flourished in the 1930s and 40s, and was so important to Paz's own writing.

Paz was responsible for finding the translators for the two editions. For the French he commissioned Guy Lévis Mano, a poet and Spanish translator who remains known as one of the great printers of the Surrealist movement, producing limited editions of texts by Breton, Tzara, Michaux, Char, and Soupault, with artwork by Giacometti, Picasso, Man Ray, Miró, and others. For the English, someone suggested Samuel Beckett, whom Paz knew slightly through their mutual publication in Max-Pol Fouchet's magazine *Fontaine*. An obstacle that would daunt lesser, or less hungry, mortals— Beckett's total ignorance of the Spanish language—was quickly overcome. Beckett had "a friend" who would help, and he had, after all, studied Latin at Trinity College.

Beckett completed his work in March or April of 1950. The original manuscript, now in Texas, includes two pages of notes, "not in Beckett's hand," on the translation of specific words, as well as corrections and additions "mostly in another hand." (No one knows to whom these hands belonged.) The French edition was published in 1952 by Editions Nagel, had one printing, and vanished. The English language edition, delayed for unknown reasons until 1958, appeared simultaneously from Thames & Hudson in the UK and the Indiana University Press. Thanks in part to its unusual collaborators, it has remained in print in paperback ever since, an extraordinarily long publishing run for what is, after all, a collection of otherwise generally arcane texts.

Years later, Beckett would write that his work on the Mexican anthology was strictly an "alimentary chore," and that the poems were "execrable for the most part." Certainly those martinets of the bilingual dictionary who normally review poetry translations would have a field day with Beckett: He drops lines from poems, writes "twenty" for "seventy." He is hopelessly lost among Mexican flora and fauna, confusing macaws and macaques, tigers and jaguars, magueys and aloes. (When the going gets really rough, in Alfonso Reyes' "Tarahumara Herbs," he randomly selects Old World plants to stand in for the Mexican.) He's clearly unfamiliar with such things as the Aztec calendar stone, which he calls "a stone of sun." Sometimes he's mysterious, as when a *sinfonía lograda* (a fully-realized symphony) becomes a "symphony of positive esthetics." Sometimes, he's just being Beckett, as when the last lines of Ignacio Rodríguez Galván's poem (which mean, literally, "Dream, be my passage through the world, / until that new dream, sweet and graceful, / shows me the sublime face of God.") are clipped to "Dream, in thy safe keeping let me come / to this world's end . . . " (Even in a translation, Godot can never arrive.) And in many of the poems he seems to be on autopilot, cruising until he can reach the next poem.

Yet Beckett's Mexican anthology is one of the liveliest English translations of the century. Its greatest achievement is its recreation of that sense of reading old texts, the distance between us and them. (One has it in one's own language, but rarely in translation, which tends to be written according to present-day usage, whatever present-day it is.) Beckett accomplishes this through a subtle mimicking—and who, besides Joyce, was a better mimic?—of the English poetry contemporary to whatever period he is translating. And he displays a stupefyingly vast command of English archaicisms that will send any diligent reader deep into the *OED*: "grateless" for ungrateful; "cramoisy" for crimson; "featly" for graceful; "ensample" for example; "cark" for anxiety or grief; "adust" for scorched; "flower-de-luce" for iris; "monachal" for monastic; "fatidic" for prophetic; "tilths" for tillable land; "popinjay" for parrot; "mede" for recompense; as well as "chalchuite"—an archaic derivative from the Nahuatl word *chalchihuite*—for turquoise, to name only some. In two cases, even the *OED* doesn't help: "wildering" for wandering; and a bird's "crawy" call. Did Beckett make them up, did someone misread his notorious crabbed handwriting, or are these actually lacunae in the definitive dictionary? With Beckett's erudition, one never knows: "Gyps" seems to be a typographical error for "gypsum," but it turns out to be an obsolete form. "Bird of Phasis" seems an odd translation of "pheasant," but the word derives from the Phasis River where the birds once abounded.

Moreover, he has created a vivid music for each poem by avoiding the end-rhymes of the Spanish (while still suggesting the original prosody through complex internal rhymes) and by breaking the lines where the English, not the original, demands it. He can take a sow's ear, like the opening two lines of Amado Nervo's "An Old Burden," and turn it, if not quite to silk, then into a purse with some inner compartments. Nervo's lines mean, literally:

Who is that siren with the voice so painful,
with flesh so white, with tresses so dark brown?

Beckett transforms this to:

Who is yonder siren so distressed
of voice, so white of flesh, so dark of tress?

The "yonder" may be a bit much, but the rhymes of "distressed," "flesh," and "tress" are more complex than the original, which doesn't rhyme at all. The poem sings, as it doesn't in Spanish. And the play between "distressed" and "tress," which Beckett made up, no doubt made his day's (or night's) work more amusing.

There are whole poems, such as the Nervo, that are far better in English than Spanish, and quite a few individual lines are simply more intense in the translation:

greeny sea-wrack coils a snaky tress
(Balbuena)

In such throng of dead forms thou didst not die
(Sandoval y Zapata)

Space is azure and the mountains bathe
in vivid azure and in azure shade
(Rodríguez Galván)

For the people the bard is grace not cark
(Díaz Mirón)

A precious pearl in the slaver of a mollusc
(Díaz Mirón)

and throughout that brooding and adust
savannah, not a path, not a track
(Othón)

what a wildering midst ruins and pits!
                    (Othón)

and many books made me all-ignorant
                    (González Martínez)

or the Yeatsian:

the tower riddled in the slinging winds
                    (López Velarde)

We will never know whether Beckett, despite later denials, was secretly enchanted with some of the poems, or whether, with a writer like Beckett, his hackwork would be anybody else's masterpiece. But no matter how or why it was written, fifty years later the book still remains the best introduction in English to classical Mexican poetry, and the repository of some remarkable poems. It stands, in some strange way, next to that other great, late 1940s invention of Mexico in English, *Under the Volcano*.

Certainly it is as impossible to imagine Beckett in Mexico as it is to imagine Malcolm Lowry anywhere else. And yet one wonders if there was not a shock of recognition when Beckett read the first page of the manuscript Paz gave him. It contained what is perhaps the first sonnet written in Mexico, by the first Mexican Spanish poet, Francisco de Terrazas. Had Beckett never translated Mexican poetry, we might never have made the connection. But because of his presence, a curious loop forms. For Mexican poetry begins not in the expected grand and tragic spectacle of the Conquest, but with a single individual in a desolate landscape, a nobody suffering in nowhere, that dismal world for which Beckett, centuries later, would be the great cartographer:

I dreamed that I was thrown from a crag
by one who held my will in servitude,
and all but fallen to the griping jaws
of a wild beast in wait for me below.

In terror, gropingly, I cast around
for wherewith to uphold me with my hands,

and the one closed about a trenchant sword,
and the other twined about a little herb.

Little and little the herb came swift away,
and the sword ever sorer vexed my hand
as I more fiercely clutched its cruel edges . . .

Oh wretched me, and how from self estranged,
that I rejoice to see me mangled thus
for dread of ending, dying, my distress!

[1994 / 2006]

SUSAN HOWE'S *My Emily Dickinson*

"I'M NOBODY!"—and it is indeed difficult to recuperate how much of a nobody Emily Dickinson once was. Take two classic literary histories: The 560 pages of Van Wyck Brooks' *The Flowering of New England* (1936) mention her only twice in passing. In the 660 oversize pages of F. O. Matthiessen's *American Renaissance* (1941), she is allotted a short paragraph: The "compressed form" of her poems "resulted from her need to resolve conflicts," which Matthiessen does not detail. "Her ideals of language, indeed her very tricks of phrase, seem indistinguishable from those" of Emerson, though she "does not have any of his range as a social critic." Even as late as 1980, she does not appear at all in John T. Irwin's *American Hieroglyphics*. D. H. Lawrence doesn't mention her in *Studies in Classic American Literature* (1923). Ezra Pound found room for John Greenleaf Whittier and James Whitcomb Riley in his anthology *From Confucius to Cummings* (1958), but did not include her. The once-important Georgian poet Harold Monro declared in 1925 that she is "intellectually blind, partially deaf, and mostly dumb to the art of poetry": "Her tiny lyrics appear to be no more than the jottings of a half-idiotic school-girl instead of the grave musings of a full grown, fully educated woman." George Whicher, who cared enough to compile a Dickinson bibliography in 1930, stated that "art forms were totally unknown to her":

> Her inadvertencies and slipshod lapses have been soberly defended as beauties beyond the comprehension of the vulgar, and her name has been invoked to support the predilections of her critics for movements in verse that she could never have heard of.

In the most influential essay of the time, Allen Tate in 1932 compared her to John Donne—the New Critics compared everyone to John Donne—in that she "*perceives abstraction* and *thinks sensation*," but writes that the difference is her "ignorance, her lack of formal intellectual training . . . She cannot reason at all. She can only *see*." Even more: "Her intellectual deficiency was her greatest distinction." Charles Olson refers to her only once, in an early draft of *Call Me Ishmael* (1947): "Dickinson loved Christ but jilted Him and married Death. Her stretch and yawn for the grave strained her nature, poisoned it."

Robert Duncan writes to Denise Levertov in 1960:

> Have you seen the new edition of Emily Dickinson's poems, restoring her punctuation? So that we see she was nearer akin than we might have suspected. The dashes (are spaces) articulate the line. And what a lovely measure, what an immediate thing comes out!

Levertov replies:

> You know, actually those dashes bother me—it seems to give a monotony of tone. I can't quite explain it. . . . There's something cold and perversely smug about E. D. that has always rebuffed my feeling for individual poems of hers extending itself to her work as a whole. She wrote some great things—saw strangely—makes one shudder with new truths—but ever and again one feels (or I do)—"Jesus, what a bitchy little spinster."

Duncan answers: "I'll not give at all on your sense of Emily Dickinson . . . her work comes thru to me without any interfering about her personality." And, a few years later, Levertov has changed her mind—at least about the dashes—and reports to Duncan on an evening with Robert Lowell:

> Imagine, it had *never occurred* to him to think of Emily Dickinson's dashes as aural notations, rests or rallentandos. He had supposed them to be merely a sort of scribbles, meaning nothing, presumably intended by E. D. to be *filled in* with "proper"

punctuation later. At first in a prideful immodest way he vigor-
ously denied they could be anything more. Eventually tho', he
evidently decided to mull over this "new idea."

Robert Creeley and Louis Zukofsky, though fellow masters of compression, did not write about her. (Zukofsky wanted three poems for his 1948
anthology, *A Test of Poetry*, but thought the permissions fee too high: $25.)
Kenneth Rexroth declared that Dickinson "is the equal of any woman poet
of the century except Christina Rosetti and the Brontë sisters." But Lorine
Niedecker—who would be compared to Dickinson far too often—included
her among the ten writers in her "immortal cupboard," and cited an 1891
letter from a prescient Alice James: "It is reassuring to hear the English
pronouncement that Emily Dickinson is fifth-rate—they have such a capacity for missing quality." Marianne Moore, in a 1933 review of the *Letters*,
praised Dickinson in her fashion:

> Dickinson has been accused of vanity. A certain buoyancy that
> creates an effect of inconsequent bravado—a sense of drama
> with which we may not be quite at home—was for her part of
> that expansion of breath necessary to existence, and unless it
> is conceited for the hummingbird or the osprey to not behave
> like a chicken, one does not find her conceited.

Others saw themselves, or what they wanted to see. Hart Crane to
Gorham Munson, 1928: "Some of Blake's poems and Emily Dickinson's
seem more incontrovertible than ever since Relativity and a host of other
ideologies, since evolved, have come into recognition." H. D. to Bryher,
1924: "Really very nice crystalline stuff." Moore again, complaining of
the characterization of Dickinson as a "rare thing, the truly unartificial
spirit": "One resents the cavil that makes idiosyncracy out of individuality." Allen Ginsberg, 1980: "a fly buzzing when you died like Emily
Dickinson brings you back mindful to the room where / you sit and keep
breathing aware of the walls around you and the endless blue sky above
your mind."

And then there is William Carlos Williams—with Olson and Susan
Howe herself, the most Americanist of American poets—whose lines from
the "Jacataqua" section of *In the American Grain* (1925) are the epigraph

to this book, and against which, we learn in the first sentence, this book is written:

> It is the women above all—there never have been women, save pioneer Katies, not one in flower save some moonflower Poe may have seen, or an unripe child. Poets? Where? They are the test. But a true woman in flower, never. Emily Dickinson, starving of passion in her father's garden, is the very nearest we have ever been—starving.
>
> Never a woman: never a poet. There's an axiom. Never a poet saw sun here.

In Williams' prose, it is often difficult to know what he means, as the sentences, passionate and enthusiastic but often abstract, tend to undermine or contradict one another. "Jacataqua," a simultaneous jeremiad and reverie on, among other things, the American woman, is no exception. Elsewhere in the essay he refers to Dickinson as "about the only woman one can respect for her clarity."

Four years later, reviewing Kay Boyle's *Short Stories*, he writes:

> Awake, Emily Dickinson was torn apart by her passion; driven back to cover she imprisoned herself in her father's garden, the mark of the injury she deplored, an opacity beyond which she could not penetrate. And in literature, since it is of literature that I am writing, it is the mark of our imprisonment by sleep, the continuous mark, that in estimating the work of E. D., still our writers praise her rigidity of the sleep walker—the rapt gaze, the thought of Heaven—and ignore the structural warping of her lines, the rhymelessness, the distress marking the place at which she turned back. She was a beginning, a trembling at the edge of waking—and the terror it imposes. But she could not, and so it remains.

In 1934, in an essay on "The American Background," he writes: "[Emerson] was a poet, in the making, lost. His spiritual assertions were intended to be basic, but they had not—and they have not today—the authenticity of Emily Dickinson's unrhymes. And she was of the same school, rebelliously." (The next sentence, beginning a new paragraph, reads: "It is impressive to experience the reflection of the American dearth in culture among women.") Two years later, in correspondence with the young poet Mary Barnard, he complains that Barnard's poems are too delicate:

> I don't ask anyone to be indelicate. That isn't it. But when a person has little actual experience of bodily contacts, when we can't get to the world hard enough or fast enough—and yet we must write—then we are likely to draw out a fund of material and make it do—and do too often—over and over—and it gets hard to keep from getting brittle. Emily Dickinson (I swore I wasn't going to use her name) succeeded by hammering her form obstinately into some kind of homespun irregularity that made it do—but even at her best—it is too far gone to heaven—too much the wish for what it might have been—to be an example for many.

[A strange conjunction: In 1979, a Japanese scholar, Hiroko Uno, claimed that the frontispiece of Volume II of Richard Sewall's *The Life of Emily Dickinson* is not a photograph of the poet, but rather of Williams' maternal grandmother, "born in England about the same time," and whose name was Emily Dickenson.]

By the time of the writing of this book, in the early 1980s, Dickinson's complexities tended to be lost, as Howe says in an interview, "in the reductive portrait of a spinster genius clothed in white à la Miss Havisham . . . a spidery recluse, a Queen at Home, sewing." Criticism concentrated on "neurosis, repression, rejection." Dickinson was, in the title of a popular feminist critique, *The Madwoman in the Attic*, driven there by the society-at-large, inhabiting the only space allowed an intelligent and sensitive woman.

Howe's mission was to avoid further psychological speculation and revisionist politics to present Dickinson in the kind of literary, intellectual, and historical context in which male poets are routinely considered. Against the cliché of Dickinson as some sort of Rousseauian natural spirit, producing quirky, unlettered effusions, Howe's Emily Dickinson is an erudite, and she tracks the poems through a vast amount of reading: Shakespeare, the Brontës, the Brownings, Spenser, Shelley, Keats, Blake, Ruskin,

Thoreau, Emerson, James Fenimore Cooper . . . the company in which, from the distance she did not perceive as a distance, Dickinson thought she was writing. Against the isolated neurotic, Howe's Dickinson is fully aware of events, including the Civil War, in the world outside. Howe goes backward, down into the roots, to show Dickinson as a sensibility and intelligence formed by Puritanism, the New England frontier, Jonathan Edwards and the Great Awakening. And against the image of the naive artist, the homebound stitcher of "inadvertent" words, Howe—as Williams had hinted at and Duncan had perceived—claims Dickinson as consciously a revolutionist of the word: with Stein, one of the two great American women avant-gardists.

It is astonishing that Howe accomplishes all this in less than 150 pages, but this is a poet's book, a classic of writers writing on writers (and others), on that short shelf with Lawrence's *Studies*, Olson's *Ishmael*, Williams' *American Grain*, Duncan's still-uncollected *The H. D. Book*, Simone Weil's *The Iliad, or the Poem of Force*, H. D.'s *Tribute to Freud*, Zukofsky's *Bottom: On Shakespeare*—all of which Howe has noted as inspirational in the writing of this book. In the endless dialogues of literature, *My Emily Dickinson* seems to be talking most to *Call Me Ishmael*. Olson/Melville and Howe/Dickinson form a yin and yang beyond male and female: Olson's Figure of Outward against the Figure of Inward and the Amherst attic where Olson's famous first sentence ("I take SPACE to be the central fact to man born in America . . .") does not apply.

Howe would go from here to the well-known essay, "These Flames and Generosities of the Heart" (in *The Birth-Mark*, 1993), which demonstrated how the standard "stanzaic" transcription of Dickinson's poems is an editorial invention quite different from the way she actually laid out the lines on the page. Poets got it immediately; the Dickinsonians found it scandalous.

The writing of writers on writers tends to last longer than standard literary criticism, and not only because it is better written. Critics explain their subjects; in writers' books, the subject is explaining the author. *My Emily Dickinson* and the later essay forever altered—at least, in certain quarters—how Dickinson is read. Yet, at the same time, it is remarkable how many passages in the book seem to be describing the poems that Susan Howe would write in the decades after.

Jean Cocteau (in the first *New Directions* anthology in 1936) called his

James Laughlin

Heir to a steel fortune, James Laughlin IV grew up in a mansion in Pittsburgh where the "inside" servants were Irish and the "outside" servants black, where, in the summer, the windows were fitted with frames of cheesecloth that had to be washed of soot every day. The Mellons lived across the street; the Carnegies nearby. Henry Clay Frick, who brought in the militia against the striking Homestead steelworkers, was a great-uncle. Strict Presbyterians, Irish who pretended to be Scottish, they were religious provincials who had found sudden wealth, much like today's oil sheikhs. "At one house," Laughlin wrote, "the butler passed chewing gum on a silver salver after the coffee." There were daily prayers and Bible readings, with the servants standing in attendance. (The Catholics were excused). The Sunday comic strips could not be read until Monday. "Books were used for decoration in the living room. The only person who ever took them off the shelves was the parlor maid who dusted them." The family traveled in its own private Pullman car.

His grandfather, James Jr., had made the money. His father, Henry, quit the business on the day James Jr. died, and devoted himself to duck-hunting and fly-fishing, yachting and golf, chemin-de-fer in the casino at Deauville, race cars at Chantilly and, in the words of his son, "the pursuit on two continents of oiselettes, whom he always treated with liberality and kindness." Stuck babysitting his two young sons on an afternoon in London, he took them to a brothel and hired one of the ladies to play checkers with the boys while he was occupied upstairs. His mother "could not wait to go to Jesus."

James III was an eccentric uncle. James IV, born in 1914, attended Le Rosey in Switzerland, where, according to his maternal grandfather, he was unfortunately overexposed to "medical knowledge"; a classmate was the future Shah of Iran ("a stinker"). At Choate he was "Best Boy" and excelled at midget football. The Laughlins were Princeton men—they had endowed a Laughlin Hall on campus and his brother in adult life had a large collection of tiger knickknacks—but James scandalized the family by choosing Harvard, where the Brahmins considered him a yokel from the "West." Harvard in those days was a place where decorators furnished one's dorm room, maids cleaned it daily, and tailors came to measure the lads for the evening wear required for the regular debutante balls. James' pal Joe Pulitzer kept a French mistress in the Boston Ritz.

At fifteen, his father gave him a thirty-foot yacht to cruise the inland waterways on their trips to Florida. At twenty-one, in the midst of the Depression, his father wrote him a check for $100,000—in today's money, many millions—to get him started in life. James grew up to be a handsome playboy and a competitive sportsman, at home in the Lichtenstein Palace, in the pages of *Town & Country*, on the golf links with Rockefellers and James Jesus Angleton, the CIA spook, or with Texas oilmen at a testimonial dinner for T. Boone Pickens. He spoke in the slangy speech of the tuxedoed screwballs of 1930s comedies, and he inhabited the kind of world where, on a ski trip in the Austrian Alps, Herbert von Karajan's chauffeured limousine would take him to the top of the mountain and, when he split his ski pants, the Queen of Holland immediately produced her sewing kit and patched them up. He founded the Alta ski resort in Utah, spent months of most years on its slopes, and received a Lifetime Achievement Award from the International Ski History Association. A registered Republican, he lived in Meadow House, a large family estate in Connecticut, where sheep grazed outside his dining room window.

That, of course, was only a fraction of the story. At Choate, under the guidance of his classics teacher, Dudley Fitts, James discovered the Moderns. He began writing in the modern style, collecting first editions from the Gotham Book Mart, and entering into ardent correspondence with writers. "Jay will not, I think, write the American *Ulysses*," Fitts commented. "He will not, so far as I am now able to judge, write anything but the world's rudest letters."

At 19, he dropped out of Harvard and went to France to work for Gertrude Stein, also of Pittsburgh, whom he called the "most charismatic pyramid ever built." His official task was writing press releases for a forthcoming lecture tour, "boiling down cerebral Steinese into simple journalese." His primary occupation, however, was to go on daily drives in the country and change the frequent flat tires while Gertrude and Alice picnicked nearby. Stein found him "extremely useful," but fired him when she caught him reading Proust: "She was deeply offended. 'J,' she asked, 'how can you read such stuff? Don't you know that Proust and Joyce copied their books from my *Making of Americans?*' "

From France he made his way to Rapallo to sit at the feet of Ezra Pound and to become the only student at what he called the Ezuversity: daily lunches, long walks, and longer monologues on everything under the Italian sun. There occurred one of the legendary moments of modernism, a story Laughlin, with his almost compulsive self-deprecation, would repeat endlessly: Pound "said I was such a terrible poet, I'd better do something useful and become a publisher, a profession which [he] inferred required no talent and only limited intelligence."

Pound persuaded Laughlin to return to Harvard so that his family would support him in his new venture and, in 1936, while he was still a student, New Directions was launched with what would be the first of more than fifty annual (and later semi-annual) anthologies. *New Directions in Prose & Poetry*, subtitled *Indirect Criticism/ Surrealism/ Dream Writing*, had no page numbers—the novice publisher forgot to include them—but it did have a hot-blooded introduction by Laughlin himself, and contributions by Pound, Wallace Stevens, William Carlos Williams (one of his greatest poems, "Perpetuum Mobile: The City"), Henry Miller, Elizabeth Bishop, E. E. Cummings, Louis Zukofsky, and Jean Cocteau, among others.

In the first five years, Laughlin brought out about forty books, selling them to bookstores out of his station wagon, and mainly concentrating on the American moderns who had nowhere else to publish: Pound, Williams, Miller, Delmore Schwartz, Kay Boyle, Kenneth Patchen. But those years also saw New Directions' entry into the Internationale of the "revolution of the word" proclaimed by *transition* magazine: Dylan Thomas, García Lorca, Kafka's *Amerika*, and Schwartz's translation of Rimbaud, based on near-total ignorance of French.

Laughlin, however, knew his French—and Italian and German—traveled to Europe frequently, and had the extraordinary knack of taking only the good advice from writers urging him to publish other writers. Beginning in the 1940s, the scope of the press expanded. One needs to take a deep breath to recite the writers for whom New Directions was an early, and usually the first, American publisher. Thomas and García Lorca were followed by Neruda, Sartre, Brecht, Camus, Céline, Mishima, Montale, Cendrars, Borges, Apollinaire, Paz, Rilke, Pasternak, Michaux, John Hawkes, Svevo, Valéry, Isherwood, Ungaretti, Nabokov, Raja Rao, Hesse, Tennessee Williams, Carson McCullers, Paul Bowles . . . the list goes on and on. In the 1940s and 1950s—it seems unimaginable now—he rescued from out-of-print oblivion *The Great Gatsby*, *Light in August*, and books by Forster, Conrad, Evelyn Waugh, Henry James, Nathaneal West, Djuna Barnes, Joyce, Lawrence, Stendhal, and Flaubert. Along with these, there was Laughlin's continuing commitment to the American poetry avant-garde. The founding fathers, Pound and Williams, were joined by H.D., Rexroth, Oppen, Olson, Ferlinghetti, Rukeyser, Creeley, Levertov, Snyder, Duncan, among many others.

The list—and one could rattle on much longer—is even more remarkable given that New Directions rarely published more than thirty books a year, and often many fewer. As an adolescent in the 1960s, I, like many others, would buy any New Directions book I saw—although I probably had never heard of the author—simply because it was published by New Directions. It was the Temple of Modern Literature, across the plaza from that other temple, the old Penguin Classics.

More than any other American publisher, New Directions had, and still has, an identity so sharply delineated that a standard topic of conversation among writers for decades has been "Why doesn't New Directions publish X or Y?" Its domain is perhaps best defined by negatives: fiction that does not rely on a strictly linear narration, poetry that is not written in traditional forms, and criticism that is non-academic and jargon-free. Its authors are too diverse to be considered a clique, yet many New Directions books have a lineage within the list, for example, Dudley Fitts to Pound to William Carlos Williams to Rexroth to Snyder to Bei Dao. Pound recommended Henry Miller, who recommended Hermann Hesse's *Siddhartha*, whose sales of a million books floated dozens of more obscure writers.

Moreover, New Directions' policy has kept it unique in the increasingly venal publishing world. It only publishes literary books. The staff remains small. It pays prompt royalties on books sold, but only minimal advances.

(This inevitably led certain novelists—Nabokov, Paul Bowles, and W. G. Sebald, among them—to follow far more lucrative offers elsewhere.) It relies more on word of mouth than on advertising or publicity. Most of all, because of Laughlin's belief that a writer of what he called "serious literature" takes twenty years to be discovered, it keeps most of its books in print forever. Laughlin's wealth let New Directions survive as a money-loser into the 1960s, until the moment when yesterday's obscure gibberish became today's course requirement. The company has generally operated at a profit since, with the backlist paying for the roster of new writers who, it believes, will be essential reading tomorrow. It is an old-fashioned, patrician way of doing business—the long-term investment—applied to the most unlikely product, avant-garde literature.

Laughlin, late in his equally long life—he died in 1997 at age eighty-three—was often urged to write an autobiography, and he worked for some years on an unfinished memoir in verse form, *Byways*. Now, Barbara Epler, the current editor-in-chief of New Directions, and Daniel Javitch, the Renaissance scholar and Laughlin's son-in law, have produced another kind of autobiography, *The Way It Wasn't*, a snazzily designed, alphabetical rummage through his files of writings, correspondence, clippings, and photographs (including one marked "Girls," where the women are clothed, and one marked "Girls: Personal and Confidential," where they are not).

"Random" was one of Laughlin's favorite words. His collected short stories was titled *Random Stories*; his collected essays, *Random Essays*. And *The Way It Wasn't* is a book to open randomly. There is a more official, extensively researched biography being written by Ian MacNiven, but in the meantime, one can browse through these pages and read it almost like a poem about Laughlin's life, one composed without chronology of the vivid moments that Pound called "radiant gists":

Tea at Renishaw Hall with Dame Edith Sitwell, who lectured him on Whitman; tea with the "Cummingses" in Patchen Place; *rotwein* with Auden in Kirchstetten; lunches with T. S. Eliot:

> There was one problem in conversing with him. He spoke very slowly . . . there were long spaces between his phrases. I would think he had finished his sentences and burst in but he hadn't, there would be more to come.

and tea with Elizabeth Bishop at a brothel in Key West:

> The madam poured from an antique tea service into flowered
> cups which were daintily grasped by the young ladies. Oreo
> cookies were served, my favorites.

Laughlin buying ballet slippers at Capezio to airmail to Céline's ballerina
wife in Denmark just after the war (and seducing the shopgirl). Jean Cocteau explaining flying saucers to him. Climbing the pyramids in Chichen
Itza with Alfred Knopf, who was outfitted in lederhosen and a pith helmet.
Baseball games with Marianne Moore ("a Livin' Doll and the Soul of Kindness, but she did go on and on when she telephoned"). Djuna Barnes, who:

> came into the ND office to tell me that the next printing of
> NIGHTWOOD was to be done on paper that would last for
> 1000 years. I called the dealers who imported Arches and FAB-
> RIANO and sech, but the best they could promise was 700
> years. She was very put out with me, declared me an idiot and
> threatened me with her cane.

Or:

> When Joyce opened the door for me in Paris he said: "I think,
> Mister Logulan, we met for the larst toime on the battlefield
> of Clontarff." Then he explained that my name meant "Dan-
> ish pirate."

(Laughlin adds: "I never saw the real JJ because I never went drinking with
him.")

Nabokov, who would stay with him in Alta, and whose life he saved
when he slid down a cliff on a butterfly-collecting expedition:

> I wanted to be his friend, but he didn't want any jejune ninka-
> poop to be his friend. He wanted big brains such as [Edmund]
> Wilson and [Harry] Levin to be his friends. . . . He would force
> a smile for me sometimes but it was a long-ways-away smile.
> The real smile was still on the flatcar that was transporting his

grandfather's carriage and horses across Europe for the summer vacation at Biarritz.

On Wallace Stevens:

> Not easy to talk to, not much bubble, a grave counselor. . . . His wife, the lady so beautiful that her head was modeled on the old Liberty dime, did not encourage literary visitors at lunch. He had to take them to the Hartford Canoe Club.

On Henry Miller:

> I wager that half the exploits in Henry Miller's *Tropics* books were imaginary. He was not Errol Flynn. He resembled the clerk in our rural general store and was equally loquacious.

Laughlin was both manic and depressive—and took various drugs for it most of his later life—both self-effacing, in the manner of the unusually tall, and aggressive. Here is the young publisher, refusing to send galleys to William Saroyan:

> Authors just have to take one look at a page of proofs to go entirely crazy and decide they are Jesus instead of Napoleon and rewrite the damn thing. I'm sorry, I just can't afford it. You authors will have to realize that we small publishers can print you but can't humor you.

Around the same time, Dame Sitwell was rapping his knuckles about a letter she had received:

> If you want to be a success as an editor and publisher, do not write this kind of letter to very eminent people. . . . I have heard a good deal about you lately; and I shall not give you 100 points for savoir faire.

Edmund Wilson called him an "impudent puppy," and the book has many zingy Laughlin lines about bookstore buyers, bankers, professors in the "beaneries," and George Bush Sr. He loathed Wyndham Lewis (who had written him "Why don't you stop New Directions, your books are crap") and Helen Vendler (who had little use for most of the American poets he published) and the notoriously impossible Edward Dahlberg and "Joke-book" Bennett Cerf of Random House—another wealthy founder of a publishing company, but one who largely abandoned his youthful literary ideals. In the 1940s, Laughlin wrote Cerf a letter that reads in its entirety:

> Dear Bennett: You have just committed one of the great crimes against American culture of our day. You have let Stendhal's *Chartreuse de Parme* go out of print. Sincerely yours.

Paul Bowles (who claimed Laughlin cheated him out of the royalties for *The Sheltering Sky*) is recalled as a "hashish-eating scum bag," a "dogs'-behind-licker," and a "vomit-drinker." Tennessee Williams, he said, had written him "affirming that dribble-pisser has the most minute membrun non-virile he has ever seen." Henry Miller, despite, or because of, all of his books that Laughlin published, called him his "arch-enemy." Lawrence Durrell replied to Miller: "I don't give a milk shake for Laughlin that shyster impresario of bad work." "The world," Laughlin wrote, "is full of a large number of irritating people."

But he loved many of the writers and—in contrast to his background and life—he particularly loved the Bad Boys in their endless varieties: Dylan Thomas, Rexroth, Pound, Mishima, Schwartz, Tennessee Williams, Ginsberg, Robert Lowell, Céline. He published many of the Beats, and many of the Beat Bibles: Rimbaud's *Illuminations* and *A Season in Hell* and Henry Miller's book on Rimbaud, *The Time of the Assassins;* Lautréamont's *Maldoror*; Baudelaire's *Flowers of Evil*, Sartre's *Nausea*. He admired the writers who were protesting the atomic bomb and the Vietnam War, and regularly sent checks—and sometimes bail money—to the alcoholic, the addicted, the depressed, and the generally cranky. It was Laughlin who had to identify Dylan Thomas, "all puffy and purple," in the morgue at Bellevue Hospital, after the final drinking bout at the White Horse Tavern:

> In the window was a little girl. She was about four feet high, and I don't think she had even finished high school yet. She filled out the forms—she couldn't spell Dylan so I spelled it

out for her. "What was his profession?" "He was a poet." That puzzled her. This little girl said, "What's a poet?" "He wrote poetry." So that is what the form says: "Dylan Thomas. He wrote poetry."

James Laughlin also wrote poetry, but no doubt under Pound's terrible pronouncement in his youth, he kept it more or less a secret until he was in his sixties. Then—perhaps inspired by New Directions poets such as Pound, Williams, H. D., Oppen, and Rexroth, who had written some of their best work late in life—he produced more than a dozen books. He typically made no claims for his poetry, calling it "light verse," though it bore no resemblance to Dorothy Parker or Ogden Nash. Rather it was, he explained in the third person:

> statements of facts as he has discerned them. Many are reports
> on perceived feelings, his own and those of others; or a plac-
> ing with imagination; or recollections from reading of matters
> with which classical writers were concerned. There is a mini-
> mum of decoration.

He wrote in the relaxed American speech of Cummings or some of Williams. Having read Latin and struggled with Greek all his life, many of the poems are translations or imitations of erotic or satiric epigrams. Some—most notably the poems in *Byways*—are long autobiographical elegies, in the manner of Rexroth's book-length poems. Most of them, however, are short poems written in a form that he invented: couplets composed on a typewriter, where no line can be more than one or two spaces longer or shorter than the previous line:

> How did you decide to translate me
> from one language to another let's
>
> say from the English of friendship
> to the French of lovers we'd known
>
> each other half a year when one day
> as we were talking (it was about one

of your drawings) suddenly you curl-
ed yourself against me and drew my

lips down to yours it was so deft
an alterance from one language to

the other as if to say yes you can
speak French to me now if you wish.

It is difficult to think of another American poet who could be both sexy and witty, take a single conceit in the manner of Donne and then present it with such a minimum of words or flourishes. Like most of the poets he revered in the Greek Anthology, he didn't write single masterpieces. He would be difficult to anthologize, as his poetry depends on the cumulative effect of an unmistakable voice. He is Satie rather than Beethoven, yet at times the despair he kept tranquilized breaks through, as in this poem written after the death of his second wife:

As he passes the open door
he can see there is no long-

er anyone in the room   no one
is lying in the bed and no

one is attending the recumbent figure   the water glass

with its bent drinking straw
is gone from the bedside ta-

ble   there are no flowers
in the vase none of her fa-

vorite red and blue anemo-
nes   the window shades have

been raised because the
room need no longer be

kept darkened   now sun-
light is flooding the

room   in its neatness
and emptiness it is for

him a scene of terror
what can he do with

what is left of his life?

The writers he published, and those he didn't publish, never stopped complaining about him and complaining to him. William Carlos Williams advised him to give up and become a novelist or a professor. Pound told Robert Duncan: "Jaz has a very long spine and he is always breaking it skiing. So when I kick his butt about what he should publish, the message does not ascend to his brain." The newest New Directions books usually sold badly and were rarely reviewed. He wrote: "I often feel I'm working in a vacuum, or in a country where few readers hear the sounds." He couldn't go on and he kept on. The writer he most regretted not publishing was Beckett.

In the era of conglomerate publishing, where the "units moved" are books, New Directions continues, the oldest independent American literary publishing house, almost exactly as Laughlin ran it. It no longer publishes the young American novelists, who expect larger advances, but it has the leading American avant-garde poets: Susan Howe, Michael Palmer, Nathaniel Mackey, Forrest Gander, among them. It is the place where one finds many of the best living foreign poets: Kamau Brathwaite, Bei Dao, Tomas Tranströmer, Inger Christensen, Aharon Shabtai, to name a few. It has had great recent success with W. G. Sebald and Roberto Bolaño, smaller success with Javier Marías and Victor Pelevin, and little success with writers who are extremely well-known elsewhere, such as Antonio Tabucchi, László Krasznahorkai, Yoko Tawada, César Aira. It has brought back into print Julio Cortázar, Clarice Lispector, Bohumil Hrabal, Muriel Spark, Eça de Queirós, and the great Chinese novel by Qian Zhongshu, *Fortress Besieged*. The books are still rarely reviewed, still wait out their twenty years depending on word of mouth among the people who still have a taste for these things. And the copyright page of every book still contains the line that was once patrician and is now commemorative: "New Directions Books are published for James Laughlin."

[2007]

Susan Sontag

A N ARTIFACT OF the times: the first issue of *The New Yorker* that followed 9/11. After the nearly all-black portrait of the Twin Towers by
Art Spiegelman; after the ads for Ralph Lauren Polo, Mercedes-Benz, and
Laurent-Perrier champagne; after eighteen pages of the usual "Goings On
About Town" ("Chef Rick Laakkonen spent his woodsy youth among Mas-
sachusetts Finns"), and before the longish articles on the Boston Red Sox,
new productions of Verdi, and the latest cookbooks, a group of writers were
asked to comment on the devastation that had just struck.

John Updike, who "happened to be visiting some kin" in Brooklyn,
raised his well-worn descriptive binoculars ("it fell straight down like an
elevator, with a tinkling shiver and a groan of concussion") and ambled to a
cheerful conclusion:

> The next morning . . . The fresh sun shone on the eastward fa-
> çades, a few boats tentatively moved in the river, the ruins were
> still sending out smoke, but New York looked glorious.

Jonathan Franzen recalled a personal "recurring nightmare," invoked "a
childish disappointment over the disruption of your day, or a selfish worry
about the impact on your finances," and lamented the "loss of daily life":
"your date for drinks downtown on Wednesday, . . . the hourly AOL updates
on J. Lo's doings." Roger Angell reminisced about World War II and "a
lifetime of bad news: your neighbor's son's car crash, your tennis partner's
blastoma, Chernobyl, or the Copacabana fire." Rebecca Mead, comparing
the National Guard barriers at 14th Street to the "velvet rope at the night-
club door," rather happily noted that "exclusivity" had been "restored" to

a lost bohemian downtown Manhattan. And then there was Susan Sontag, blasting in her first sentences through the cluelessness and *The New Yorker* style-must-go-on prose:

> The disconnect between last Tuesday's monstrous dose of reality and the self-righteous drivel and outright deceptions being peddled by public figures and TV commentators is startling, depressing. The voices licensed to follow the event seem to have joined together in a campaign to infantilize the public. Where is the acknowledgment that this was not a "cowardly" attack on "civilization" or "liberty" or "humanity" or "the free world" but an attack on the world's self-proclaimed superpower, undertaken as a consequence of specific American alliances and actions?

Widely assailed in the prevailing jingoism of the moment—particularly for lines such as "Let's by all means grieve together. But let's not be stupid together."—Sontag's three paragraphs were yet another instance of the singular position she held in American culture. She might not have been the only one to say or think these things, but she was the only one who could get them aired in a mainstream magazine. Her death in December of 2004 created a genuine absence that no one has filled.

She was that unimaginable thing, a celebrity literary critic. Most middle- and highbrow readers probably would have been able to recognize her on the street, as they would not, say, George Steiner. An icon of braininess, she even developed, like Einstein, a trademark hairdo: an imperious white stripe, reminiscent of Indira Gandhi, as though she were declaring a cultural Emergency. Most readers probably know a few bits about her life, as they do not of any other critic: The girl Susan Rosenblatt—Sontag was her stepfather—in her junior high class in Arizona, with Kant, not a comic book, hidden behind her textbook. Her teenaged marriage to Philip Rieff that was her entry into egghead society. ("My greatest dream was to grow up and come to New York and write for *Partisan Review* and be read by 5,000 people.") Her trip to Hanoi in 1968. The miniskirted babe in the frumpy Upper West Side crowd and her years as the only woman on the panel. The front-page news in 1982 when, after years of supporting various Marxist revolutions, she declared that communism was "fascism with a human face." Her months in Sarajevo in 1993, as the bombs fell, bravely or foolishly attempting to put on a production of *Waiting for Godot*. Her struggle with cancer. Her long relationship with the glamour photographer Annie Leibovitz. We even know—from Leibovitz's grotesque "A Photographer's Life" exhibition and book—what Sontag looked like in the last days of her life and after her death.

At thirty, she had indeed become a regular contributor to the *Partisan Review*, as well as the *New York Review of Books*. At thirty-three, she collected her essays into *Against Interpretation* (1966), surely the best-known book of cultural criticism of its time, a dizzying, intimidating simultaneous celebration of asceticism (Simone Weil) and absurdism (Eugène Ionesco), suicidal suffering (Cesare Pavese), physical self-loathing (Michel Leiris) and physical delight (Norman O. Brown), the criminal (Jean Genet) and the transgendered (Jack Smith), the minimal (Nathalie Sarrraute) and the maximal (happenings, *Marat/Sade*), the films New York intellectuals were talking about (Godard, Resnais, Bresson) and the films French intellectuals were talking about (*The Incredible Shrinking Man, The Rise and Fall of Legs Diamond*). The book ended with a declaration of a "new sensibility," first proclaimed in the pages of *Mademoiselle* magazine, most of which sounded like the manifestoes of a half-century before:

> Art today is a new kind of instrument, an instrument for modifying consciousness and organizing new modes of sensibility. And the means for practicing art have been radically extended . . . Painters no longer feel themselves confined to canvas and paint, but employ hair, photographs, wax, sand, bicycle tires, their own toothbrushes and socks. Musicians have reached beyond the sounds of the traditional instruments to use tampered instruments and (usually on tape) synthetic sounds and industrial noises.

The new sensibility is rooted in "new sensations such as speed," the new crowds of people and the proliferation of material things. It blurs the distinction between high and low art, refuses to be sentimental, views the artwork as an object and not an "individual personal expression," and does not believe it should be a vehicle for meaning or moral judgment. "The new sensibility understands art as the extension of life."

Against Interpretation was a bombshell partially because, cloaked in a familiar and unthreatening critical discourse, it finally brought the tenets of Dadaism and Futurism and Surrealism to Riverside Drive, where the modern had been Joycean and Eliotic, a territory patrolled by New Critical, Freudian, and Marxist exegetes. What was missing in the book was any sense that Sontag was raising the revolutionary banner in a very tiny kingdom. When, in a famous sentence—the entire last section of her title essay—she declared, "In place of a hermeneutics we need an erotics of art," the first-person plural reflected how isolated that kingdom was. It was already forty years after the first Surrealist manifesto or, closer to home, seven or eight years after "Howl" or *On the Road*. "We" could have taken the subway downtown.

Against Interpretation also contained, of course, "Notes on 'Camp,'" which remained Sontag's best-known shorter essay, and the one cited in nearly all the obituaries. It has dated badly, especially as the word "camp" (let alone "to camp") has long since reverted to its summer leisure connotations, and its subtleties, so meticulously detailed by Sontag, have been reduced to the "Cult" section of the video store. Yet "Notes on 'Camp'" inadvertently became Sontag's most influential essay. Its 53-point structuralist analytic overkill on a minor pop phenomenon—in this case, an ironic fad among certain witty gay men—was something new in the US, though the French had been doing it for years. From that seed, to her dismay, grew the vine that would eventually overrun the English Department, producing a thousand deconstructionist dissertations on *Batman*. But it was also—in a climate where the literary establishment passed over homosexuality in polite silence and the left was largely hostile—one of the earliest attempts, and surely the most important, to illuminate (and even praise!) a gay sensibility.

Most of the qualities of Sontag's work as a critic were in place in that first book of essays. Her prose style barely changed over the next forty years. As much of literary criticism sunk into an imported techno-jargon, she was notable for the clarity of her heavily-worked phrases that seemed to have been written under Walter Benjamin's dictum that every sentence should contain a thought. (She had a fondness for the unnecessarily italicized word and, like Edward Said, a tendency to string together three nouns, verbs, or adjectives—a tic perhaps picked up from Robert Lowell's poems.) One always knew exactly what Sontag was saying, even if one didn't think it was true. And each essay was extensively researched and elegantly argued with her University of Chicago training in philosophy, full of precisely apt quotations that apparently came from a photographic memory. Describing Roland Barthes, she described herself:

> [His work] has some of the specific traits associated with the style of a late moment in culture—one that presumes an endless discourse anterior to itself, that presumes intellectual sophistication: it is a work that, strenuously unwilling to be boring or obvious, favors compact assertion, writing that rapidly covers a great deal of ground.

The essays are ruminative, utterly humorless—her favorite word was "serious"—and unlike the work of many of the writers she most admired, in that she never attempted to do anything new or different, formally, with her critical prose. She did not, or could not, follow another Benjamin dictum she cited: "All great works of literature found a genre or dissolve one." She was a celebrant of transgression, but there was nothing transgressive about her writing. Brilliant syntheses of what were often continental ideas unfamiliar to American audiences, her best literary essays were unmatched models in the art of the introduction.

Fashioning herself after the European (especially Eastern European), Russian, and Latin American literary writers who had become intellectual consciences in their societies, Sontag began her role as an often-inflammatory political commentator the year after *Against Interpretation*, in the Winter 1967 issue of *Partisan Review*. Another artifact of its age, it was dedicated to a symposium on "What's Happening to America." ("There is a good deal of anxiety about the direction of American life. In fact, there is reason to fear that America may be entering a moral and political crisis.") Participants were asked to answer seven questions on Lyndon Johnson, inflation, foreign policy, the role of the intellectual, the "activities of young people today," and so on. Although one of the questions was "Is white America committed to granting equality to the American Negro?" it did not occur to anyone to ask any actual American Negroes. Only two women were invited: Sontag and Diana Trilling, then sixty-two.

Sontag's response was a full-scale bombardment of H. L. Mencken's Yahooland, not excluding "John Wayne chawing spareribs in the White

House," the genocide of the American Indian, and "box architecture." Amazingly, in 1967, she is (with Jack Newfield, in passing) the only participant to mention sex, drugs, and rock & roll. She even admitted to taking drugs herself, though her cultural references reveal her as somewhat less than groovy: her primary example of the sounds of the counterculture is the hopelessly showbiz—the word then was "plastic"—Supremes. Her response also contained the lines that set off a long apoplectic reply from Sidney Hook in the next issue, and were among her most notorious at the time:

> The truth is that Mozart, Pascal, Boolean algebra, Shakespeare, parliamentary government, baroque churches, Newton, the emancipation of women, Kant, Marx, Balanchine ballets, *et al.*, don't redeem what this particular civilization has wrought upon the world. The white race *is* the cancer of human history . . . [her italics]

She came to regret that last phrase, and wrote a whole book against the use of illness as metaphor, and yet this sentiment never led to any public curiosity about those who are not cancerously white. In her collected critical writings there are only a few pages—some program notes for a Japanese Bunraku puppet performance and a passage on photography in China— that deal with the cultural products of the majority of the world. Her one published entry into the third world—the 1968 "Trip to Hanoi"—shows her trying to put on a brave face, but utterly at sea, and her early short story, "Project for a Trip to China," is an embarrassing bit of Chinoiserie, however dismantled and self-consciously postmodern. Like the old joke about the Oxford don, she knew everything, and nothing about everything else. It's too bad. One would have thought, to take only one example, that Yukio Mishima would have been a perfect subject for her—a counterpart to her essay on Leni Riefenstahl—with his conjunction of authoritarianism, militarism, the cult of the body, and self-destructive narcissism.

She may well have been the last unashamed Eurocentrist. Even the Americas barely appear in her taste for writers. There are three essays on American writers of any stripe: a review of Norman O. Brown (1961), an obituary for Paul Goodman, "quite simply the most important American writer" of the last twenty years (1972), and an appreciation of Glenway

Wescott (2001). Latin America is confined to Machado de Assis (1990), three pages on Juan Rulfo (1994), and a very slight "Letter to Borges" in 1996. Unexpectedly, though she is taken to be an ur-feminist, she rarely wrote on women writers: Weil and Sarraute in *Against Interpretation*, Pauline Réage (now-forgotten author of *The Story of O*) as part of a long essay on pornography in 1967, an introduction to Marina Tsvetayeva in 1983 (that says little about Tsvetayeva and much about Joseph Brodsky), a few pages on Elizabeth Hardwick in her essay on Wescott, and Anna Banti in 2003. In the early years, this was perhaps to avoid ghettoization as a woman writer on women writers, a need to be taken as one of the guys in what was essentially a guy-world, but this was not the case later on, when her fame allowed her to write on anything she chose. Her lack of generosity to other women writers was most baldly apparent in the uncollected and unpleasant speech she gave in 2003, accepting the Prince of Asturias Prize, which she was obliged to share with the Moroccan writer Fatema Mernissi, whom she indirectly belittled as a mere ethnic token.

She had no apparent interest in poetry, other than Rilke, Auden, and a few friends. And though she was considered the trendiest critic, the one who was up on everything happening right now, she largely stopped writing about the living—particularly living writers—after the 1960s. There was an essay on Elias Canetti, then seventy-five, in 1980; one on W. G. Sebald twenty years later; and one on Adam Zagajewski in 2001.

The critic of the current always faces the problem that, in the next generation, taste will have moved on and the subject no longer of great interest (Resnais, Bergman), or the subject will be seen as entirely of its moment and now quaint ("camp," happenings), or the critic's initial perceptions will have become so absorbed into received thought that they are no longer vital (Godard). But the risk in writing exclusively on the past, even the recent past, is that the critic will be seen at best as nostalgic, at worst as sour. Sontag had been one of the first American highbrow literary critics to write on the movies ("*the* art of the twentieth century"—her italics) and her example had paved the way for the strange idea and practice of the incorporation of Film Studies into the English Department. But by 1995, marking "A Century of Cinema" in *Where the Stress Falls*, she was lamenting the passing of a golden age of cinephilia in the 1960s and early 1970s—which was of course her period of intense moviegoing—and its "profusion of masterpieces." She complained that "one hardly finds anymore, at least among the young, the distinctive cinephilic love of movies" (which seems completely untrue) and concluded: "If cinephilia is dead, then movies are dead." In 1979, writing on Hans-Jürgen Syberberg, she claimed, somewhat ridiculously, that "lately, the appetite for the truly great work has become less robust." Twenty-one years later, her essay on Sebald began: "Is literary greatness still possible?" And in her 2004 essay on Victor Serge (reprinted in *At the Same Time*), she writes:

> To read Serge's memoirs is to be brought back to an era that seems very remote today in its introspective energies and passionate intellectual quests and code of self-sacrifice and immense hope: an era in which the twelve-year-olds of cultivated parents might normally ask themselves [as Serge did]: "What is life?"

Throughout Sontag's writings, the literary figures she admires from earlier in the 20th century are described as "heroes," "giants," even "gods." We, implicitly, are midgets, and may produce no great art again. Even our children—though it is unlikely Sontag talked to many—no longer wonder.

Much of her best writing was done in the 1970s. *On Photography* (1977), her contentious love-hate letter to the "quintessential art of affluent, wasteful, restless societies," remains the best introduction to the subject, not only a fairly comprehensive brief history, but Sontag's finest display of her synthetic skills, managing to incorporate nearly everything that has been thought or said on photography into a free-flowing argument that would become one of her perennial themes: how photographs—and by extension films and television—those "clouds of fantasy and pellets of information" have become a "pseudo-presence" more real than the real itself in a world dependent on their production and consumption. (In 2003, she returned to the subject of the "modern experience" of "being a spectator of calamities" in *Regarding the Pain of Others*, an elaboration, partial repetition, and partial refutation of the earlier book. One reads it again now almost as a creepy prophecy, knowing that Sontag's own suffering would be turned, via Leibovitz, into a media mix of photographic images to be displayed next to images of half-clothed movie stars.)

Her next book, *Illness as Metaphor* (1978), probably more than anything else she wrote or said, made a genuine difference in the world. Its thesis, bolstered by Sontag's usual extraordinary range of historical facts and citations, was simple: Cancer is not a metaphor for anything. Cancer is not the result of repressed emotions or of personality disorders, as was widely believed at the time. Cancer should not be a dirty secret. Cancer is "just a disease—a very serious one, but just a disease. Not a curse, not a punishment, not an embarrassment." Her apt comparison throughout the book was with tuberculosis, once a similarly metaphorical affliction and now merely physiological. This was a revelation—and, like most revelations, perfectly obvious after the fact. That we now live in an era where presidential candidates and their wives openly discuss their cancer, complete with medical diagrams in the newspapers, is the result of a shift in thinking that clearly began with both Betty Ford's openness about her own condition while still in the White House and Sontag's book. In 1988, Sontag brought out a sequel, the excellent *AIDS and Its Metaphors.*

This period ended with *Under the Sign of Saturn* (1980), surely the best collection of her shorter essays, the ones that many people remember first when thinking of Sontag: the portraits of Artaud and Canetti, the memoir of Barthes, the celebration of Syberberg's *Hitler* (an enthusiasm few shared), the great studies of Benjamin and melancholy, and of Riefenstahl and the sexual allure of fascism.

After that, she concentrated on novels, of which—like many critics who write fiction—she was the greatest champion. A famous writer with numerous friends and varied interests, she became, as is often the case, bogged down in ephemera and favors: speeches, statements, responses; program notes for performances of dance, theater, and opera; short texts for art catalogs; something on grottoes for *House and Garden*; something on *Don Quixote* for the Spanish Tourist Board. *Where the Stress Falls* (2001), her first collection in more than twenty years, contained only a few essays in the book's 350 pages that seemed like major efforts, most notably her second, and much longer, appreciation of Barthes.

At the Same Time is a similar miscellany, drawn from the last four years of her life: introductions, political responses, short essays, keynote addresses, prize acceptance speeches. The book opens with "An Argument About Beauty," which is an argument against the word "interesting" as a replacement for "beautiful":

One calls something interesting precisely so as not to have to commit to a judgment of beauty (or of goodness). The interesting is now mainly a consumerist concept, bent on enlarging its domain: the more things become interesting, the more the marketplace grows.

Sontag had a tendency to blame everything on consumerism, though surely one could also say: "the more things become beautiful, the more the marketplace grows." And she herself was frequently not immune to the use of "interesting" as a catch-all, as in (on Barthes) "everything he wrote was interesting."

There is a section of mainly slight political pieces, beginning with her notorious contribution to the 9/11 issue of *The New Yorker*. In the version published in *At the Same Time*, her first sentence is now considerably softer: "To this appalled, sad American, and New Yorker, America has never seemed farther from an acknowledgment of reality than it's been in the face of last Tuesday's monstrous dose of reality." And, in an interview for an Italian newspaper a few weeks later, she is already backtracking from her initial comment that the attack was a "consequence of specific American alliances and actions":

> But the view I detect among some American intellectuals like [Gore] Vidal and many *bien-pensant* intellectuals in Europe— that America has brought this horror upon itself, that America itself is, in part, to blame for the deaths of these thousands upon its own territory—is not, I repeat, not a view that I share.

She declares that she is "guardedly optimistic," and seems uncharacteristically delusional—not only in hindsight: it would have seemed like a fantasy at the time—as she imagines "strenuous debates in the highest government-military circles":

> Clearly, our masters of war have realized that we face an exceedingly complex "enemy" who cannot be defeated by the old means. . . . One can only hope that something intelligent is being planned . . . that the Bush administration, Tony Blair, et al. have really understood that it would be useless or, as they

say, counterproductive—as well as wicked—to bomb the op-
pressed people of Afghanistan and Iraq . . .

A year later, she was writing in the *New York Times* of the War on Terror
as a "pseudo-war," a metaphor more than a war, and decrying the patriotic
blather attending the first anniversary of September 11. In May 2004, in
what is evidently the last piece she wrote, she returned to themes in *On Photography* and *Regarding the Pain of Others* to consider the pornography of
the torture photographs from the Abu Ghraib prison, and both the official
and media responses to them. Although she is adamantly opposed to the
war in Iraq, it is startling that she now refers to the invasion of Afghanistan,
without elaboration, as "quite justified."

Five formal speeches are included, which will be of interest mainly
to Sontag completists. "The Conscience of Words" (the title, uncredited,
taken from Canetti) was written for her controversial acceptance of the
Jerusalem Prize in 2001 from then Mayor Ehud Olmert. It is alternately
bland and testy ("To accept an honor is to believe, for a moment, that one
has deserved it. . . . To refuse an honor offered seems boorish, unconvivial,
pretentious."), platitudinous until near the end, when, in two perfunctory
paragraphs, she criticizes Israeli treatment of the Palestinians and calls for
the dismantlement of the settlements. This is somewhat expanded, along
with some words against the war in Iraq, in "On Courage and Resistance,"
the Oscar Romero Award Keynote Address, honoring the Israeli soldiers
who have refused to serve in the Occupied Territories.

"The World as India," the St. Jerome Lecture on Literary Translation, invokes St. Jerome, gathers the usual suspects whenever translation
is discussed (Goethe, Schleiermacher, Benjamin, the Tower of Babel) and
oddly ends up in a Bangalore call center. This is the world as India: the
few thousand who answer 1-800 numbers with trained American accents,
and not the billion other people on the subcontinent. In "Literature Is
Freedom," accepting the German Freedom Prize, she invokes her love
of German literature, responds to Donald Rumsfeld's recent characterization of "old Europe," and runs through some familiar notions on the
differences and similarities between Europe and the United States, the old
and the new.

In the cranky "At the Same Time: The Novelist and Moral Reason-
ing," the Nadine Gordimer Lecture, she invokes Nadine Gordimer, and

then defends the novel by launching into an attack on the global world of mass media and the internet. Even translation gets its lumps, for it "entails a built-in distortion of what the novel is at the deepest level," which is "the perpetuation of the project of literature itself." (Why translation distorts the perpetuation of literature—one would think the opposite is true—she doesn't say.) There are predictable statements against televison:

> Literature tells stories. Television gives information. . . . The so-called stories that we are told on television satisfy our appetite for anecdote and offer us mutually canceling models of understanding . . . a lesson in amorality and detachment that is antithetical to the one embodied by the enterprise of the novel.

And so on, based on the assumption that fiction is Dostoyevsky and television is *Baywatch*, when of course most fiction is Danielle Steele and some television—to take one of Sontag's favorites—is Fassbinder's *Berlin Alexanderplatz*. She laments at length the impending triumph of hypertext—strangely making this, the penultimate piece she wrote, among the most dated. And along the way, she makes some false pronouncements on poetry: Time is not "essential" for poetry (rather like saying time is not essential for music). "Poetry is situated in the present." The metaphor is *"necessary"* (her italics) for poetry, and "a great poet is one who refines and elaborates the great historical store of metaphors." Obviously a great poet is more than a metaphor-machine, and some employ no metaphors at all.

The best and worst essays in the book are a section of five introductions. An unusually weak one on the letters of Rilke, Pasternak, and Tsvetayeva: "a god and two worshippers, who are also worshippers of each other (and who we, the readers of their letters, know to be future gods)."

> Today, when "all is drowning in Pharisaism"—the phrase is Pasternak's—their ardors and their tenacities feel like raft, beacon, beach.

An unconvincing one on Anna Banti's *Artemisia*, where Sontag seems more interested in the figure of the painter Artemisia Gentileschi herself, and the fact that Banti had to write the manuscript twice, the first version having been lost when Banti's house in Florence was blown up by the retreating

German army in 1944. With Halldór Laxness' *Under the Glacier,* she seems far off her turf, contextualizing as best she can with everything from *Steppenwolf* to Buster Keaton. (And disbelief does not get willingly suspended when she declares, twice, that this book is "like nothing else Laxness ever wrote," considering that he produced some sixty volumes, most of them as yet untranslated from the Icelandic.)

There are two superb introductions: One on *Summer in Baden-Baden,* " a crash course on all the great themes of Russian literature," the single, posthumously published novel by Leonid Tsypkin, a Russian doctor who died in 1961. Sontag—as with so many books—was responsible for bringing the novel back into print, which itself belies the claim in her opening sentence that it is "unlikely that there are still masterpieces" to be discovered from the second half of the 20th century, written in major languages.

Then, the finest essay in the book, an introduction to Victor Serge's *The Case of Comrade Tulayev,* also a Sontag rediscovery. Serge (1890-1947), a Russian who wrote in French, a militant who spent some ten years in jail, is another one of Sontag's heroes, transparently a person she would have liked to have been: a novelist and a revolutionary, reviled by both the left and right, who in his anticommunism still had "not given up on the idea of radical social change," someone in the middle of the major struggles of the first half of the century, someone who knew everyone:

> There was nothing, ever, triumphant about his life . . . unless one excepts the triumph of being immensely gifted and industrious as a writer; the triumph of being principled and also astute and therefore incapable of keeping company with the faithful and the cravenly gullible and the merely hopeful; the triumph of being incorruptible as well as brave and therefore on a different, lonely path from the liars and toadies and careerists; the triumph of being, after the early 1920s, right.
>
> Because he was right, he has been punished as a writer of fiction. The truth of history crowds out the truth of fiction . . .

It is equally transparent that Sontag, who frequently referred to herself as primarily a fiction writer, a "storyteller," is talking about herself. On the previous page she had written:

Finally, he was a lifelong practicing intellectual, which seemed to trump his achievement as a novelist, and he was a passionate political activist, which did not enhance his credentials as a novelist either.

There are too many examples of intellectual novelists and activist novelists to make this statement true, and it seems to apply mainly to Sontag's perception of herself. It is the aspect of Sontag that is most difficult to take: the longing, or the pretense, to be a witness, a melancholic standing in the ruins of history, despite the circumstances of her life. As a critic, she was a Roland Barthes who dreamed of being a Walter Benjamin, and moreover, a Walter Benjamin who dreamed of being a Russian novelist. But she was born too late, and in the wrong place.

She had written on Canetti, "He is preoccupied with being someone *he* can admire," (her italics), and the same seems true of the girl Susan Rosenblatt from nowhere in Eisenhower America. The quintessential cosmopolitan, there was something provincial in her unabashed idolatry of the great, in her need—though she railed against American consumerism—to consume every book, play, opera, ballet and dance performance, or art exhibit she thought worth reading or seeing. A sign of boundless energy—the jacket of *At the Same Time* reproduces a scrap from her notebooks, which reads: "Do something. Do something. Do something."—but, one also suspects, a sign of a certain insecurity, as though she still needed to prove that she had arrived and that she was the best informed in the room. It was evident in her predilection for pronouncements, in her belief—she is again describing Canetti—that "to think is to insist." In Sontag there is always the insistence that she is, like Serge, "right," even when that rightness contradicts—as it did in so many political matters over the years—the right things she had said before.

In the end, there are three Sontag books to read: *On Photography, Illness as Metaphor*, and a third, invented volume, drawn from the other books, of her *Selected Portraits* (Artaud, Benjamin, Barthes, Canetti, Cioran, Godard, Leiris, Lévi-Strauss, Pavese, Riefenstahl, Sebald, Serge, Tsypkin), for, as an idolizer, she wrote her best essays on single figures, rather than larger tropes. Three good books is a lot, more than most writers achieve, though perhaps not what she imagined of herself, or for herself. In 1967, she had written in her journal:

My image of myself since age 3 or 4—the genius-schmuck . . .
Sartre (cf. "Les Mots") the only other person I know of who
had this "certainty" of genius.

(By "schmuck" she meant her personality flaws, and her inability, at the
time, to form long-lasting relationships.) It is a Hollywood cliche that a
beautiful actress needs an element of ugliness to become a great star, and
one might say that a genius needs an element of stupidity, or something
wrong, to become a great imaginative writer. Sartre certainly had his. But
Sontag seems to have had nothing stupid about her at all. Arguably the most
important American literary figure or force of the last forty years, she may
ultimately belong more to literary history than to literature.

[2007]

ALTER AND THE PSALMS

*O*UT OF THE *mouths of babes; apple of the eye; fire and brimstone; out of joint; sleep the sleep of death; sweeter than honey and the honeycomb; whiter than snow; oh that I had wings like a dove for then I would fly away; the meek shall inherit the earth; tender mercies; clean hands and a pure heart; I have been young and now am old; my cup runneth over; many a time; clean gone; the days of old; I am a worm and no man; his heart's desire; the heavens declare the glory of God; go down to the sea in ships; at their wits' end; the valley of the shadow of death; make a joyful noise; go from strength to strength . . .*

The 1611 King James Authorized Version of the Book of Psalms—and of course of the entire Bible—is so deep in the English language that we no longer know when we are repeating its phrases. Inextricable from the beliefs and practices of its faithful for four hundred years, it has been transformed from the translation of a holy book into a holy book itself. Poets, however, know from experience that there are no definitive texts, and over the centuries an assembly of angels has been singing the Psalms in its own ways: Wyatt, Sidney, the Countess of Pembroke, Campion, Milton, Crashaw, Vaughan, Smart, Clare, Hopkins, and Kipling among them. Some were setting lyrics to new tunes; some were performing metrical exercises with familiar material; some were expressing private prayer; some were simply writing a poem. St. Augustine said that all things written in the Psalms are mirrors of ourselves, and it was inevitable that, when English poets were still largely Christian believers, they would look into the mirror of this foundational anthology of poetry, as Chinese poets looked into the Confucian *Book of Songs*.

In the modernist era, the poets, as Pound wisecracked, have been more interested in Muses than Moses, and though bits of the Psalms have inevitably been embedded in poems, new translations have become the province of theologians and academics. The latest is a handsome edition, complete with the requisite red ribbon, by Robert Alter, the best-known Jewish Biblical scholar of the moment, and it has arrived accompanied by a joyful noise, widely acclaimed in the press as the Psalms for Our Time.

New translations of a classic text are either done as a criticism of the old translations (correcting mistakes, finding an equivalent that is somehow closer to the original, writing in the language as it is now spoken) or they are a springboard for trying something new in the translation-language, inspired by certain facets of the original (such as Pound's Chinese or Anglo-Saxon versions, Paul Blackburn's Provençal, Louis Zukofsky's Latin). Alter, whose concern is Biblical Hebrew and not contemporary American poetry, is in the former camp. As he explains in the introduction, his project is to strip away the Christian interpretations implicit in the King James and later versions, and restore the context of the archaic Judaism of the half-millennium (roughly 1000-500 BCE) in which the Psalms were written. His poetics is an attempt to reproduce the compression and concreteness of the Hebrew, "emulating its rhythms" and "making more palpable the force of parallelism that is at the heart of biblical poetry." As for mistakes, it is surprising that the King James apparently has so few. Alter corrects very little, sometimes unconvincingly, though he is more specific on flora and fauna.

His de-Christianization is largely in the avoidance of frequent King James terms such as "salvation," "soul," "mercy," "sin" and its sister, "iniquity." He translates the KJ line "my soul thirsteth for thee" (63) (Psalm 63) as "my throat thirsts for you," explaining in the introduction that, although the Hebrew word *nefesh* "means 'life breath' and, by extension, 'life' or 'essential being'. . . by metonymy, it is also a term for the throat (the passage through which the breath travels)"—a translation, in other words, more literal than the original. Elsewhere, "my soul" becomes "my being," or sometimes merely "I." For "sin" he prefers "offense"; for "mercy," "kindness." For "iniquity," he often chooses "mischief," which, in American English, is more likely to be associated with frat-boy pranks on Halloween than treachery in the desert. Thus the KJ "They cast iniquity upon me" (55) becomes "They bring mischief down upon me" and the KJ "Iniquities prevail against me" (65) becomes "My deeds of mischief are too much for me." The strangest choice of all is the replacement of the often reiterated "salvation" and its cognates with "rescue" (the noun), in ways that seem to have no connection with English as it is spoken: "rescue is the LORD's" (3) or "the cup of rescue I lift" (116) or the KJ "An horse is a vain thing for safety" (33) that becomes the incomprehensible "The horse is a lie for rescue."

The parallelism that is the organizing principle of the psalmodic line (and of much archaic poetry) has been plain in English since the translations of Miles Coverdale in 1535. Coverdale marked the division into hemistiches (or what Alter, following Benjamin Hrushovski, calls "versets") with a colon, a practice followed, inconsistently, by the King James. Bishop Robert Lowth explained it in detail in 1753 at Oxford, and inspired Christopher Smart, who attended the lectures, to use the form for his *Jubilate Agno*. Alter emphasizes this by dividing the line into two, with the second one indented, giving the poem a more "modern" look, but it is hard to see why this is "more palpable" than previous versions. Open any page of the KJ version and the parallelism is quite clear: "Let the floods clap their hands: let the hills be joyful together" (98)—a line I picked at random—seems little different from:

.

> Let the rivers clap hands,
> > let the mountains together sing gladly

though Alter is, characteristically, slightly more awkward.

To illustrate how he has rendered the condensed language of the original, Alter, in the introduction, takes an unfortunate example, the famous line from Psalm 23: "Yea, though I walk through the valley of the shadow of death, I will no fear no evil." He explains that the Hebrew has eight words and eleven syllables, but the King James translation "weighs in" at seventeen words and twenty syllables. Alter has brought this down to thirteen words and fourteen syllables, an admirable diet, but there are few who wouldn't prefer the chubbier version to this:

> Though I walk in the vale of death's shadow,
> > I fear no harm.

Over the last century, there have been many translation strategies for giving a sense of the denseness of classical languages such as Chinese or Sanskrit: layout on the page, enjambment, the dropping of articles when possible, a reliance on Anglo-Saxon rather than Latinate words. Alter tends to use the possessive. The opening line of Psalm 19 in the King James, "The heavens declare the glory of God" becomes "The heavens tell God's glory"; if nothing else, cutting three syllables. Its concluding lines, which are repeated thrice daily by observant Jews, "Let the words of my mouth, and the meditation of my heart, be acceptable in thy sight, O LORD, my strength, and my redeemer" are turned into lines that would have the prayerful stumbling:

> Let my mouth's utterances be pleasing
> and my heart's stirring before You,
> LORD, my rock and redeemer.

Considering that the Psalms are meant to be spoken or sung, many of Alter's lines are difficult to say: "Your throne stands firm from of old, / from forever You are" (93) is one for elocution class, and the KJ "Make haste, O God, to deliver me; make haste to help me, O LORD" (70) has been turned into a stammer: "God, to save me, / Lord, to my help, hasten!"·

Translation comes from somewhere, the language and literature of the original, but it also goes somewhere, into the language and literature of the translation-language. Far too often, the experts of one know very little about the other. The cliché that only poets can translate poetry is only half true. More exactly, only poetry-readers can translate poetry: those familiar with the contemporary poetry of the translation-language, the context in which the translation will be read. Based on the evidence here, Alter seems to know very little about the last hundred years of English-language poetry.

He is partial to Victorian language, perhaps in the belief that it is more "poetic." The result is that, at times, he sounds more dated than the King James. He's in "death's vale" where the KJ was in "the valley of death." His Lord is "my crag and my bastion" (18) where the KJ's is "my rock, and my fortress." He has a "people aborning" (22) where the KJ has a "people that shall be born," and a "sojourner" (94) for the KJ's "stranger." The KJ's "I have considered the days of old" (77) is now "I ponder the days of yore." And the famous line "I have been young, and now am old" (37) has been turned into A. E. Houseman: "A lad I was, and now I am old."

Worse, like many writing poems for the first time, he is in love with inverted syntax: the trees "fresh and full of sap they are" (92); "they fix to the string their arrow" (11); "His handiwork sky declares" (19, better known as "the firmament sheweth his handywork"); "orphans they murder" (94). Sometimes he merely inverts the King James phrases: "For I am poor and needy" (86) becomes "for lowly and needy am I"; "The sea is his, and he made it" (95) turns into "His is the sea and He made it"; or similarly, "Thy way is in the sea" (77) is now "In the sea was Your way." There are inversions on nearly every page, and after a while, wonder, one does, if it's not the swamp of Yoda the Jedi Master we're in. That sinking feeling hits bottom as early as Psalm 23:

> The LORD is my shepherd,
>   I shall not want.
> In grass meadows He makes me lie down (23)

(And, almost needless to say, for "He restoreth my soul," Alter has "My life He brings back.") The incessant inversion, combined with the predilection for possessives, leads to many examples of the kind where *La plume de ma tante* would become "My aunt's is the pen" The first line of Psalm 24 is straightforward in the King James: "The earth is the LORD's, and the fullness thereof." Alter's line needs to be diagramed: "The LORD's is the earth and its fullness."

He seems to have no ear for American English, from the alpha (2: "Why are the nations aroused, / and the peoples murmur vain things?") to the omega (150: "Let all that has breath praise Yah"—a construct rather like "All who is going should get on the bus."). He is oblivious to American slang, not realizing that Psalm 66 (KJ: "Make a joyful noise unto God . . . Say unto God, How terrible art thou in thy works!") in his version ("Shout out to God . . . Say to God, '"How awesome your deeds.'"") sounds like a Christian Rock band warming up the crowd. He sometimes slips out of register: "The wicked man borrows and will not pay, / but the just gives free of charge" (37). And he apparently can't hear that the line "Free me, LORD, from evil folk" (140) is best spoken in the voice of George Bush.

Inversion, the possessive, the unpronounceable, and an unfortunate word-choice all converge in Psalm 18, where he transforms what is a dull line in the King James ("As soon as they hear of me, they shall obey me: the strangers shall submit themselves unto me.") into: "At the mere ear's report they obeyed me, / aliens cringed before me." There are many other lines that would cause the meek to tremble, though perhaps not aliens to cringe. Among them: "With their dewlaps they speak haughty words" (17); "All day long I go about gloomy" (38); "Like sheep to Sheol they head" (49, KJ: "Like sheep they are laid in the grave"); "All the wrongdoers bandy boasts" (94); "For all gods of the peoples are ungods" (96); "I hate committing transgressions" (101); "I resemble the wilderness jackdaw" (102); "for we are sorely sated with scorn" (123); and, perhaps the worst of all, the anatomically perplexing "The wicked backslide from the very womb" (58). But fortunately, as Edward Dahlberg once remarked, "There are many psalms that even the droning of a priest cannot kill."

As one reads along, the suspicion grows that perhaps this book is not about the poetry at all, but about the commentary. Usually half, and sometimes more, of every page is taken up by Alter's notes. Certainly there are many editions where the notes are more interesting than the texts, but the commentary here divides between lexical minutiae, of interest largely to Hebraicists (though this is a heavily promoted mass-market book) or a running exegesis for freshman, in a relentless reiteration of the obvious. The line "my being like thirsty land to you" (143) is glossed:

> Rain in this climate and therefore in this body of literature is characteristically thought of as a desperately needed blessing. Hence God's responsive presence is metaphorically represented as the rain the parched land awaits to quicken it with growth.

though one presumes that, by page 493, the reader has already figured out that these people are living in the desert. "Sing to the LORD a new song" (149) needs this explanation:

> The idea of a "new song" is highlighted in several psalms. In this sense, this is a kind of self-advertisement of the psalmist, as if to say "here is a fresh and vibrant psalm that you have never heard before."

It is remarkable that, in some two thousand of such notes, most of them longer than these, very little outside of Alter's own interpretations is ever mentioned. He takes issue with some of the King James readings, and very occasionally disputes some (usually unnamed) Biblical scholars, but not once does he cite any of the translations from the history of English poetry, the uses to which individual psalms have been put, the detailed Christian exegeses of everyone from St. Augustine to John Donne (and only rarely the Jewish exegeses of Avraham Ibn Ezra and Rashi), or even—except where there are specific references—other passages in the Bible. (This is contrary to Jewish tradition, which tends to pile up citations and defer to authorities from the long transmission of wisdom.) There is one far-fetched mention of Mallarmé, unconvincingly explaining why, in Psalm 65, Alter translates a certain word as "silence." And he defends his transformation of the well-known line "sweeter also than honey and the honeycomb" (19) into "and sweeter than honey, / quintessence of bees"— despite his own injunction against multisyllabic Latinate words and the inappropriate alchemical term—by modestly noting: "The English equivalent offered here may sound like a turn of phrase one might encounter in the poetry of Wallace Stevens, but it offers a good semantic match for the Hebrew." (The Hebrew had merely put together two words that both mean "honey.")

St. Hilary said that the Book of Psalms is a heap of keys that can open every door in a great city, but that it is hard to find which key opens which lock. For translation, the opposite has been true: Many poets have discovered many different keys to unlock certain doors.

For emotional power, Sir Thomas Wyatt, circa 1536:

> From depth of sin, and from a deep despair,
> From depth of death, from depth of heart's sorrow,
> From this deep cave, of darkness' deep repair,
> Thee have I called, O Lord, to be my borrow;
> Thou in my voice, O Lord, perceive and hear
> My heart, my hope, my plaint, my overthrow,
> My will to rise, and let by grant appear
> That to my voice thine ears do well intend. (130)

("Borrow" here means "deliverer from prison.")

For concision and straightforward speech, Arthur Golding—whose translation of Ovid was loved by Pound and plagiarized by Shakespeare—in 1571:

> My heart is boiling of a good word.
> The work that I indite shall be of the King.
> My tongue is the pen of a swift writer. (45)

(Alter: "My heart is astir with a goodly word. / I speak what I've made to the king. / My tongue is the pen of a rapid scribe.")

The lute music of Sir Philip Sidney in the 1580s:

> How long (O Lord) shall I forgotten be?
>   What? ever?
> How long wilt thou thy hidden face from me
>   Dissever? (13)

And Sidney's sister, the Countess of Pembroke, ten years later, bringing in the whole orchestra:

> Lord, crack their teeth! Lord, crush these lions' jaws!
>   So let them sink as water in the sand;
> When deadly bow their aiming fury draws,
>   Shiver the shaft ere past the shooter's hand. (58)

Thomas Campion in 1612, similarly alliterative, but restoring the psalm to the clarity of a single human voice singing:

> Aloft the trees that spring up there
> Our silent Harps we pensive hung:
> Said they that captiv'd us, Let's hear
> Some song which you in *Sion* sung. (137)

(Alter: "On the poplars there/ we hung up our lyres./ For there our captors had asked of us / words of song, / and our plunderers—rejoicing: / 'Sing us from Zion's songs.'")

Milton, in 1653, the master of syntactical inversion:

> Rise, Lord, save me, my God, for thou
>   Hast smote ere now
>   On the cheek-bone all my foes,

Of men abhorred
Hast broke the teeth. This help was from the Lord;
Thy blessing on thy people flows. (3)

The sheer goofiness of Richard Crashaw in 1648, translating "The LORD is my shepherd" as:

Happy me! O happy sheep!
Whom my God vouchsafes to keep; (23)

(And later, "He leadeth me besides still waters" becomes, in part: "At my feet the blubb'ring Mountain / Weeping melts into a fountain.")

Isaac Watts in 1719, making an entirely new song out of "O sing unto the LORD a new song":

Joy to the world—the Lord is come!
Let earth receive her King:
Let every heart prepare him room,
And heaven and nature sing. (98)

Christopher Smart in 1765, turning a single line (KJ: "He giveth snow like wool: he scattereth the hoarfrost like ashes") into one of his typically bright and idiosyncratic stanzas:

His snow upon the ground he teems,
Like bleaching wool besides the streams,
To warm the tender blade;
Like ashes from the furnace cast,
His frost comes with the northern blast
To pinch and to pervade. (147)

Thomas Merton, who as a Trappist monk recited them every day, wrote that "The Psalms teach us the way back to Paradise." And more: "Indeed, they are themselves a Paradise."

Curiously, many of Alter's goals were achieved in the 1960s in *The Jerusalem Bible*, an English translation by an anonymous committee—though the translation of Jonah has been attributed to J. R. R. Tolkein—directed by Alexander Jones, of a decades-long French project by the (Catholic) School of Biblical Studies in Jerusalem. It is entirely without literary pretension, and its strictly literal, plain-spoken minimalism takes one far from the courtly elegance of the King James and into the world of the desert tribes. Its narratives, at times, seem as straightforward and unadorned as Icelandic sagas, those other great tales of vengeful shepherds. And its deadpan translation of the interminable and detailed rules and prohibitions underscores how selective the so-called fundamentalists of our age are:

> When two men are fighting together, if the wife of one intervenes to protect her husband from the other's blows by putting out her hand and seizing the other by the private parts, you shall cut her hand off and show no pity. (Deuteronomy 25: 11-12)

Moreover, it manages, in the Bible's deepest strata, to summon up the archaic world where Yahweh was not the only God, but the chief among many gods—Canaanite and other eclipsing figures—simply by naming him. (Alter refuses to do this, in deference to the orthodox Jewish taboo against saying the name, and resorts to the standard "Lord" in small capital letters.) Here are a few lines from Psalm 29, in the *Jerusalem Bible* translation:

> The voice of Yahweh over the waters!
> Yahweh over the multitudinous waters!
>
> The voice of Yahweh in power!
> The voice of Yahweh in splendor!
>
> The voice of Yahweh shatters the cedars,
> Yahweh shatters the cedars of Lebanon,
> making Lebanon leap like a calf,
> Sirion like a young wild bull.
>
> The voice of Yahweh sharpens lightning shafts!

The anonymous JB translators, who make no claim for poetry, have inadvertently written a Beat poem—by Allen Ginsberg or Anne Waldman or

Michael McClure—a reminder that it is the Psalms that have set the tone and standard for what an oracular and ecstatic poem should sound like: in English, from the King James to Whitman to Ginsberg; and in the rest of the world from Whitman to Neruda and Senghor, among so many others. Moreover, where the usual "Lᴏʀᴅ" carries millennia of evolving interpretations, and an inherent benevolence, calling Yahweh by his name—as we would a Greek or Hittite or Hindu god—presents a mythological otherness, an unsophisticated warrior god of the neolithic Hebrews, far from the deity now invoked in suburban synagogues.

We tend to remember the songs of praise and of thanksgiving, but most of the psalms are preoccupied with vengeance. The psalmist is surrounded by enemies who slander him, bring lawsuits against him, cheat him in the marketplace, and he calls on Yahweh to destroy them. Or the Hebrews are surrounded by hostile tribes and they call on Yahweh to destroy them. Everyone knows Psalm 137, the beautiful song of exile ("By the rivers of Babylon, there we sat down, yea, we wept, when we remembered Zion") but few remember how it ends, here in Alter's translation:

> Daughter of Babylon the despoiler,
>   happy who pays you back in kind,
>   for what you did to us.
> Happy who seizes and smashes
>   your infants against the rock.

Alter comments that the psalm "ends with this bloodcurdling curse pronounced on their captors, who, fortunately, do not understand the Hebrew in which it is pronounced." A cheerful thought, but language is more than the meaning of words, and somehow one suspects that if this curse was indeed once spoken aloud, the Babylonians, knowing nothing of the original, would still have been able to translate it.

[2008]

THE T'ANG

I.

WOMEN IN THE courts of the T'ang Dynasty (618-907) painted their eyebrows green; the standard of beauty was brows as delicately curved as the antennae of moths. Foreheads were powdered yellow with massicot, a lead oxide, for yellow was the color of vitality. Plumpness, as in many societies where the masses are hungry, was the ideal and useful, men claimed, in winter: in the poorly heated palaces, a prince or minister could huddle his heftiest concubines around him to protect him from drafts. There are at least twenty-four hairstyles mentioned in the poetry, some a foot high, held together by lapis lazuli hairpins clattering with pearls, with silk flowers and birds of gold perched on the top. As the empire was crumbling, the most popular styles had names such as "Deserting the Family" and "Uprooting the Grove." Yang Kuei-fei, the emperor Hsan Tsung's beautiful courtesan whose machinations set off a civil war, kept a tiny jade fish in her mouth.

The empire, expanding and contracting with conquests and defeats, at its height stretched east to the China Sea, south to Annam, and west along the Silk Route as far as Samarkand. The Grand Canal, a massive feat of construction 1,200 miles long, linked north and south, and a network of highways and waterways connected 1,859 cities, twenty-two of them with populations of at least half a million. The capital, Ch'ang-an (present-day Xi'an) was the largest city in the world, some thirty square miles, laid out in a grid pattern with wide avenues lined with fruit trees and patrolled by unforgiving policemen, the Gold Bird Guards. Nearly two million inhabitants were apportioned into 108 walled wards, including two vast markets with hundreds of lanes, strictly organized according to goods and services; parks with artificial lakes and artificial mountains and imported birds and game; and an extensive Pleasure Quarters of banquet halls and brothels.

Every aspect of life was codified and enforced by imperial edict: the length of tunics, the price of every item in the market, the colors that may be worn by ministers of certain ranks, the number of blows with a thin rod that a speeding coachman should receive. There were prohibitions against eating a white sheep that had a black head or a dish of pheasants with wal-nuts. Censuses of every village were taken to ensure an exact collection of taxes and to fill the ranks of compulsory labor and conscription. The coun-try was converted to a cash economy and the foundation of imperial wealth became its tax on salt, a commodity everyone needed. Under the T'ang, the system of strict examinations on the classics as a requirement for entering the civil service became universal; one census listed 130,000 students. Al-though this hardly resulted in a total meritocracy, it meant that some young men who did not come from well-connected families could rise to powerful positions in the government and an increasing number of talented—or, at least, educated—people entered the bureaucracy.

The T'ang became rich on trade, promoted by a new merchant class along the Silk Route (where Sogdian was the lingua franca) or on the sea routes that led to the port of Canton, where the sailors spoke Persian. Coral from the Mediterranean or Ceylon; golden peaches from Samarkand; car-damon from Tonkin; "thousand-year" jujubes from Tabaristan; ostrich-egg cups from Bukhara; various peppers from Burma; feathers from the white egrets, peacocks, and kingfishers of Annam (one princess had a dress en-tirely made from feathers); pistachios from Persia; furs of sable, ermine, miniver, steppe foxes, and martens . . . The list of T'ang imports is endless, and T'ang coins have been found as far west as the coast of Somalia.

The masses, who rarely saw these treasures, told tales of strange objects with magical powers, brought from abroad: a single bean that was sufficient food for weeks; a certain wheat that made the body so light that one could fly; a crystal pillow that gave the sleeper visions of strange lands; a piece of rhinoceros horn that could heat a palace; hairpins that turned into drag-ons; pots that cooked without fire; the translucent stone that emitted a cool breeze; the plant that was always surrounded by darkness.

All things foreign were the rage. Aristocrats learned to sit in chairs, the "barbarian beds." Dandies preferred to speak Turkish, and set up blue felt nomadic tents in their urban courtyards, where they dressed like Khans and ate chunks of lamb that they cut off with swords. Courtesans sang songs with titles like "Watching the Moon in Brahman Land," playing melodies on foreign instruments adapted from Indian, Turkish, Korean, and Persian tunes. Entertainment was provided by dancers from Tashkent or the Sogdian "twirling girls" who performed balancing on giant balls. Saffron-flavored wine, made from grapes imported from Turkey, was served in agate cups, poured in the Pleasure Quarters by blue-eyed hostesses. "When I drink this," said the Emperor Mu Tsung, "I am instantly conscious of harmony suffusing my four limbs—it is the true Princeling of Grand Tranquility"— the latter being an honorific for Lao Tzu, the Taoist sage.

It was a time of inordinate leisure. Mandarins were given fifty-eight days off during the year to celebrate twenty-eight holidays. There were holidays for viewing the moon and to outshine it. (At the latter, one emperor erected a lantern tree two hundred feet tall with 50,000 oil cups lit by a thousand palace women costumed in brocade.) Periodically the emperor would declare a three-day carnival in the streets, with floats five stories high carrying acrobats swinging on poles, musicians, and singers. In the palace, the bureaucratic office known as the Service of Radiant Emolument was in charge of imperial banquets; the cooking alone was handled by a staff of two thousand, preparing such rare dishes as steamed bear claw, Bactrian camel hump, jellyfish with cinnamon, proboscis monkey soup with five flavors, barbequed elephant trunk, and, in summer, melons that were kept cool in jade urns of ice brought down from the mountains. They wanted it all to last forever, and they drank strange elixirs concocted by Indian charlatans and Taoist alchemists that would promote longevity or even ensure immortality. It is said that five of the T'ang emperors died from these potions.

In Ch'ang-an there were churches, temples, and mosques for Nestorian Christians, Manicheans, Zoroastrians, and Muslims. Jewish merchants probably passed through. But by far the most popular of the imported religions was Buddhism, which had been brought from India some centuries before and was actively promoted in the T'ang by the notoriously ruthless Empress Wu, the only woman emperor in Chinese history and perhaps second only to Elizabeth I as the most powerful woman who ever lived. (Her Buddhism was more calculating than spiritual, for Confucianism would never have permitted a woman on the throne.) Chinese pilgrims spent years on the long journey to India to visit the sacred places and gather scrolls, and hundreds of scholar monks were installed in the imperial palace to translate and interpret the texts—one catalog lists translations of 2,487 different works. Poets and intellectuals preferred the asceticism and the enlightenment through nature in the Ch'an school, which became Zen in Japan. The masses venerated the Buddha Amitabha and the compassionate bodhisattva Kwan-yin, hoping to be reborn in the paradise of the Pure Land on the way to nirvana. The vast wealth accumulated by the temples and monasteries, channeled into enterprises like mills and oil presses, money lending and the opening of agricultural lands, further expanded the economic boom. It is a measure of Buddhism's reach that when, toward the end of the dynasty, the emperor Wu Tsung turned against the religion as an economic rival to the state, 4,600 monasteries and 40,000 shrines were destroyed, and a quarter of a million monks and nuns were defrocked. Buddhism in China never recovered.

The T'ang invented printing, for Buddhists believed that one gathered karmic merit by the ceaseless repetition or reproduction of the sacred texts. (A single monastery in Ch'ang-an had a thousand copies of the *Lotus Sutra*). The imperial library had some 200,000 books and scrolls, classified and labeled under four categories: Classics, Histories, Philosophers, and Collections. Individual scholars had private libraries with tens of thousands of books.

They invented toilet paper, which was viewed with disgust by the foreign visitors. They invented gold plating, true porcelain, and the magnetic needle; they excelled, as might be expected, at cartography. During the T'ang, the Chinese acquired their taste for tea, which quickly—and typically—became so refined that one connoisseur wrote a treatise on the sixteen ways of boiling water and their particular effects on brewing the leaves.

The best and worst of times: There were forty-two recorded famines, and wars with the Tibetans, the Uighur Turks, the Khitan of Manchuria, the southern nation of Nan-Chao (now in Yunnan province), the Koreans, and the Annamese. Emperors rose by assassinating their siblings, children, parents, uncles, cousins, and were assassinated themselves in turn. Eunuchs staged attempted coups, killing thousands of officials. In the civil war known as the An Lu-shan Rebellion (755-763), tens of millions died. The poet Tu Fu writes of fields overrun with nettles, for there were no men left to work the land; of fifteen-year-olds sent off to war who return as old men, if they return at all; of white bones bleached in the sun on the far western borders, where the lamentations of the living mingle with the eerie whimperings of ghosts.

2.

Magnificent examples of T'ang (and some earlier) art were on display this spring at the Palazzo Strozzi in Florence—one Renaissance paying tribute to another—in an exhibition called "China: At the Court of the Emperors." The installation, created by the fashion designer Romeo Gigli, placed the dramatically lit pieces on red clay-colored simulacra of dunes, as though the objects had just been unearthed. With the Chinese penchant for classification, one could categorize most of the works as Horses, Beauties, Buddhas, and Exotics (with some inevitable overlap, such as Beauties on Horses.)

The T'ang emperors, descended from nomads, were horse-crazy. They began the dynasty with five thousand horses; at its height they had a million, mainly imported from the West. Only aristocrats and the military were permitted to ride, and men and women alike played the Persian game of polo. The Emperor Hsan Tsung was particularly proud of his hundred dancing horses who, decked in embroidery with jewels in their manes, performed every year on his birthday next to the Tower of Zealous Administration, along with trained elephants and rhinoceroses, orchestras, acrobats, and a legion of elaborately dressed showgirls pounding on "thunder drums."

In the Strozzi there was a whole room of ceramic horses, most of them fired with the tri-colored glaze (yellow, green, and ochre) that the T'ang invented. Musicians played drums on horseback; Central Asian grooms in tall conical—to us, comical—hats led horses by bridles that are now lost; a dancing horse raised a hoof. And Beauties rode, dressed in men's clothes or in what must have been Nomad Chic, with wide-brimmed or cascading hats and riding boots. (It was later, during the Sung Dynasty, that foot-binding was introduced and languorous inactivity became the feminine erotic ideal; the T'ang aristocratic male apparently preferred equestrian and acrobatic women.)

Among the horseless Beauties were court ladies with Churchillesque jowls and pinched rosebud mouths and the lower-class, slender and graceful dancers, with waving sleeves that extended far beyond their hands.

One of the most beautiful objects in the show is simply identified as a "dancer," but seems to be some sort of other-worldly being, thin as a mantis, wearing a strange dress that evokes both beetles and old science-fiction movies. A foot tall, her fists are clenched in front of her, with both index fingers mysteriously pointing upward. Her hair has been shaped into two enormous wheels, which the catalogue unhelpfully states was "poetically described"—it does not say by whom—as "double-ring-shaped, gazing at the immortals."

The Exotics included both people and objects. There were foreign men with beards and bulging round eyes, strange hats and leopard-skin trousers, and—the liveliest piece—a haughty camel-driver on a kneeling camel with an identically arrogant expression. During the T'ang, animation came to sculpture, and many of the non-religious figures seemed like snapshots, motion momentarily arrested. (Particularly beautiful, though not an Exotic, was a kowtowing official dissolving into a puddle of his robes.) It is a curiosity that, at the same historical moment, the Moche in Peru were also vividly portraying ordinary life in ceramics.

Exotic objects included a plate with the figure of Dionysus and another made of Islamic blue glass; a ewer with six, probably Indian, faces; a Roman-style amphora with handles of Chinese dragons drinking from the lip; a candle holder in the arms of what may have been an African slave, crouched on top of an elephant. In a silver "box of the seven countries," Mongolia is represented as a fat man sitting on a rug, Tibet is two shepherds chasing a yak, India is mendicant monks. In a circular ceramic tomb guardian, a man turns into a quadruped that turns into a serpent that turns into a woman; the man is a foreigner, the woman Chinese. It is, in its way, a metaphor for the metamorphoses of the whole era.

Although there are still murals in the tombs—a few fragments were included in the exhibition, including a wonderful portrait of a woman playing with a goose—and in the famous Tunhuang Caves, almost no T'ang paintings or drawings on paper or silk survive. Remarkably, however, much is known about the artists and their work from contemporary and later writings. That is, there is an extensive art history without the art.

For the first time, artists were considered as belonging to schools, rather than as isolated individual talents; occasionally contests were held where representatives competed to depict an identical scene. There were painters who specialized in women or horses, of course, but also in hawks, flowers, insects, and wild animals. Foreign emissaries had their portraits painted to create a kind of catalog of the peoples of the world, and there were painters whose forte was imaginary scenes in foreign lands, including one series, alas now lost, on life in the Kingdom of Prom, which was known elsewhere as Rome.

As in any era, there were businessmen-artists, obsequious to the wealthy, and bohemian eccentrics. One of the latter was Mo Wang, known as Ink Wang, who only painted when he was drunk. After countless cups of wine, he would throw ink on a piece of silk and then, in the words of a T'ang critic:

> He would kick at it, smear it with his hands, sweep his brush about or scrub with it, here with pale ink, here with dark. Then he would follow the configurations thus achieved, to make mountains or rocks, or clouds or water.

The T'ang invented a genre that would remain popular for centuries: a landscape where the artist inserts a portrait of himself admiring the scene, the painting or drawing accompanied or surrounded by a first-person text, often lengthy, written by the artist himself. Chinese art historians call this "scholarly painting," but in the West, the current combinations of the visual and the textual are "postmodern."

3.

The T'ang was, above all, a time of poetry. It is universally considered their golden age, unmatched since, perhaps because golden ages of poetry nearly always occur when the nation becomes international, when new things and new ideas flood in. And, until quite recently, this was never quite the case again in China, absorbed in its own vastness.

Since Ezra Pound's 1915 *Cathay*, T'ang poetry has been an inextricable element of Anglo-American modernism—as it is not in the other Western languages—and hugely popular among general readers. Many of its greatest poets have become familiar: Li Po through Pound, Po Chü-i through Arthur Waley, Tu Fu through Kenneth Rexroth, Han Shan through Gary Snyder, and these and others through Witter Bynner and Kiang Kang-hu's 1929 *The Jade Mountain* (a translation of the classic *300 Poets from the T'ang* anthology) and a shelf of books by the great Sinologists Burton Watson and, lately, David Hinton. It was the kind of poetry that, in English, poets

wanted: a poetry about everything, from stomach aches to the collapse of
the empire; a poetry of precise observation and concrete images of everyday
life and of nature, where the transcendent or the sublime and a range of
human emotions were expressed by not expressing it at all, where they were
shown and not told.

Moreover, it was a poetry of the individual at home in the city, or in
exile or reclusion in the wilderness, where war and the burdens of history
were always on the horizon. For the moderns, China a thousand years ago
seemed like today. And equally attractive to a poetics promoting concision
and compression, the T'ang poets seemed able to cover a lot of ground and
to say it all with very few words. Here is Tu Fu, as translated by Kenneth
Rexroth, in a poem that, in Chinese, has eight lines:

I PASS THE NIGHT AT GENERAL HEADQUARTERS
A clear night in harvest time.
In the courtyard at headquarters
The wu-t'ung trees grow cold.
In the city by the river
I wake alone by a guttering
Candle. All night long bugle
Calls disturb my thoughts. The splendor
Of the moonlight floods the sky.
Who bothers to look at it?
Whirlwinds of dust, I cannot write.
The frontier pass is unguarded.
It is dangerous to travel.
Ten years wandering, sick at heart.
I perch here like a bird on a
Twig, thankful for a moment's peace.

The publication of A. C. Graham's anthology *Poems of the Late T'ang* as
a Penguin paperback in 1965 was an event, in that most of the poets I knew
avidly read it. Some fifty thousand poems by 2,200 T'ang poets survive, but
English-language readers, after a half-century of extraordinary translations,
had assumed they were more or less familiar with the turf. But this was another kind of Chinese poetry, one without cups of wine in the moonlight, or
nostalgia for old friends:

The wind in the *wu-t'ung* startles the heart, a lusty man despairs;
Spinners in the fading lamplight cry chill silk.
Who will study a bamboo book still green
And forbid the grubs to bore their powdery holes?
This night's thoughts will surely stretch my guts straight:
Cold in the rain a sweet phantom comes to console the writer.
By the autumn tombs a ghost chants the poem of Pao Chao.
My angry blood for a thousand years will be emeralds under
    the earth!

Not only was the imagery bizarre, but the translation was utterly unlike
the relaxed American speech of Rexroth or Snyder or Watson, which had
become—and largely remains—the standard idiom for Chinese poetry in
English translation, a stripping away of rhetorical flourishes as a way of suggesting the extreme compression of the classical Chinese. This, however,
was something else: "spinners in the fading lamplight cry chill silk" seemed
more like Hart Crane than William Carlos Williams.

The poet was Li Ho, who did not fit any of the traditional categories
assumed for Chinese poets. He was neither a Confucian civil servant restoring meaning to language nor a Taoist adept out in nature, neither a libertine
nor a Buddhist monk. He was a Crazy Poet—the Chinese refer to him as the
"ghostly genius"—who rode his donkey all day and wrote scattered lines
that he tossed into a bag. At night, he emptied out the bag and put the lines
together as poems, which he threw into another bag and forgot. His mother
complained that "this boy will spit his heart out," which he did at age twenty-
six. Here he imagines himself being welcomed into the land of the dead:

The Southern hills, how mournful!
A ghostly rain sprinkles the empty grass.
In Ch'ang-an, on an autumn midnight,
How many men grow old before the wind?
Dim, dim, the path in the twilight,
Branches curl on the black oaks by the road.
The trees cast upright shadows and the moon at the zenith
Covers the hills with a white dawn.
Darkened torches welcome a new kinsman:
In the most secret tomb these fireflies swarm.

The book opens with the last poems of Tu Fu, in old age and in exile ("There's always a place kept for an old horse / Though it can take no more to the long road.") as the hinge between High T'ang and Late T'ang. Graham then presents six poets of what was called the New Style, a poetry, he writes, "which explores the Chinese language to the limit of its resources." A poetry of often strange images and dense, sometimes impenetrable allusions, only one of its prosodic complexities can be approached in English translation: the parallelism of many of its couplets, where nearly every word had a complement or opposite in the accompanying line.

Among the poets—all of them quite different and clearly demarcated in Graham's translation—is Meng Chiao, who gave up his life as a Ch'an Buddhist recluse to become an impoverished poet in the eastern capital, Lo-yang. (He wrote, in a poem not included here: "A poet only suffers writing poems. / Better to spend your life learning how to fly.") The selection includes an excerpt from Meng Chiao's hallucinatory long poem, "Sadness of the Gorges"—the same gorges that are now under water, flooded by dams—of which these couplets are typical:

> The rays between the gorges do not halt at noon;
> Where the straits are perilous, more hungry spittle.
> Trees lock their roots in rotted coffins
> And the twisted skeletons hang tilted upright.

His perceived "coldness" and violent imagery were too much for many later Chinese poets. The great Sung poet Su Tung-p'o wrote (in Burton Watson's translation), "My first impression is of eating little fishes— / what you get's not worth the trouble," and said it was better to "lay aside the book / and drink my cup of jade-white wine." It was some centuries until changing taste would discover him again.

Han Yü, a militant Confucianist who held various important official posts and helped lead the ideological campaign against Buddhism, had a predilection for the grotesque in both its realistic and fantastic manifestations, whether a description of a state execution or of demons feeding on vomit. Graham includes excerpts from "The South Mountains," a poem of 204 lines ending in identical rhymes, with forty-six similes, all beginning with "like," packed into sixty of them. The mountains, Han Yü writes, are:

Scattered like loose titles
Or running together like converging spokes,
Off keel like rocking boats
Or in full stride like horses at the gallop;
Back to back as though offended,
Face to face as though lending a hand,

and so on. As far as I know, this combination of trance-inducing repetitive rhyme and hyper-similitude would not be attempted again for another 1,100 years, until the Chilean poet Vicente Huidobro's modernist extravaganza, *Altazor*.

Tu Mu, although a downwardly mobile bureaucrat, is the most cheerful of the lot. "There is more joy in him," writes Graham, "than in any T'ang poet later than Li Po." Wine-drinker, observer of nature, nostalgist, he is the closest, in the book, to the traditional image of the Chinese poet, though he saw himself as occupying a middle ground between what he called the "intricate beauty" of Li Ho and the "familiar and commonplace" of older poets, such as Po Chü-i:

By river and lakes at odds with life I journeyed, wine my
    freight:
Slim waists of Ch'u broke my heart, light bodies danced into
    my palm.
Ten years late I wake at last out of my Yang-chou dream
With nothing but the name of a drifter in the blue houses.

(The blue houses are brothels.)

The leading figure of the late T'ang is undoubtedly Li Shang-yin, a Taoist who worked as a proofreader in the Imperial Library. It is said that he is second only to Tu Fu in the number of critical commentaries on his work; the thickly stacked allusions have kept the exegetes busy for centuries. Stephen Owen, in a recent encyclopedic survey of the period, writes that Li Shang-yin's poetry "gestures toward concealed meaning while simultaneously keeping the meaning hidden."

He is both the most sensualist and scholarly poet of the T'ang. On one side, in Graham's words, the "silken, flower-decked, phoenix-infested imagery . . . glittering with pearls and jades, heavily scented with cassia or incense, dripping with the tears of wax candles," with women "at the center of this sumptuousness." On the other, "abrupt transitions in which an allusion provides the unmentioned bridge, delicate variations on commonplace references, oblique glimpses of historical events, direct presentation of a scene before his eyes in which one senses elusive parallels with a scene in history or poetry." We, of course, are completely clueless in this labyrinth of references; annotation may explain a little but ultimately doesn't help. What remains is a kind of presence: like most great poetry, Li Shang-yin's is always on the verge of being understood and is never quite understood:

PEONIES
The brocade curtains have just rolled back. Behold the Queen
    of Wei.
Still he piles up the embroidered quilts, Prince O in Yüeh.
Drooping hands disturb, tip over, pendants of carved jade:
Snapping waists compete in the dance, fluttering saffron
    skirts.
Shih Ch'ung's candles—but who would clip them?
Hsün Yü's braziers, where no incense fumes.
I who was given in a dream the brush of many colors
Wish to write on petals a message to the clouds of morning.

A Sung Dynasty critic, attempting to find a Confucian social function for this poetry, wrote: "People see only that his poems delight in talking about women and do not see that they were a mirror of and a warning for the age." They may not have been a warning, but they were certainly a mirror, much like the T'ang mirror that was on display in the Palazzo Strozzi: bronze with mother-of pearl, turquoise, and malachite inlay set in lacquer, with an eight-petalled lotus depicted at the center. From each petal another lotus sprouted, creating the illusion of a dome; around the flowers, pairs of Mandarin ducks flew, the Chinese symbol for lovers. Li Shang-yin was both the epitome and the culmination of an era of refined excess and the exotic.

A few decades after his death, in the last years of the dynasty, warlords ravished the country. One of them, Huang Ch'ao, a salt merchant who had failed the civil service exams, captured Ch'ang-an in 881. A satiric poem was posted on the wall of a government building, criticizing the new regime. (As, eleven hundred years later, the Democracy Movement would begin with the poems that Bei Dao and other young poets glued to the walls in their capital, Beijing.) Huang Ch'ao issued orders that everyone capable of writing such a poem be put to death. Three thousand were killed.

[2008]

II.

POSTCARD FROM CHINA

I HAD VOWED never to go to China until my friend, the exiled poet Bei Dao, was able to travel freely there, but when I received a last-minute invitation to the Century City First International Poetry Festival in Chengdu, he urged me on: "If you wait for me, you'll be too old to enjoy it."

The international perspective of the festival was to be limited to two Americans. Luckily, they asked me to choose the compatriot, and I easily picked Forrest Gander—excellence and congeniality being a rare combination in American letters. Tracking him down in an artists' retreat somewhere in the Texas desert, I fulfilled a lifelong dream of reenacting Eric Newby's famous telegram to his friend in Buenos Aires: "ARE YOU AVAILABLE NURISTAN JUNE." I had rehearsed the casual tone: "Hi Forrest, want to go to Sichuan Province next week?"

As we staggered off the plane and rode into the city, the young poets assigned to meet us evaded casual questions: "They'll tell you at dinner." We were driven to a Las Vegas-style extravaganza, complete with rows of spouting dolphin fountains, called the Hotel California—China, in the 1970s, having had a Cultural Revolution that evidently saved them from Top 40 radio. Ignoring the department store, multiplex cinema, ice skating rink, conference center, Opera House, ten banquet halls, Shunxing Venison Restaurant, Fisherman's Wharf ("old bar from San Francisco"), Seine River Left Bank Grill Room, Blue Danube Night Club, food supermarket, and art gallery ("biggest indoor sculpture in China"), we were hurried into the basement to Chengdu Famous Snacks Town, a recreation of a "street in Old China" with oversize paper lanterns, soy sauce and rice wine in antiqued barrels, medicinal herb sellers, calligraphers, and shadow puppeteers, where a large group of poets was waiting for us in the Authentic Tea

House. As the endless delicacies spun around on the lazy Susan at the center of the table, there were veiled allusions and exchanged glances, but only exhortations to eat more. Finally, when we appeared suitably stupefied by too much food and too little sleep, our host, the poet Zhai Yongming—now 50, her name was always followed by the epithet, the Most Beautiful Woman in Sichuan—with great embarrassment broke the news: The police had cancelled the festival.

Government intervention in a provincial poetry event was the only thing in China that would turn out to match my expectations. I knew of course about its capitalist boom, but I had imagined the cities to look like those in the Third World, with high-rises and shopping malls around the corner from shantytowns. Moreover, I assumed I'd see a collage of New New China and Old New China: Calvin Klein here and Chairman Mao there. Instead, it appeared that the conversion to Calvinism was complete. The capitalist-roaders were on the Autobahn.

"Boom" does not begin to describe it. In the cities we visited, most of the old neighborhoods had been torn down and replaced with buildings of a futuristic massiveness. Everything was new, or under construction or renovation; everyone looked busy; everything was highly organized and efficient; the streets were spotless, the air filthy from the factories and traffic; human energy and natural resources were being consumed at blast-furnace rates. Unbelievably, though we wandered far off the tourist track, we didn't see any slums, or more than a handful of evidently poor people. Perhaps this was chance, but it was utterly unlike, say, Bombay or Bogotá, where the immediate presence of poverty is overwhelming, and penthouses overlook ruins.

Since 1990, the average annual per capita growth in China has been 8.5%. (In India, with which China is invariably compared, it is 4%. In the US, averaging the 1990s boom with the Bush bust, it is 2%.) It is the ultimate capitalist dream: 1.3 billion consumers who don't yet own an i-Pod. And even more: they themselves are making all this stuff, for themselves as well as for the world. Japan's economic "miracle" was dependent on exports, and became less miraculous when they had to go abroad for cheap labor. It is not difficult to imagine China thriving without having to export anything at all, the goods for its expanding middle class supplied by the bottomless pool of labor in the villages. As it has been throughout most of its history, China barely needs the rest of the world.

This is development in hyperdrive. An hour outside of Chengdu, we were taken to the Mrgdava Museum of Stone Sculpture Art. (Mrgdava being the Deer Park where the Buddha delivered his Fire Sermon.) "Supervised and sponsored," according to the catalog, by Zhong Ming, described to me as a formerly penniless poet, this was a magnificent private collection of over a thousand large pieces, mainly from the T'ang and Sung Dynasties, housed in a beautiful museum designed by one of China's best architects, Liu Jiakun. The American robber barons had taken 50 or 75 years to make their money, amass their collections, and build their museums. Zhong Ming had done it in ten. No one could explain how he had managed.

The received wisdom is that the Chinese cities are thriving at the expense of the countryside. Certainly it is true that farmers are not allowed to migrate to the cities, and there are countless stories of corrupt officials expropriating peasant lands, as the archetypal greedy landlords of Maoist propaganda once did. But the government statistics say that only 3.1% of the rural population is below the poverty line, most of the poor belonging to the largely Muslim minorities in the western provinces. (In the US, the equally semi-credible official statistics are 12.7% of the general population, including 24.4% of African-Americans and 21.9% of all children.) A further 6% are listed as "low income," somewhat above the poverty line. According to UNICEF, primary school enrollment is 93% (the same as the US). In 1990, 43% of the villages had telephones, now 92% do—and China must be the only place in the world where cell phones work in remote mountain fastnesses. The literacy rate is 90%; in India it is 57%. Life expectancy for a newborn is now 71 years; in the US it is 77; in India it is 64. The villages we happened to see in Sichuan and Yunnan provinces appeared to be self-sustaining farming communities, without the visible suffering of similar hamlets in India or Latin America. The Tibetans in these provinces, unlike, by most accounts, those in Tibet, seemed to be thriving—no doubt because they are an unthreatening minority in Han Chinese areas—and were building elaborate temples and stupas.

Everywhere we went was packed with middle-class Chinese tourists— urban people are now completely free to travel without permits. We were told beforehand that the festival would arrange to take us on a 4-day jeep trip deep into the mountains, and I had come prepared with all my Greenland gear. The expedition turned out to be a five-bus caravan with 150 people who had attended an art festival in Chengdu, and our destination was not a pup tent above the treeline but Jiu Zhai Paradise Holiday Resort, a Disneyland version of a Qiang minority village under an enormous glass stately pleasure dome, evidently modeled on Biosphere—and, like Biosphere, with most of its trees dying—surrounded by 1,100 guest rooms. A visit to the nearby national park was like a horror movie produced by the Sierra Club, as we became stuck, immobile with no escape on a narrow mountain trail with about 10,000 other hikers. The sheer number of human beings in China is ungraspable, like the distances in the universe. The relatively low percentage of the poor translates into a 100,000,000 people. My favorite factoid—perhaps apocryphal, but still believable—is that if China becomes an entirely middle-class country, and every Chinese person decides to spend only one week of his or her life visiting Paris, there will be an extra 400,000 people a day trying to get into Les Deux Magots.

It is inexplicable why, as hundreds of millions are in an orgy of laissez-faire capitalism, the government still cares about poetry. Bei Dao, China's best-known poet, is a case in point. After the Tiananmen Square massacres in 1989, he went into exile in northern Europe and the United States, traveling on "stateless citizen" papers (which drove immigration officials crazy, as there was nothing to stamp). For nine years, his wife and daughter were not allowed to leave the country to visit him, and his books were, of course, banned. A few years ago, now a US citizen, he was allowed to visit his dying father, as long as he stayed at home in Beijing and made no public appearances or statements. He was permitted a few more visits, none longer than a month, and was once allowed to travel to Shanghai. A book of his poems was published, sold out its first printing of 50,000, and then was not allowed to be reprinted. He has now remarried to a woman who lives in Beijing, whom he met in the US. He was able to go to China for one week last December for the birth of their child, but has been refused a visa since. His wife is free to travel, but the baby has deliberately been given no identity papers, and cannot go abroad. The family remains suspended in bureaucratic limbo.

Unlike in Maoist China, however, censorship is now random and de-centralized. A book will be banned at one publishing house and appear from another. In the case of our poetry festival, the venue was simply changed and the events declared "private," though anyone could attend. Some thirty poets from around the country had shown up anyway—everything had been paid for by the owner of the Hotel California, Ju Zhai Paradise, and a dozen skyscrapers in various cities apparently copied from *Metropolis* and *The Jetsons*. (A reputed poetry lover, he never materialized, nor did I learn his name.) So we had a few long panel discussions at a local university and an all-night reading at a trendy bar owned by Zhai Yongming, the Most Beautiful Woman in Sichuan.

As at all poetry festivals, it was later difficult to remember what anyone had said on the panels, but the types were familiar: the poet-professor, inordinately pleased with his apposite quotations from Mark Twain and Thomas Hardy; the passionate youth who didn't want to read anything at all, so that his feelings and insights would remain pure; the shy, spiritual poet who, when, asked how Buddhism had informed his poetry, replied, "I like the silences"; the energetic and charming young grant-getter; the two or three women invitees rightfully angry at the scarcity of women; the untranslated poet who claimed poetry could not be translated; the polymath, equally at home discussing the latest American poetry or Shang Dynasty numismatics; the senior poet, too drunk to say much at all. The writer most mentioned was Borges, and there were quite a few references to Harold Bloom, who had recently been translated into Chinese. Everyone was surprised that Forrest and I were rather tepid on the Western Canon; they assumed that this was the Universal Gospel, and couldn't quite believe our assertions that it was more like a dying cult in New Haven. They were also lately enamored with the "anxiety of influence" version of literary history, though it is largely inapplicable in the Chinese tradition, which never had anxiety about influence; perhaps the Oedipal drama had particular resonance in a nation of single children. All in all, one wondered why the police had bothered to shut the whole thing down.

Strangely, the visual artists seem to be able to do whatever they like. In Beijing, the "Post-Sense" group is escalating the Actionism of Vienna in the 1960s: nailing themselves into coffins full of animal entrails, cutting off pieces of their own skin and sewing them on to a live pig, etc., etc., and—no one knows if this is true or not, but it's all over the American fundamentalist Christian websites—cooking and eating an aborted human fetus. I briefly met one of them, a pretty, smiling young woman named Peng Yu, who, with her husband Sun Yuan, largely works, as they say, in severed human heads and the cadavers of children. The couple caused a scandal on BBC Channel 4, pouring blood on the actual corpse of Siamese twins. A more recent work is a 4-meter-high pillar of human fat, collected from clinics that perform liposuction. It is not titled "Would You Like Fries with That?"

I spent a day and a long evening in Da Shan Zi, a Beijing district of small factories and machine shops, half of them still in operation and half turned into huge and funky artists' studios, galleries, and the inevitable cafes and restaurants, much like those in the former East Berlin. Happily, the artists I visited were at the quirkier end of art and performance art. Ye Fu had built a huge bird's nest at the top of a tower and lived in it for a month without leaving. Cang Xin likes to lick things and has had himself photographed licking the Great Wall, the sidewalk outside of the House of Commons, and statues in Rome. Chen Wenbo paints large canvasses depicting blank sheets of paper. Many of the painters openly parodied Mao and Maoist propaganda. When I asked how the artists were avoiding censorship while poetry was still being banned, they replied: "Oh, no one cares about artists."

It's almost impossible to understand what's happening in China, and those I asked had no answers. Rural and urban people seem to live under two separate governments. In the cities, money is the only ideology. People are largely free to do what they want, and say what they want, though they can't always say it in print or on the Internet. (I was surprised by the openness with which opinions were expressed in conversation, even in large groups where not everyone was known to each other. In Albania last winter, it was notable at dinner parties that no one said much of anything at all, although it was years after the end of the dictatorship; they passed the evening telling very long jokes.) Except in Tiananmen Square, the police and the army are invisible in the cities—of course they are there, but their low profile was unexpected. The last bastion of Maoism seems to be a soap opera about the Long March that runs every night on television—swamped by music videos and game shows—featuring a kindly, avuncular Mao helping old soldiers cross streams and sharing his rice with peasant children. Otherwise, what used to be called "Marxist-Leninist-Mao Zedong thought" is now a get-rich scheme for Party members.

In the villages, movement is strictly controlled, to keep the cities from be-coming, like Mexico City or Lagos, junkheaps of the uprooted. But peasant unrest has always led to the fall of empires in China, and the government is frantically applying bandages: eliminating taxes for farmers, building roads and power grids and schools and hospitals. The policy toward the minori-ties seems to have changed, encouraging cultural identity rather than sub-suming it into nationhood. In the parts of Yunnan Province that I saw, the Naxi people and Naxi everything were ubiquitous, the Naxi language with its truly pictographic writing was now being taught in schools, and Joseph Rock—the first Western Naxi scholar, whose writings haunt the last Cantos of Ezra Pound—has been canonized as a local saint. Where the government remains stubbornly unaccommodating is in the case of Falun Gong, a spiritual practice, popular in the villages, that officials see as a subversive force, and which is being hopelessly suppressed—martyrdom always being the best recruitment. This seems inexplicable, especially when Taoist and Buddhist temples are being built or restored everywhere, and are filled with practitioners.

Perhaps the greatest surprise for me was that the hundred-year Chinese inferiority complex toward the West appears to be over. They have gone from desiring the things of the West, to making the things for the West, to owning the companies that make the things (including the "IBM" computer on which I am typing). China is the one place in the world where the Pax Americana seems far away, where almost no one asks about Bush. It's holding the chits for much of America's trillion-dollar debt; in China, the US is Little Brother. At the cancelled Century City First International Poetry Festival, I never figured out where Century City is, but it was clear where the century is going.

[2005]

Oranges & Peanuts For Sale
(A Photograph by Anton Bruehl)

O RANGES COME FROM Asia, but no one knows exactly where. The Chinese mention them in their earliest writings; the word is Sanskrit: *naranga.* Some say they were grown in Mesopotamia; some say the Egyptians ate them; some say there are oranges in the Bible, but some say those are not oranges at all. The Romans got them from the Persians, and built the first greenhouses with sheets of mica to protect them: "orangeries." Jupiter gave Juno an orange on their wedding day, as a symbol of eternal love, but oranges died out in most of the Mediterranean with the fall of the Empire. The Moors kept them cultivated in Spain; the Crusaders brought them back to Italy. Columbus carried orange seeds with him on his second voyage. The Portuguese took them to Brazil; not many years later, no one knows why, the first Western travelers deep in the interior reported seeing wild orange trees growing. Bernal Díaz del Castillo himself planted the first orange seeds in Mexico, in Tonalá, in the week of 12-20 July 1518. The orange is not a fruit, but a berry; I don't know why. *La mar no tiene naranjas,* the sea has no oranges.

The peanut is not a nut, but a legume. It came from Brazil, or it came from Peru, or it came from Brazil to Peru, or it came from the Guaraní region of Paraguay and Bolivia to Brazil and Peru; no one knows. The Spanish brought it to the Caribbean, where the Arawaks called it "mani"; then they brought it from the Caribbean to Mexico, where the Aztecs called it "cacahuete"; both words are still used in Spanish. The Portuguese brought it to Africa, where it was called "nguba"; the slaves brought it to the American South, where it was called "goober" or, as in the song, "goober pea." The Spanish brought it to the Philippines, and it spread to China, where it was called the "foreign bean." The Chinese brought it to Japan, where it was called the "Chinese bean." Someone, no one knows who, brought it from Africa to India, where it was called the "Mozambique bean." In the gold rush of the 1870s, the Chinese brought it to Australia, where, a few decades later, Anton Bruehl was born. The idiosyncratic American delight, peanut butter, was invented by a physician in St. Louis in the 1890s, but no one knows his name.

During the Second World War, it became difficult for Brazil to export oranges. The groves were neglected, and nearly every orange tree in the country, some forty million of them, died from a disease no one had known before, which they called La Tristeza. *La naranja es la tristeza*, the orange is sadness.

La naranja es la tristeza del azahar profanado, the orange is the sadness of its violated blossom, *pues se torna fuego y rojo que antes fue puro y blanco*, for what was once pure and white turns fire and red. In England and Sicily, it was the symbol of the victim's heart; you pinned the name to an orange and hid it in the chimney until the person died. The peanut has never been a symbol of anything, though some African tribes believed it was one of the few plants to possess a soul.

The peanut is mysterious. It is small, with leaves on the top and flowers on the bottom. The flowers pollinate themselves, lose their petals, and then the ovaries enlarge, grow away from the plant, turn into long stems that burrow into the earth and form peanuts at their tips. The peanut is the only plant that forms its fruit underground. It is a metaphor for something, but I don't know what. García Lorca never mentioned a peanut.

An orange is green, and only turns orange when the weather cools. The color is named after the fruit; the fruit is not named after the color.

The botanist George Washington Carver, who devoted his life to the domestication of peanuts, once had a dream. God appeared to him and said, "Ask me anything." "Tell me everything there is to know about the peanut." And God replied: "Your mind is too small to comprehend the peanut."

I.

ON A SHIP off the coast of Java in October 1904, a young French doctor, Victor Segalen, makes a note to himself: "Write a book on exoticism." Fourteen years later, he is still writing notes for that book, which in 1908 he had predicted would be published in 1918 and cost exactly 3.50 francs. In the meantime, he has lived for two years in a kind of sexual paradise in Tahiti; gone to Djibouti to find people who knew Rimbaud; collaborated with his close friend Claude Debussy on unrealized operas about Orpheus and the Buddha; published a novel based on Maori mythology; learned Chinese; led archeological expeditions in China and written a book on its stone statuary; published a now-classic novel, *René Leys*, based on his audience with the Emperor; written a book of prose poems inspired by Chinese steles and another that is a commentary on imagined Chinese paintings; fought in World War I; and returned to China to recruit workers for French munitions factories. In the months before his accidental death in 1919 at age 41, he will suffer a nervous breakdown and have a long convalescence in Algeria. The last entry for his book on exoticism considers a final sentence for the foreword to the book.

Segalen's *Essay on Exoticism*, as it remains, is an essay on writing an essay on exoticism, the things that need to be discussed (sex, time, space, individualism, nature, race, painting, Hinduism, morality, travel, extraterrestrials, French literature, the future) and the things that need to be avoided: "It cannot be about such things as the tropics or coconut trees, the colonies or Negro souls, nor about camels, ships, great waves, scents, spices, or enchanted islands . . . nor about any of the preposterous things that the word 'Exoticism' commonly calls to mind." True exoticism, he writes in italics, is the "*manifestation of Diversity.*" It is a "spectacle of Difference": everything that is "foreign, strange, unexpected, surprising, mysterious, amorous, superhuman, heroic, and even divine, everything that is *Other.*"

Exoticism is "not an adaptation to something; it is not the perfect comprehension of something outside oneself that one has managed to embrace fully"—he is thinking of contemporaries such as Paul Gauguin or Pierre Loti, notorious for "going native"—"but the keen and immediate perception of an eternal incomprehensibility." Exoticism is not "the vision of the tourist or of the mediocre spectator, but the forceful and curious reaction to a shock felt by someone of strong individuality in response to some object whose distance from oneself he alone can perceive and savor." Too enamored with Nietzsche, he writes that only an Artist has the sensibility to understand and savor exoticism's "aesthetics of diversity." And he coins a new word for this new type of artist: the Exote.

2.

Exoticism is dependent on a kind of ignorance; clearly, that which is known and familiar is not exotic. Exoticism brings the shock of non-recognition. And photography, with its real documentation of the seemingly unreal unknown—far more than paintings or poems or novels, which blurred the boundaries between the exotic and fantasy—has been both exoticism's primary vehicle and a source of its partial dissolution.

It began by making the familiar exotic: Fox Talbot taking photographs of books and leaves and china to see how they would look as these strange new objects, photographs. But it quickly moved into making the unfamiliar exotic, as photographers packed off with their heavy equipment to the corners of the earth. It was a fortuitous conjunction of technique and aesthetics. Long exposures necessitated that the subject had to be posed in isolation, and the isolation of the subject, its decontextualization, meant that the photographs carried the requisite aura of the exotic. There is nothing known, and nothing to know, about the world inhabited by the "noble savage" American Indians of Edward Curtis or the languid North African odalisques of Lenhert and Landrock. Like the subjects of pornography, they are surfaces, objects of curiosity or desire detached from the rest of life, theirs or ours.

The invention of the reflex camera, of course, froze humans in motion, presenting a moment from that real life. Merely by presenting a context—that is, much more information—it became a force for anti-exoticism, revealing that those italicized *Others*, despite their dress and surroundings, were not all that different from unitalicized us. What Cartier-Bresson, to take the obvious example, finds around the world is a common humanity: in Urumqi, a mother chastises her daughter; in Noboribetsu, businessmen sleep on a train; in Bali, a girl gets her hair done. The *Face of Asia* is a human face, recognizable to all.

Exoticism, in the 20th century, with the rise of universal travel, tended more toward spectacle or class than geography. Spectacle—panoramas of vast numbers of people all engaged in the same thing—was uncommon outside of Chinese or North Korean political celebrations or Salgado's famous Brazilian gold miners. So, with the advent of computer technology, it began to be invented rather than reported, most notably in Andreas Gursky's enormous photographs of endlessly repeated images. As simulacra, they were objects of a kind of *faux* exoticism for an age of *faux* everything.

Class meant the very rich or niche groups on the fringes of humanity. Yet however bizarre the subjects, their exoticism—if they were exotic at all—was more dependent on the form of the image than its content. The subject was posed, almost always staring directly at the camera; interior or exterior surroundings were minimal or non-existent, unless they were as unusual as the subject. The prevailing sentiment was the wonder of the weird. In contrast, a photograph of anyone doing anything was reportage, a slice of life, and not especially exotic, however equally voyeuristic. A transvestite photographed by Arbus or Mapplethorpe was exotic; a transvestite photographed by Brassai or Goldin was not. Or was not until time had passed: In the rapid acceleration of change on earth, the new version of old-fashioned exoticism is nearly anything that happened the day before yesterday.

3.

Segalen writes: "There are born travelers or *exotes* in the world. They are the ones who will recognize . . . those unforgettable transports which arise . . . from the moment of Exoticism." Mitch Epstein has always struck me as an exote, one who does not normally photograph traditionally exotic subjects, yet often somehow discovers exotic moments.

Some representative photographs:

A crowd of typical New York City policemen on the street. Except that one of them appears to be wearing lipstick.

A young couple standing on a littered sidewalk, gazing into a shoddy store window at some ugly landscape paintings. Except that one of the paintings is quite crooked.

A driver in Gujarat, India, photographed from the back seat, sitting calmly smoking. Except that he and the interior of the car are completely covered in dust.

An unremarkable window with chiffon curtains in a town called Cheshire, Ohio. Except that there are two surveillance cameras on the window ledge.

A luxurious suburban house by a pond in California, surrounded by thick trees and a verdant lawn. Except that behind the house stretches an expanse of desert wasteland.

An audience of smiling, ordinary-looking Americans, who could be at a school play. Except that they are watching a half-naked woman being spanked by a man in leather.

Beautiful swirling clouds, worthy of one of Constable's cloud studies. Except that they are issuing from two smokestacks at a coal power plant.

Epstein does not photograph extraordinary events, nor does he create events for the photograph, nor does he "manipulate" (as they now say) the image. All of his moments are real and ordinary, except that there is often an "except that."

Sometimes the mystery of the photograph depends on the juxtaposition of two incongruent elements:

A cloth bundle (someone sleeping?) on the ground in a beautiful flowering garden; two rows of magnificent trees leading like a processional way to an oil refinery; a high school football team practicing on the field, with a huge power plant belching smoke in the distance; a battered briefcase on a pristine mattress in an apparently empty room; an American flag on a hanger in a plastic dry-cleaning bag; a typical Middle American grandma, holding a handgun on the arm of her easy chair.

Sometimes it is a single incongruous element:

A Vietnamese still life, with a shirtless man in the background. A lamp, a red plastic bucket, a vase with a forlorn spray of flowers, a voltage regulator with a cat sleeping on it, and a pig's foot in a plastic bag.

Sometimes the mystery is in the subtle variations of elements:

Four identical statues of Ho Chi Minh on a shelf; two wrapped in newspaper, one partially unwrapped, one entirely unwrapped. (We understand the wrapped and the unwrapped, but why is one partially unwrapped?)

Two Vietnamese girls wearing similar but not identical, elaborate, somewhat ridiculous hairpieces. The face of one of them, though no cigarette is visible, is obscured by smoke.

(Segalen writes: "All interest resides in Difference. The finer the Difference . . . the greater the awakening and stimulation of the feeling for Diversity. Red and green? Not at all! Red and reddish, then red and another red with an infinite number of gradations. . . . Separated from each other, the objects might seem vaguely similar, homogenous; placed side by side, they are opposed to each other, or, at least, they "exist" with all the more force because matter, richer and more supple, has more means and nuanced modalities.")

Sometimes there is a spectacle of incongruity:

A burly policeman or security guard sitting at a table with a shotgun, a stun gun, a heavy-duty flashlight, and a box of plastic "examination gloves," peering straight at us through binoculars. And more: he is sitting in the New Orleans Museum of Art, in front of an abandoned information desk. And even more: he has a large tin of cookies on his table.

A group of women, young and old, looking for something—a lost earring or contact lens—on a sidewalk in New York. And more: they are all wearing impossibly bright polyester dresses. And more: one is holding a magazine whose back cover is a liquor advertisement with a single large word: "Authentic."

Four hippie chicks in Topanga Canyon in 1974, one with a requisite tambourine, another with requisite feathers in her hair. And more: they sit together on bales of hay, fondling an enormous boa constrictor. And even more: behind them, in the upper right of the photograph, a baby lies unattended in the dirt, next to an overturned bottle of milk.

A simple exoticist would have framed the four young women and the snake. An exote like Epstein transforms the merely strange into mystery—Segalen's "eternal incomprehensibility"—by including the element that lies in a corner of the frame.

In the century since Segalen wrote, the word "diversity" has, ironically, constricted, and now largely refers to matters of ethnicity, gender, sexual preference. It has become difficult to separate his *"manifestation of Diversity"* from an advertising campaign with representatives of various races. And yet, Mitch Epstein's photographs are evidence that the dream of a genuine exoticism remains possible in a world where we think we already know what everything in the world looks like. It is not that Epstein travels to odd corners of the globe. His "spectacle of Difference" is that what he sees there are ordinary things and scenes that seem not quite ordinary, and ordinary people who are not quite like ordinary people like us.

[2006]

In Blue

I.

G O BACK far enough and there is no blue.

Blue, black, blonde, blaze, the French *blanc,* and even *yellow* all derive from one proto-Indo-European word: **bhel*—that which is shining, burning, flashing, or that which is already burnt.

Homer's sea is notoriously *wine-dark.* Odysseus' hair is the color of a hyacinth. (Milton, in turn, blind and a classicist, gave his Adam "hyacinthine locks.")

In most of the languages of Asia, Africa, and the pre-Columbian Americas, there is one word for blue and green. Linguists, with no ear for language, call that word *grue.*

Thoreau: "Walden is blue at one time and green at another, even from the same point of view. Lying between the earth and the heavens, it partakes of the color of both."

Go back far enough and Africans, in the European languages, are blue. Ravens, in the Icelandic sagas, are blue.

In Welsh, *glas* is the color of the sky, grass, and silver; *glas* is also vigor, the life-force. In Middle English, *blewe* is the color of both the sea and of burnt-out ashes.

The primary colors for the Mayas and Aztecs were yellow, red, white, and black: the colors of the various kinds of corn they grew.

2.

Kandinsky said that blue creates the feeling of supernatural rest. "When it sinks almost to black, it echoes a grief that is hardly human. When it rises toward white . . . it grows weaker and more distant."

Kandinsky cites a Doctor Freudenberg of Weimar, who had a patient who could not eat a certain sauce without tasting blue. Kandinsky does not specify the sauce.

Kandinsky writes:

"There are pale blue spots on the yellow glare. Only my eyes saw the pale blue spots. They did my eyes good. Why didn't anyone else see the pale blue spots on the yellow glare?"

3.

Blue is a sound.

Amy Beach said an A-flat is blue. Rimsky-Korsakov said an E-sharp is blue. Franz Liszt, rehearsing in Weimar in 1842, implored the orchestra to add a little blue.

Scriabin said that both a G-flat and an F-sharp are an intense blue; B-natural an ordinary blue; and E-natural a sky blue.

Painting, said Arthur G. Dove, is "music of the eyes."

Blue is a sound: blues.

Kandinsky said that the sound of a flute is light blue, a cello a darker blue, a double bass an even darker blue, and the organ darkest of all.

Thoreau: "All sound heard at the greatest possible distance produces one and the same effect, a vibration of the universal lyre, just as the intervening atmosphere makes a distant ridge of earth interesting to our eyes by the azure tint it imparts to it."

Blue is the color of Visuddha, the chakra located in the throat.

4.

Blue is a snail.

In Biblical Hebrew, the word for blue is *tekeleth*, the name of the snail from which a blue dye was derived.

The Talmud says these snails appear only once every seventy years.

5.

Raoul Dufy: "Blue is the only color that maintains its own character in all of its tones . . . it will always stay blue."

Blue is the color of the Persian paradise.

6.

Questioned by an anthropologist, a Huichol shaman identified Pantone 301C as the blue that is sacred.

7.

Shepherds in northern Iraq and remote valleys in the Caucasus Mountains of Armenia, the Yezidis speak Kurdish but do not consider themselves Kurds. They say they come from India, which is why they believe in reincarnation and have strict castes. It is unknown how many there are, for if you ask someone if he is Yezidi, he will not reply. They worship Satan, whom they call Malek Taus, the Peacock King, who was forgiven by God and is not evil.

They have two sacred books. The only copy of one of them, the Black Book, was stolen centuries ago and taken, they say, to England; but there are men called the Talkers who can recite every word of it, and they pass it on to their sons.

They are forbidden to eat lettuce.

They loathe, or fear, the color blue. The worst curse in their language is: "May you drop dead dressed in blue."

8.

Malevich: "I have broken the blue boundary and have come out into the white."

[2008]

PHOTOGRAPHY AND ANTHROPOLOGY
(A CONTACT SHEET)

I.

S IBLINGS: both born in the late 1830s or early 1840s, both growing up—and, in a way, still spending their lives—pulled from side
to side in a contentious, unresolvable custody battle between objectiv-
ity and subjectivity, truth and fiction, science and art, reason and the
imagination.

Both preoccupied with time: Photography as an art, perhaps the only
art, that always reaches us in the past tense, the record of a moment that will
not return; an art that is inextricable from nostalgia, and one that has particularly appealed to melancholics. Anthropology as a social science that was
based on the urgency that its objects of study would soon be lost—indeed
the mere presence of the anthropologist was a sign of that loss—that it all
must be recorded now, in word or image; a discipline that has appealed to
the discontents of technological civilization, those who long for something
else, a something forever receding.

Henri Cartier-Bresson, in 1952, could be speaking in the voice of an
anthropologist: "We photographers deal in things that are continually van-
ishing, and when they have vanished there is no contrivance on earth that
can bring them back again."

2.

In the 1890s, in the pages of the *Journal of the Anthropological Institute of
Great Britain and Ireland*, there is no doubt that photography is useful for
anthropologists. C. H. Read maintains that photographs "deal with facts
about which there can be no question," unlike the "timid answers of natives

to questions propounded through the medium of a native interpreter [that] can be but rarely relied upon, and are more apt to produce confusion than to be of benefit to comparative anthropology."

Photographic facts are clearly facts, a more solid foundation for a new science than the information provided by subjective informants, who are not unlike the unreliable narrators in the contemporaneous fictions of Henry James. (There is as yet no consideration of the unreliable human clicking the shutter of the disinterested recording instrument.) But it is debatable how these facts should be obtained. M. V. Portman insists that "for ethnology, accuracy is required." This means that the natives "should be stark naked, a full face and profile view should be taken of each, and the subject should touch a background painted in black and white chequers, each exactly two inches square. All abnormalities, or deformations, whether natural or intentional, should be photographed." Furthermore, "delicate lighting and picturesque photography are not wanted." Portman produces eleven volumes of anthropometric photographs of Andaman Islanders, and an additional four volumes of statistics for each individual: pulse, respiration rate, body temperature, weight, etc., as well as tracings of his or her hands and feet.

For Everard im Thurn, who has spent many years in the jungles of Guyana, the "use of the camera" for "an accurate record" is "not of the mere bodies of primitive folk—which might indeed be more accurately measured and photographed for such purposes dead than alive, could they be conveniently obtained when in that state—but of these folk regarded as living beings." Im Thurn—recapitulating early photography's own move from studio to field—recommends taking pictures in local settings where the subjects would be comfortable. He may well be the first to think about the feelings of the "uncharacteristically miserable natives" portrayed in contemporary photographs, whom he compares to "badly stuffed and distorted birds and animals." Among his few surviving photographs are some "natural poses" that look like snapshots and (possibly unconsciously) homoerotic portraits of native lads lounging.

With its third, 1899 edition, *Notes and Queries*—the handbook for English anthropologists—includes extensive information on photographing in the field.

3.

At the turn of the century, anthropological photography fell into two categories. For those who considered themselves anthropologists, the visual was merely the means to a scientific end. Their concern was strictly documentation: surveys of "types" with anthropometrical measurements; inventories of tools, weapons, ornaments, shelters; and surveillance: step-by-step records of ceremonies, tool-making, food preparation, and so on. For the others—travelers and professional photographers producing work for books, magazines, and the postcard trade—it meant an aesthetic of exoticism largely presented in the reigning pictorialist mode. The two would come together in 1900 in the figure of Edward Curtis, who meticulously collected vast amounts of ethnographic material and information about American Indians while simultaneously creating manipulated situations and "reenactments" for his romanticized images—a conscious effort to recuperate a past glory from the actual deracination and squalor he was seeing.

The question, then or now, was whether truth (this "science of man") was better served by the photos of sullen natives standing naked next to measuring rods, or by the portraits of noble savages posed like Roman orators. Beyond some visual details, did either convey much actual information? Or was it another kind of "information"?

George Hunt, the first Native American photographer (he was half-English and half-Tlingit, and raised as a Kwakiutl) assisted both Curtis and Franz Boas. He, for one, believed that the camera, as he wrote in a letter to Boas, "will show you everything Plainer than writing it alon." But he complained about Curtis that "he Dont know what all the meaning and the story of it. . . . Mr Curtice did not take the story or did not care as long as he get the picture taken."

4.

A photograph, like a line of poetry, has no fixed meaning. On the one hand, it does not exist without a caption, mentally provided by the viewer when the subject or context is recognizable or by the photographer when it is not. We either know what we are seeing or need to be told. On the other hand, it cannot be paraphrased; no words can convey all that we are seeing. A photograph tells us something, but never enough; much of its power is precisely in that it gives us some undefinable sense of the subject matter while propelling us to imagine the rest, the world outside the literal frame. This is especially true in anthropological photography, where the subject, by definition, is an unfamiliar culture, whether that culture lives in longhouses or hangs out in malls.

A monograph may give us the facts of social organization, myths, ceremonies of birth and initiation and death, but a photograph, as the old Kodak slogan goes, "puts you in the picture." It has a tangible immediacy. You are, after all, looking at someone who is often looking at you; or you are watching, at a slight distance, people doing something, with a glimpse of the unknown landscape they inhabit. Unlike the data of a monograph, a photograph induces response. George Hunt had said that Curtis took the photograph but did not "take the story." It's always the case: the viewer makes the story, the narrative of which the photograph is a scene. A kind of television "docudrama": fiction, written by the viewer, "based on actual events" seen by the photographer.

5.

Too easy to say, as is often said, that anthropological photography began as an institutionalized contempt: the colonialist "shooting" the natives. For it also began as curiosity, fired by the belief, in the social Darwinism of the time, that tribal cultures represented the "childhood" of our technological society, that what we were looking at was our unevolved selves.

After the Second World War, in reaction to the horrors and human evils, this turned into empathy, epitomized by Edward Steichen's 1955 *The Family of Man*, a kind of pop anthropology, the most successful photo exhibition ever, and a book that was on the coffee tables of seemingly every middle-class Stevenson Democrat. Based on Steichen's conviction that "photography is a major force for explaining man to man," its message was that we are all just like us. In the Orinoco or in Kansas, a mom is a mom. Or, in the words of the title of the Magnum series that ran in the *Ladies' Home Journal* in the late 1940s, "People Are People the World Over," as nearly everyone, from Freud and Jung to Lévi-Strauss, had been saying in more elaborate terms for most of the 20th century.

More recently, the reigning academic dogmas of identity politics and deconstruction have intersected to assert the ineluctable Otherness of the Other and our doomed incomprehensibility in the tangle of differences. Turgenev's famous line that "the heart of another is a dark forest" now applies to the people of the dark forest. Apparently the only acceptable response to this post-colonial and post-structuralist critique is self-consciousness. The subject of a photograph or film or monograph is not the culture, but the photographer or filmmaker or anthropologist making an artifact about the culture. After more than a century of trying to suppress autobiography, it all ends up becoming nothing but autobiography.

6.

Anthropological photographs are boxes within boxes. Most tribal cultures are dependent on the control of knowledge, the presence of secrets that are known only to initiates or to a priestly caste. (Our "seeing is believing" is their "not seeing is believing.") Western society, outside of the military, believes that knowledge must be shared and accessible to all; it gets a particular thrill when secrets are revealed. In the 19th century, the response to the veiled women of Islam was the popularity of postcards showing half-naked Muslim women—anyone with a dime could enter the harem. But of course these photos, literal unveilings, revealed nothing under the skin of the women themselves. "A photograph is a secret about a secret," said Diane Arbus. "The more it tells you the less you know."

In the 1890s, the Arrernte people in central Australia, fearing that the encroachment of white settlers would ultimately doom them, astonishingly grasped the workings of Western media and decided their only hope was in telling their story to the world. They enlisted the head of the local telegraph station, Frank Gillen, who spoke some Arrernte; he, in turn, cleverly brought in Baldwin Spencer, a hyperenergetic professor of biology, who was friendly with Sir James Frazer in Cambridge. The Arrernte not only provided detailed information about many aspects of their lives, they also allowed Spencer and Gillen to witness and photograph their secret ceremonies.

The Arrernte were not saved in the manner they had hoped, but Spencer and Gillen's books, articles, and illustrated lectures were a sensation in Europe, providing a living example of a society still in its "childhood" stage. Out of Spencer and Gillen came, among many other books, Durkheim's theories of religion and society in *The Elementary Forms of Religious Life* and Freud's foundational patricide myth in *Totem and Taboo*. Malinowski launched his career debunking the theories based on European inventions of the Aborigine.

In recent years, with somewhat heightened sensitivity to the aboriginal peoples, the photographs of the secret Arrernte ceremonies taken by Spencer are generally not published. Not, as might be expected, so that white people won't see them. The Arrernte do not want them available to their own uninitiated men and women—the people to whom this knowledge would matter, a knowledge on which a world depends.

7.

The pictorialist Roland Reed, late in life, recalling his early years photographing in the American West, said, "An Indian was really an Indian in those days." It need hardly be said that Indians are still Indians in these days, that no culture was, as in utopian dreams, timeless and unchanging before its "first contact" with the West. The subjects of anthropological photographs may now be more likely to be wearing t-shirts than body paint, but they too, like their ancestors in the early photographs, belong to a culture in perpetual flux and a moment that is always receding. In one of his letters, George Hunt wrote, "oh Mr Boas, What I have seen over there I will never see again." It's as true now, anywhere, as it was on the Northwest Coast more than a hundred years ago.

The cultures once imagined as living in a timeless present from the beginning of history have entered history. Even more, they have entered photographic history, as the Indian of these days looks at the Indian of those days. The Seminole/Muskogee/Navajo woman photographer Hulleah J. Tsinhnahjinnie has recorded a beautiful dream of George Trager's famous 1891 photograph of Big Foot, lying frozen in the snow after the massacre at Wounded Knee:

> In my dream I was an observer floating—I saw Big Foot as he is in the photograph, and my heart ached. I was about to mourn uncontrollably when into the scene walked a small child, about six years old. She walked about the carnage, looking into the faces of those lying dead in the snow. She was searching for someone. Her small mocassin footprints imprinted the snow as she walked over to Big Foot, looking into his face. She shakes

his shoulders, takes his frozen hand into her small, warm hand, and helps him to his feet. He then brushes the snow off his clothes. She waits patiently with her hand extended, he then takes her hand and they walk out of the photograph.

8.

Some Australian aboriginal groups do not allow photographs of deceased people to be shown. Across the Tasman Sea, the opposite is the case. The Maori early on adopted photography in their reverence for ancestors as the source of a group's knowledge and authority, and incorporated them as part of the *whakapapa*, the genealogy that is the continuing "story of ourselves." Photos hang in the meeting-houses next to the carved wooden images of earlier ancestors; photos are displayed at funerals and sometimes attached to headstones.

Some Australian aboriginal groups do not allow photographs of the living to be taken. A sign at Uluru (Ayer's Rock) warns tourists: "Having one's photograph taken is considered culturally inappropriate as the image captured on film, believed to be part of one's spirit, is removed from that person's control forever."

The Yoruba believe that twins are blessed, more closely connected to the spirit world; a family that has twins proudly displays their photographs. But if the twins are two boys (or two girls) and one dies before the picture can be taken, they photograph the survivor and print the negative twice in the same frame. If the twins are a boy and a girl and the girl dies, they photograph the boy twice, once in girl's clothing, and put the two negatives together. (Or vice-versa if it is the boy who dies.)

From culture to culture, a photograph is inextricable from spirit—the "aura" Benjamin thought was missing in reproducibility—a power to be maintained or avoided.

9.

With the universality of the camera, we are in an era of self-representation. These images are compelling subjects of anthropological inquiry, like arts or crafts, the products of a certain culture's sensibilities: the way, for example, that the Yoruba photograph their patriarchs seated in the exact same position as their traditional sculpture. But they may not be anthropological photographs, which traditionally have depended on a crossing of cultures, a true "outsider art."

A photographer told me, some years ago, about waiting in line at B & H, the famous New York camera store, behind a group of Papua New Guinea tribesmen, in full-feathered regalia, who had been brought to the city for the opening of a museum exhibition. They were served by the legendarily cranky Hasidic Jews who run the place, themselves in native costume, and who were utterly nonplussed: a customer is a customer.

The next chapter in the history of traditional anthropological photography might well begin with those Papuan New Guinean photos of indigenous New York.

IO.

The Aymara in the southern Andes believe that one can only speak of what one has personally experienced. Thus, you cannot say, "Lincoln was assassinated," only "I have heard that Lincoln was assassinated."

Unlike nearly everyone else, they believe that the past is in front of you and the future behind you, for the past has been clearly seen and the future is unknown.

[2008]

QUESTIONS OF DEATH
(1892)

1. Is the cause of death recognized (wounds, disease, etc.), or is it assigned to some act of commission or of omission of the defunct?

2. Do the friends or relations attend upon the sick man until his death, or is it considered unlucky to be present at the supreme moment?

3. What is done with the body immediately after death? Are the limbs straightened or bent up?

4. Is ordinary clothing left upon the body, or is any special dress used?

5. Is the body left in the house, or removed to any other locality, before burial?

6. Is embalming practiced, and what preservatives are used? Are portions of the body treated in any way?

7. Is there any funeral procession, and who composes it?

8. Are hired mourners known?

9. Are signs of mourning worn, such as shaving the head, wearing clothes of unusual colors, etc.?

10. Is self-mutilation practiced by the mourners?

11. Are speeches (eulogies of the deceased, etc.) made at the grave? Are these pronounced by public orators, or by friends of the defunct?

12. What is the mode of burial: in trees, on platforms, in the earth?

13. Is any coffin used?

14. Are the remains left undisturbed, or are the bones removed when decay is complete?

15. What is buried with the body: any implements, weapons, food, or eating utensils, and why?

16. Are wives, servants, slaves, or favorite animals buried with the body, and what reason is assigned for this practice?

17. Are any images of wood or pottery buried with the body?

18. What is the posture of the body in the grave?
18a. Is it regarded as of importance whether the head is directed to any point of the compass? Are there any ceremonies at the digging of the grave?

19. Is a grave or coffin ever re-opened for the interment of a near relation?

20. Is an interment ever made in a canoe, and is the latter provided with all necessary apparatus?

21. Are heads of friends preserved by smoking or otherwise?

22. How are these regarded, as a protection or as mere souvenirs? Will the owners readily part with them?

23. In burials by inhumation, is any mound or prominent memorial raised above the grave?

24. Are fetishes placed on the graves?

25. Are these for the good of the deceased or as a protection against him (to keep his spirit quiet)?

26. Are there any superstitious ideas about graveyards? Will the natives visit them at all times?

27. Are objects of value buried in the grave, and are they considered safe from theft?

28. What is the difference between the burial of a chief and of a common man or woman? Does it differ only in degree of cost?

29. Are individuals buried in their houses, and are these houses then deserted?

30. Are the persons who have handled a corpse regarded as unclean? For how long? How do they purify themselves?
30a. In what posture is the body carried to the grave?

31. Is cremation practiced as well as inhumation, tree burial, etc., and why? How is the body burnt, on a specially prepared pyre or in the house of deceased?

33. Are there any ceremonies observed, or special instruments used, at the lighting of the funeral fire?

34. Are any living creatures, inanimate objects, incense, etc., burnt in it?

35. Is a mound erected over the pyre, or are the bones collected and preserved or buried?

36. If buried, what is the method (form of grave and of the cinerary urn, accompanying objects, attendant ceremonies, etc.)?

37. If the calcined bones are kept above ground, who keeps them, and how are they regarded? Is the fate of surviving relations bound up in their preservation?

38. Is desiccation of the dead body practiced?

39. Are mummies made?
    (Describe the process and the nature of preservatives used.)

[2008]

III.

"POETRY IS NEWS"

I AM BOTH pessimistic and optimistic about what's happening and briefly, or not so briefly, I'd like to say why:

First, I take the word "politics" in a very narrow sense: that is, how governments are run. And I take the word "government" to mean the organized infliction or alleviation of suffering among one's own people and among other peoples.

One of the things that happened after the Vietnam War was that, in the US, on the intellectual left, politics metamorphosed into something entirely different: identity politics and its nerd brother, theory, who thought he was a Marxist, but never allowed any actual governments to interrupt his train of thought. The right however, stuck to politics in the narrow sense, and grew powerful in the absence of any genuine political opposition, or even criticism, for the left had its mind elsewhere: It was preoccupied with finding examples of sexism, classism, racism, colonialism, homophobia, etc.—usually among its own members or the long-dead, while ignoring the genuine and active racists/ sexists/ homophobes of the right—and it tended to express itself in an incomprehensible academic jargon or tangentially referential academic poetry under the delusion that such language was some form of resistance to the prevailing power structures—power, of course, only being imagined in the Foucauldian abstract. (Never mind that truly politically revolutionary works—Tom Paine or the Communist Manifesto or Brecht or Hikmet or a thousand others—are written in simple direct speech.) Meanwhile, Ronald Reagan was completely dismantling the social programs of the New Deal and Johnson's Great Society—creating the millions of homeless, the 25% of American children who live in poverty, the obscene polarization of wealth, and so on. (And the poets, typically, were only moved to speak up when he cut the NEA budget.) Clinton might have had a more compassionate public face, but essentially the political center had shifted so far right that today the Democratic party is to the right of any European conservative party, and the Republicans just slightly to the left of a European national front party.

The main result of almost thirty years of these so-called politics on the left is that there are now more women and minorities in the Norton anthologies, and we all know how to pronounce "hegemony"—surely a great comfort to the 4 million people, predominately black men, currently in the prison system, or the teenage girls in most places in America who need an abortion and there's nowhere to get help, or the parents and babies who create the statistics of by far the highest infant mortality rate among the technological nations, or the teachers and kids in public school buildings, 95% of which need major repair.

The good news about the monstrosity of the Bush administration is that it is so extreme and so out of control that it has finally woken up the left, and once again we're talking about politics as the rest of the world knows it, about people getting slaughtered, people being hungry, and people deprived of basic human rights—and not about language as a capitalist construct or queer musicology. The best news of all is that very young people—the generation of the Zeroes—after the decades of MTV and Nintendo somnambulism, are being politicized by the collapsed economy, the prospect of a reinstituted draft, and the realization that their sneakers are made by child-slaves in the Third World. Every political youth movement has its own culture—look at the 30s, the 60s, or radical Islam today. It will be extremely interesting to see, and utterly unexpected to find, what culture this youth movement produces: What will be their ideals and practices, their music and poetry, or even their dress? I have a feeling that we won't have a clue, and that their response may well be a sort of iconoclastic asceticism, not unlike radical Islam, impervious to corporate takeover, and completely alien to their parents. [One of the hardest things for people my age to understand is that this is not 1967 all over again, that things are going to be very different, and that, if we don't learn to listen, we are going to end up being, as our old formula goes, part of the problem and not part of the solution.]

I take this gathering as a kind of union meeting—the union of writers, mainly poets—and it seems to me the primary question for us is: things are going to be happening with or without us, are we going to be part of it, or are we going to continue to talk about essentialism at the MLA and finding your voice at the AWP?

Poets in times of political crises basically have three models. The first is to write overtly political poems, as was done during the Vietnam War. 95% of those poems will be junk, but so what? 95% of anything is junk. It is undeniable that the countless poems and poetry readings against the Vietnam War contributed to creating and legitimizing a general climate of opposition; they were the soul of the movement. And it also resulted in some of the most enduring poems of the 20th century, news that has stayed news indeed.

The second model is epitomized by George Oppen, who as a Communist in the 30s, and a poet uncomfortable with the prevailing modes of political poetry, decided that poets should not be treated differently from others, that the work to be done was organizing, and so he stopped writing and became a union leader.

The third model is César Vallejo, also a Communist in the 20s and 30s. He refused to write propaganda poems—he wanted to write the poems he wanted to write—so to serve the cause he wrote a great deal of propaganda prose.

The first model (political poems) is the most common, and no doubt the one we'll be seeing the most, and frankly it will come as a relief from all those anecdotes of unhappy childhoods and ironic preoccupations with "surface." Oppen, of course, was a kind of secular saint—and most of us are too egotistical to take a vow of silence. But it is the example of Vallejo that seems to me the least explored.

People who are poets presumably know something about writing. So why does it never occur to them to write something other than poems? There are approximately 8,000 poets registered in the Directory of American Poets—are there even four or five who have written an article against the Bush Administration? Most of us can't get onto the Op-Ed page of the *Times*, but most of us do have access to countless other venues: hometown newspapers, college newspapers, professional newsletters, specialist magazines, websites, and so on. All writers have contacts somewhere, and all these periodicals must fill their pages. Even poetry magazines: Why must poetry magazines always be graveyards of orderly tombstones of poems? How many of them in the 1980s, for example, even mentioned the name "Reagan"? How many of them today have any political content at all?

I've been writing articles since Bush's inauguration for translation in magazines and newspapers abroad and, if nothing else, they at least help to demonstrate that the US is not a monolith of opinion. (Foreign periodicals can't get enough of Americans critical of Bush.) In English, I send my articles out via e-mail. It's one of the best ways, and certainly the easiest, to publish political writing in this country. Send it to your friends and let the friends, if they want, send it on. Let the readers vote, not with their feet, but with the forward button.

The last time I was here at St. Marks, in 1994, I was practically laughed off the stage, and widely derided later, for saying that the major organizing force of political opposition in the future was going to be the internet. Now of course, it's a banality. The internet has completely changed all the rules. It's how the like-minded instantly find each other; it's the one national and international forum that has been—so far—impossible to control; and it's practically the only source of opposition information and opinions from everywhere in the world: not only immediate access to the foreign press, but also, to find out what's happening on the other side, to the endless reports available from the Dept. of Defense and right-wing think tanks. That still-unrecognized prophet, Abbie Hoffman, said, almost forty years ago, that if you want to start a revolution, don't bother to organize, seize a television station. With the internet, we all have our own tv stations and publishing companies and newspapers; we are all our own columnists and investigative reporters. The potential is limitless: Trent Lott was brought down by a blog; all the doubts about the war that are seeping into the general public began online; and just this week even Lovely Laura's Poetry Tea got canceled thanks to an e-mail petition.

There are 8,000 poets in the Directory, and Anne Waldman and Ammiel Alcalay, a month ago, had trouble coming up with a list to invite to speak here. One eye may half-open when, like Laura's party, it directly involves them, but most American writers have lost the ability to even think politically, or nationally, or internationally. In all the anthologies and magazines devoted to 9/11 and its aftermath, nearly every single writer resorted to first-person anecdote: "It reminded me of the day my father died . . ." "I took an herbal bath and decided to call an old boyfriend . . ." Barely a one could imagine the event outside of the context of the prison cell of their own expressive self. (Or, on the avant-garde, it was a little too real for ironic pastiche from their expressive non-self.)

We are where we are in part because American writers—supposedly the most articulate members of society—have generally had nothing to say about the world for the last thirty years. How many of those 8,000 poets have ever been to a Third World country (excluding beach vacations)? How many think it worthwhile to translate something? How many can name a single contemporary poet, not living in the US, from Latin America or Africa or Asia? In short, how many know anything more about the world than George Bush knows?

After thirty years of self-absorption in MFA and MLA career-mongering and knee-jerk demography and the personal as political and the impersonal as poetical, American writers now have the government we deserve. We were good Germans under Reagan and Bush I; we were never able to separate Clinton's person from his policies and gave him a complacent benefit of the doubt; and the result is Cheney and Rumsfeld and Ashcroft and Perle and Wolfowitz and Scalia and Rice and their little president. They can't be stopped, but I do think they can be slowed down.

[St. Mark's Poetry Project, New York, February 2003]

Anonymous Sources
(A Talk on Translators & Translation)

SOME YEARS AGO, Bill Moyers did a PBS series on poetry that was filmed at the Dodge Festival in New Jersey. Octavio Paz and I had given a bilingual reading there, and I knew that we would be included in the first program. The morning of the broadcast, I noticed in the index of that day's *New York Times* that there was a review of the show. This being my national television debut, I naturally wondered if their tv critic had discovered any latent star qualities, and quickly turned to the page. This is what he wrote: "Octavio Paz was accompanied by his translator,"—no name given, of course—"always a problematic necessity."

"Problematic necessity," while not yet a cliche about translation, rather neatly embodies the prevailing view of translation. I'd like to look at both terms, beginning with the one that strikes me as accurate: necessity.

Needless to say, no single one of us can know all the languages of the world, not even the major languages, and if we believe—though not all cultures have believed it—that the people who speak other languages have things to say or ways of saying them that we don't know, then translation is an evident necessity. Many of the golden ages of a national literature have been, not at all coincidentally, periods of active and prolific translation. Sanskrit literature goes into Persian which goes into Arabic which turns into the Medieval European courtly love tradition. Indian folk tales are embedded in *The Canterbury Tales*. Shakespeare writes in an Italian form, the sonnet, or in the blank verse invented by the Earl of Surrey for his version of the *Aeneid*; in *The Tempest*, he lifts a whole passage verbatim from Arthur Golding's translation of Ovid. German fiction begins with imitations of the Spanish picaresque and *Robinson Crusoe*. Japanese poetry is first written in Chinese; Latin poetry is first an imitation of the Greek; American poetry in the first half of the 20th century is inextricable from all it translated and learned from classical Chinese, Greek, and Latin; medieval Provençal and modern French; in the second half of the century, it is inextricable from the poetries of Latin America and Eastern Europe, classical Chinese again, and the oral poetries of Native Americans and other indigenous groups. These examples could, of course, be multiplied endlessly. Conversely, cultures that do not translate stagnate, and end up repeating the same things to themselves. Classical Chinese poetry, perhaps the best literary example, is at its height during the T'ang Dynasty, an age of internationalism, and then becomes increasingly moribund for almost a millennium as China cuts itself off from the world. Or, in a wider cultural sense of translation: the Aztec and Inkan empires, which could not translate the sight of some ragged Europeans on horseback into anything human.

But translation is much more than an offering of new trinkets in the literary bazaar. Translation liberates the translation-language. Because a translation will always be read as a translation, as something foreign, it is freed from many of the constraints of the currently accepted norms and conventions in the national literature.

This was most strikingly apparent in China after the revolution in 1949. An important group of modernist poets who had emerged in the 1930s and early 1940s, greatly under the influence of the European poets they were translating, were now forbidden to publish and were effectively kept from writing. All the new Chinese poetry had to be in the promoted forms of socialist realism: folkloric ballads and paeans to farm production and boilerplate factories and heroes of the revolution. (The only exceptions, ironically, or tragically, were the classical poems written by Mao himself.) Yet they could continue to translate foreign poets with the proper political credentials (such as Eluard, Alberti, Lorca, Neruda, Aragon) even though their work was radically different and not social realist at all. When a new generation of poets in the 1970s came to reject socialist realism, their inspiration and models were not the erased and forgotten Chinese modernists—whose poems they didn't know, and had no way of knowing—but rather the foreign poets whom these same modernists had been permitted to translate.

Translation liberates the translation-language, and it is often the case that translation flourishes when the writers feel that their language or society needs liberating. One of the great spurs to translation is a cultural inferiority complex or a national self-loathing. The translation boom in Germany at the turn of the 19th century was a response to the self-perceived paucity of German literature; translation became a project of national culture-building: in the words of Herder, "to walk through foreign gardens to pick flowers for my language." Furthermore, and rather strangely, it was felt that the relative lack of literary associations in the language—particularly in contrast to French—made German the ideal language for translation, and even more, the place where the rest of the world could discover the literature it couldn't otherwise read. Germany, they thought, would become the Central Station of world literature precisely because it had no literature. This proved both true and untrue. German did become the conduit, particularly for Sanskrit and Persian, but it also became much more. Its simultaneous, and not coincidental, production of a great national literature ended up being the most influential poetry and criticism in the West for the rest of the century. [And perhaps it should be mentioned that, contrary to the reigning cliché of Orientalism—namely that scholarship follows imperialism—Germany had no economic interests in either India or Persia. England, which did, had no important scholars in those fields after the pioneering Sir William Jones. Throughout the 19th century, for example, Sanskrit was taught at Oxford exclusively by Germans.]

In the case of the Chinese poets, their coming-of-age during the Cultural Revolution meant that they had been unable to study foreign languages (or much of anything else) and thus were themselves unable to translate. But to escape from their sense of cultural deficiency, they turned to the translations of the previous generation, and began to discover new ways of writing in Chinese, with the result that Chinese poetry experienced its first truly radical and permanent change in centuries.

Among American poets, there have been two great flowerings of translation. The first, before and after the First World War, was largely the work of expatriates eager to overcome their provinciality and to educate their national literature through the discoveries made in their own self-educations: to make the US as "cultured" as Europe. The second, beginning in the 1950s and exploding in the 1960s, was the result of a deep anti-Americanism among American intellectuals: first in the more contained bohemian rebellion against the conformist Eisenhower years and the Cold War, and then as part of the wider expression of disgust and despair during the civil rights movement and the Vietnam War. Translation—the journey to the other— was more than a way out of America: the embrace of the other was, in the

1960s, in its small way, an act of defiance against the government that was murdering Asian others abroad and the social realities that were oppressing minority others at home. Foreign poetry became as much a part of the counterculture as American Indians, Eastern religions, hallucinatory states: a new way of seeing, a new "us" forming out of everything that had not been "us." From 1910 to 1970, it is difficult to think of more than a very few American poets who didn't translate at least something, and many translated a great deal. It was one of the things that one did as a poet, both a practice for one's own work and a community service.

By the early 1970s, of course, this cultural moment was over, and the poets became detached from the intellectual and cultural life of the country, as they vanished along career paths into the creative writing schools. There were now more American poets and poetry readers than in all the previous eras combined, but almost none of them translated. The few who continued to do so, with two or three notable exceptions, were all veterans of the 1960s translation boom.

The obvious result was that we were simply not getting the news. In the 1960s—to take only Latin America—works by Neruda, Paz, Parra, and many others were being translated as, or shortly after, they were being written. There was a lively international dialogue among the living. But for the next thirty years or so, the subsequent generations remained invisible. At various times I was asked to edit anthologies of Latin American poetry, but I realized that at least half of the poets I would want to include had never been translated, and there were simply not enough poet-translators to take on the work.

Paradoxically, the rise of multiculturalism may have been the worst thing to happen to translation. The original multiculturalist critique of the Eurocentrism of the canon and so forth did not lead—as I, for one, hoped it would—to a new internationalism, where Wordsworth would be read alongside Wang Wei, the Greek anthology next to Vidyakara's *Treasury*, Ono no Komachi with H. D. Instead it led to a new form of nationalism, one that was salutary in its inclusion of the previously excluded, but one that limited itself strictly to Americans, albeit hyphenated ones. Freshman literature courses began to teach Chinese-American writers, but no Chinese, Latinos but no Latin Americans. In terms of publishing, if you were a Mexican from the northern side of the Rio Grande, it was not very difficult to get published; if you were from the southern side, it was almost impossible. Co-

incident with an explosion of Chicano Studies departments, Chicano literary presses, special collections at libraries, literary organizations, and so on,
readers in the US had far less contemporary Mexican literature available to
them than they did in the 1960s.

   This complacent period—nationalist without overt flag-waving, isola-
tionist without overt xenophobia, and uninformed—came to an end with
9/11, the rise of the Cheney-Bush administration, and the wars in Afghanistan and Iraq. Once again, Americans were ashamed to be American, were
fed up with America, and began looking abroad just to hear the sound of
someone else's voice. The first years of the 21st century have seen a boom in
new presses that publish translation, grants and prizes, courses in translation, international festivals, websites. Relative to publishing in other countries, the situation is still pathetic: the total number of translated literary
books with any sort of national distribution is still in the low hundreds. But
an awareness has changed—and, for the first time, there is actually some interest in Arabic literature, an almost entirely unexplored library of wonders.
George Bush may be the best thing that happened to literature.

   The necessity of translation is evident; so why is it a problem—or, as they
now say, problematic? Milan Kundera famously considered the poor translations of himself as—and only a man would write this—a form of rape,
and he characterized the bad translations of Kafka as betrayals in a book
called *Testaments Betrayed*. All discussions of translation, like 19th century
potboilers, are obsessed with questions of fidelity and betrayal. But in the
case of a writer like Kundera, who came of age in a society dominated by the
secret police, "betrayal" carries an especially heavy weight. We know what
a translation is supposedly a betrayal of, but is it unfair to ask to whom the
text is being betrayed?

   And one can never mention the word "translation" without some wit
bringing up—as though for the first time—that tedious Italian pun *tradut-
tore traditore*. Luckily, the Italian-American philosopher Arthur Danto has
recently and I hope definitively laid it forever to rest:

   Perhaps the Italian sentence betrays something in the cultural
   unconscious of Italy, which resonates through the political and
   ecclesiastical life of that country, where betrayal, like a shadow,
   is the obverse side of trust. It is an Unconscious into which the

lessons of Machiavelli are deeply etched. Nobody for whom
English is a first language would be tempted to equate translation and treason.

The characterizations of translation as betrayal or treason are based on
the impossibility of exact equivalence, which is seen as a failing. It's true:
a slice of German pumpernickel is not a Chinese steam bun which is not
a French baguette which is not Wonder Bread. But consider a hypotheti-
cal line of German poetry—one I hope will never be written, but probably
has been: "Her body (or his body) was like a fresh loaf of pumpernickel."
Pumpernickel in the poem is pumpernickel, but it is also more than pumpernickel: it is the image of warmth, nourishment, homeyness. When the
cultures are close, it is possible to translate more exactly: say, the German
word *pumpernickel* into the American word *pumpernickel*—which, despite
appearances, are not the same: each carries its own world of referents. But
to translate the line into, say, Chinese, how much would really be lost if it
were a steam bun? (I leave aside sound for the moment.) "His body (her
body) was like a fresh steam bun" also has its charm—especially if you like
your lover doughy.

It's true that no translation is identical to the original. But no reading
of a poem is identical to any other, even when read by the same person.
The first encounter with our poetic pumpernickel might be delightful; at a
second reading, even five minutes later, it could easily seem ridiculous. Or
imagine a 14-year-old German boy reading the line in the springtime of
young Alpine love; then at 50, while serving as the chargé d'affaires in the
German consulate in Kuala Lumpur, far from the bakeries of his youth;
then at 80, in a retirement village in the Black Forest, in the nostalgia for
dirndled maidens. Every reading of every poem is a translation into one's
own experience and knowledge—whether it is a confirmation, a contradic-
tion, or an expansion. The poem does not exist without this act of translation. The poem must move from reader to reader, reading to reading, in
perpetual transformation. The poem dies when it has no place to go.
Translation, above all, means change. In Elizabethan England, one of its
meanings was "death": to be translated from this world to the next. In the
Middle Ages *translatio* meant the theft or removal of holy relics from one
monastery or church to another. In the year 1087, for example, St. Nicolas
appeared in visions to the monks at Myra, near Antioch, where his remains

were kept, and told them he wished to be translated. When merchants arrived from the Italian city of Bari and broke open the tomb to steal the remains, Myra and its surroundings were filled with a wonderful fragrance, a sign of the saint's pleasure. In contrast, when the archdeacon of the Bishop of Turin tried to steal the finger of John the Baptist from the obscure church of Maurienne, the finger struck him dead. (Unlike dead authors, dead saints could maintain control over their translations.) Translation is movement, the twin of metaphor, which means "to move from one place to another." Metaphor makes the familiar strange; translation makes the strange familiar. Translation is change. Even the most concrete and limited form of translation—currency exchange—is in a state of hourly flux.

The only recorded example of translation as replication, not as change, was, not surprisingly, a miracle: Around 250 BCE, 72 translators were summoned to Alexandria to prepare, in 72 days, 72 versions of the Hebrew Bible in Greek. Each one was guided by the Original of all Original Authors and wrote identical translations. 72 translators producing 72 identical texts is an author's—or a book reviewer's—dream and a translator's nightmare.

A work of art is a singularity that remains itself while being subjected to restless change—from translation to translation, from reader to reader. To proclaim the intrinsic worthlessness of translations is to mistake that singularity with its unendingly varying manifestations. A translation is a translation and not a work of art—unless, over the centuries, it takes on its own singularity and becomes a work of art. A work of art is its own subject; the subject of a translation is the original work of art. There is a cliché in the US that the purpose of a poetry translation is to create an excellent new poem in English. This is empirically false: nearly all the great translations in English would be ludicrous as poems written in English, even poems written in the voice of a *persona*. I have always maintained—and for some reason this is considered controversial—that the purpose of a poetry translation into English is to create an excellent translation in English. That is, a text that will be read and judged *like* a poem, but not *as* a poem.

And yet translations continue to be measured according to a Utopian dream of exact equivalences, and are often dismissed on the basis of a single word, usually by members of foreign language departments, known in the trade as the "translation police." They are the ones who write—to take an actual example—that a certain immensely prolific translator from the German "simply does not know German" because somewhere in the vastness of *Buddenbrooks*, he had translated a "chesterfield" as a "greatcoat." Such examples, as any translator can tell you, are more the rule than the exception. One can only imagine if writers were reviewed in the same way: "the use of the word 'incarnadine' on page 349 proves the utter mediocrity of this book."

This is the old bugbear of "fidelity," which turns reviewers into television evangelists. Obviously a translation that is replete with semantical errors is probably a bad translation, but fidelity may be the most overrated of a translation's qualities. I once witnessed an interesting experiment: Average 9-year-old students at a public school in Rochester, New York, were given a text by Rimbaud and a bilingual dictionary, and asked to translate the poem. Neither they nor their teacher knew a word of French. What they produced were not masterpieces, but they were generally as accurate as, and occasionally wittier than, any of the existing scholarly versions. In short, up to a point, anyone can translate anything faithfully.

But the point at which they cannot translate is the point where real translations begin to be made. The purpose of, say, a poetry translation is not, as it is usually said, to give the foreign poet a voice in the translation-language. It is to allow the poem to be *heard* in the translation-language, ideally in many of the same ways it is heard in the original language. This means that a translation is a whole work; it is not a series of matching *en face* lines and shouldn't be read as such. It means that the primary task of a translator is not merely to get the dictionary meanings right—which is the easiest part—but rather to invent a new music for the text in the translation-language, one that is mandated by the original. A music that is not a technical replication of the original. (There is nothing worse than translations, for example, that attempt to recreate a foreign meter or rhyme scheme. They're sort of like the way hamburgers look and taste in Bolivia.) A music that is perfectly viable in English, but which—because it is a translation, because it will be read as a translation—is able to evoke another music, and perhaps reproduce some of its effects.

But to do so requires a thorough knowledge of the literature *into which* one is translating. Before modernism, poems, no matter from where, were translated into the prevailing styles and forms: the assumed perfection of the heroic couplet could equally serve Homer, Kalidasa, or the Chinese folk songs of the *Book of Odes*. The great lesson of modernism—first taught by Ezra Pound, but learned, even now, only by a few—was that the unique form and style of the original must in some manner determine the form and the style of the translation; the poem was not merely to be poured into the familiar molds. Thus, in Pound's famous example, a fragment of Sappho was turned into an English fragment, ellipses and all, and not "restored" or transformed into rhyming pentameters.

This was based on a twofold, and somewhat contradictory, belief: First, that the dead author and his or her literature were exotic, and therefore the translation should preserve this exoticism and not domesticate it. Second, that the dead author was our contemporary, and his or her poems—if they were worth reading—were as alive and fresh as anything written yesterday. An unrestored Sappho was "one of us" precisely because she was not one of us: a foreign (in the largest sense) poet pointing to a way that our poems could be written today.

Modernism—at least in English—created extraordinary works in translation because they were written *for* modernism: written to be read in the context of modernist poetry. The cliché that the only good poetry translators are themselves poets is not necessarily true: the only good translators are avid readers of contemporary poetry in the translation-language. All the worst translations are done by experts in the foreign language who know little or nothing about the poetry alongside which their translations will be read. Foreign-language academics are largely concerned with semantical accuracy, rendering supposedly exact meanings into a frequently colorless or awkward version of the translation-language. They often write as though the entire 20th century had not occurred. They champion the best-loved poet of Ruthenia, but never realize that he sounds in English like bad Tennyson. Poets (or poetry readers) may be sometimes sloppy in their dictionary-use, but they are preoccupied with what is *different* in the foreign author, that which is not already available among writers in the translation-language, how that difference may be demonstrated, and how the borders of the possible may be expanded. Bad translations provide examples for historical surveys; good translations are always a form of advocacy criticism: Here is a writer one ought to be reading and here is the proof.

Translation is an utterly unique genre, but for some reason there is a perennial tendency to explain it by analogy. A translator is like an actor playing a role, a musician performing a score, a messenger who sometimes garbles the message. But translation is such a familiar and intrinsic part of almost any culture that one wonders why there is this need to resort to analogies:

we do not say that baking is like playing the violin. One analogy, however, is *why* exact: translators are the geeks of literature.

Translators are invisible people. They are often confused with simultaneous interpreters—even at bilingual poetry readings. According to a survey of my own clippings—which I happen to have, but any translator could tell you the same story—90% of book reviews never mention the translator's name, even when they are talking about the author's so-called style. When they do, the work is usually summed up in a single word: *excellent, mediocre, energetic, lackluster.* Discussions of the translation longer than one word are nearly always complaints about the translation of a word or two.

Translators sometimes feel they share in the glory of their famous authors, rather like the hairdressers of Hollywood stars, but authors tend to find them creepy. As Isaac Bashevis Singer said:

> The translator must be a great editor, a psychologist, a judge of human taste; if not, his translation will be a nightmare. But why should a man with such rare qualities become a translator? Why shouldn't he be a writer himself, or be engaged in a business where diligent work and high intelligence are well paid? A good translator must be both a sage and a fool. And where do you get such strange combinations?

"Why shouldn't he be a writer himself?" is the great and terrible question that hangs over the head of every translator, and of every author thinking about his translator. One might say that the avoidance of the question—not the response to it—has created the recent flood of publications in which translators explain themselves.

Some translators now claim that they are authors (or something like authors), which strikes me as a Pirandellesque (or Reaganesque) confusion of actor and role. It began some thirty years ago in the US as a tiny microcosm of the larger social currents. Translators began to come out of their isolation and anonymity to form groups, such as the Translation Committee of the PEN American Center, where they could share the tales of misfortune of their underpaid, entirely unrecognized, and often exploited occupation. This led to demands, as a group, for thoroughly justified material concessions: the translator's name prominently featured on the book and in all notices of the book, a share in the author's royalties and subsidiary rights (rather than a flat fee—degradingly known as "work for hire"—with no subsequent rights or income), and some sort of "industry standard" for translation fees. Simultaneous to the slow acceptance of these demands was a proliferation of conferences and lectures on translation as an art. This in turn coincided with the rise of so-called theory in the universities, and there is, perhaps, no subject in literature more suited for theoretical rumination in its current modes than translation: the authority of the author, the transformation of the sign, the tenuousness of signifier and signified, the politics of what is/isn't translated and how it is translated, the separation of text and author, the crossing (or impossibility of crossing) cultural barriers, the relativism of the translation as discourse, the translator as agent of political/cultural hegemony, and so on. All of which are sometimes interesting in themselves, but generally unhelpful when one actually translates. (As Borges said, "When I translate Faulkner, I don't think about the problem of translating Faulkner.")

With this preoccupation with the translator—and the self-evident and now excessively elaborated corollary that everything is a form of translation—the translator has suddenly become an important person, and explaining translation a minor but comfortable academic career and a source of invitations to conferences in exotic climes. Small wonder, then, that the advance guard of translators and their explainers are now declaring that the translator is an author, that a translated and original text are essentially indistinguishable (because an original text is a translation and/or a translation is an original text) and, most radically, that the sole author of a translation is the translator (who should therefore have 100% of the rights and royalties to the books). This strikes me as presumptuous, if not hubristic; and it may well be time to raise the banner of the translator's essential and endearing anonymity. In the US, we can no longer use the word "craft," which has been taken over by the creative writing schools, where the "craft" is taught in "workshops." So let us say that translation is a trade, like cabinet-making or baking or masonry. It is a trade that any amateur can do, but professionals do better. It is a trade that can be learned, and should be (though not necessarily institutionally) in order to practice. It is a trade whose practitioners remain largely unknown to the general public, with the exception of a few workers of genius. It is a trade that is essential to a literate society, and—let's raise another banner—whose workers should be better paid.

For me, the translator's anonymity—his role as the Man Without Qualities standing before the scene, a product of the *zeitgeist* but not a direct maker of it—is the joy of translation. One is operating strictly on the level of language, attempting to invent similar effects, to capture the essential, without the interference of the otherwise all-consuming ego. It is the greatest education in how to write, as many poets have learned. It is a prison in the sense that everything is said and must now be re-said, including all the author's bad moments—the vagaries, the repetitions, the clichés, the clinkers—while strictly avoiding the temptation to explain or improve. It is a prison, or a kind of nightmare, because one is in a dialogue with another person whom you must concede is always right. But it is also a liberation. It is the only time when one can put words on a page entirely without embarrassment (and embarrassment, it seems to me, is a greatly underrated force in the creation of literature). The introspective bookworm happily becomes the voice of Jack London or Jean Genet; translation is a kind of fantasy life.

Translators are often asked to talk about their relationships with the authors they translate, and they tend to reply with sometimes amusing intertextual anecdotes. Authors, however, never talk about their translators, beyond a few passing complaints. This is because the author-translator relationship has no story. Or more exactly, the story has only one real character: the author. The translator, as translator, is not a fully-formed human being; the translator, in the familiar analogy, is an actor playing the role of the author. Sometimes we, the audience, are aware of the actor "doing" the role brilliantly or poorly, sometimes we forget he is an actor at all (the "invisibility" that is often still considered the translation ideal, particularly for prose). But in either case, reflections on that role remain one-sided: Olivier may write a memoir of his Hamlet, but Hamlet, if he existed, would never write of his Olivier.

Translation is the most anonymous of professions, yet people die for it. It is little known that the *fatwa* against Salman Rushdie and its subsequent global mayhem, riots, and deaths were the result of a mistranslation. Rushdie's book was named after a strange legend in Islamic tradition about the composition of the Quran, which was dictated to Muhammad by Allah Himself through the angel Jibril. According to the story, Muhammad, having met considerable resistance to his attempt to eliminate all the local gods of Mecca in favor of the One God, recited some verses that admitted three popular goddesses as symbolic Daughters of Allah. Later he claimed that the verses had been dictated to him by Satan in the voice of Jibril, and the lines were suppressed. The 19th century British Orientalists called these lines the "Satanic verses," but in Arabic (and its cognate languages) the verses were known as *gharaniq*, "the birds," after two excised lines about the Meccan goddesses: "These are the exalted birds / And their intercession is desired indeed." In Arabic (and similarly in the cognate languages) Rushdie's title was literally translated as *Al-Ayat ash-Shataniya*, with *shaytan* meaning Satan, and *ayat* meaning specifically the "verses of the Quran." As the phrase "Satanic verses" is completely unknown in the Muslim world—which Rushdie apparently didn't know—the title in Arabic implied the ultimate blasphemy: that the entire Quran was composed by Satan. The actual contents of the book were irrelevant.

Translators were among those who paid for this mistake: In July of 1991, the Italian translator of *The Satanic Verses*, Ettore Caprioli, was stabbed in his apartment in Milan, but survived. Days later, the Japanese translator, Hitoshi Igarashi, an Islamic scholar, was stabbed to death in his office at Tsukuba University in Tokyo.

As far as I know, Rushdie has never made any extended comment on Hitoshi Igarashi. It would take another kind of novelist—Dostoyevsky perhaps—to untangle the psychological, moral, and spiritual meanings and effects of the story of these two: the man who became the most famous writer in the world at the price of what seemed, for some years, to be life imprisonment, and the anonymous man who died for a faithful translation of an old mistranslation, paying for the writer's mistake.

Translation is the most anonymous of professions, yet people—to paraphrase William Carlos Williams on poetry—die from the lack of it. The first World Trade Center bombing, in 1993, might have been averted if the FBI had bothered to translate the boxes of letters, documents, and tapes it had already seized in the course of various investigations, which specifically detailed the plot. But those were in a foreign language—Arabic—and who could be bothered?

After 9/11 however, they began to bother, and there is now something called the 300th Military Intelligence Brigade. 1,500 language experts, most of them Mormons trained for missionary work in heathen lands, housed in six sites in the state of Utah, are frantically trying to translate the mountain of documents that have been gathered by the various agencies. Their commander, Col. Dee Snowball, rallied the troops with these words: "You will not garner the glory that the combat soldier receives, but you will make a huge impact in the defense of your country." It is the military version of what all translators feel.

Translation is an obvious necessity that is somehow considered to be a problem. (There are never conferences on the "pleasures of translation.") Yet it is a problem that only arises in the interstices when one is not casually referring to some translated bit of literature: the Bible, Homer, Kafka, Proust . . . Could it possibly be that translation essentially has no problems at all? That it only has successes and failures? There is no text that cannot be translated; there are only texts that have not yet found their translators. A translation is not inferior to the original; it is only inferior to other translations, written or not yet written. There is no definitive translation because a translation always appears in the context of its contemporary literature, and the realm of the possible in any contemporary literature is in constant flux—often, it should be emphasized, altered by the translations that have entered into it. Everything worth translating should be translated as many times as possible, even by the same translator, for you can never step into the same original twice. Poetry is that which is worth translating, and translation is what keeps literature alive. Translation is change and motion; literature dies when it stays the same, when it has no place to go.

[2001–2008]

"The Post-National Writer"

S AUL BELLOW'S recent death was a sad reminder of his unfortunate defense, years ago, of Western Civilization:"Where is the Zulu Tolstoy? Where is the Proust of Papua New Guinea?" (Bellow being perfectly fluent in all 700 languages of Papua New Guinea.) At the time, I was ranting to my old friend Lydia Davis that there may or may not be a Papuan Proust, but there certainly is a Bengali one, Nirad Chaudhuri, author of *Autobiography of an Unknown Indian*. Decades later, when she was commissioned to do a new translation of *Swann's Way*, Lydia happened to remember my rant and read the book. It turned out to be inspirational for her, not only as a great book itself, but for the way Chaudhuri handled long sentences in an old-fashioned, turn of the century diction, which she thought perfect as a kind of foundation for Proust in English. She told me the book was continually at her side throughout the writing of her brilliant and acclaimed translation. Literature, contrary to most literary critics, rarely moves in a straight line.

Post-national, like any "post-" phrase that does not refer to an actual chronology, is essentially meaningless. We all sort of know what it means. This is, of course, the age of mass migration and global consciousness. It is obvious that, despite the last stands of certain reactionary forces, mutual isolationism—after a long and slow process that began in the 19th century—has vanished forever. Not only in the metropolises, but almost anywhere in the world. Go into any peasant village in the Third World and you'll find people who have been to Europe or the US, or have relatives there, who are fans of a mass culture that is not, as it is usually demonized, exclusively American, but which equally includes such things as Brazilian soap operas or Hong Kong martial arts movies—things that are strangely not attributed to Brazilian or Hong Kong hegemony. The images may be exaggerated, but, for the first time in history, people in the villages of the world have images of what a lot of the rest of the world looks like.

And of course we are at the beginning of the age of the internet. Ten years ago, the future seemed more dismal than usual, heading toward a near-complete corporate takeover of all the means of conveying information; dissident political voices and what James Laughlin used to call "serious literature," among other things, would be forced to retreat to the monasteries of tiny presses and magazines struggling in an inflated economy. The internet has changed all that, practically overnight. Suddenly, like-minded souls who share specialized interests—and serious literature will always be a specialized interest—can easily find one another. Suddenly, there is access to everything. The sensitive youth in a small town in the hinterlands doesn't have to move to Paris or New York to discover the latest writing, or buy the books, or communicate with others who are reading the same things. The writer in Bangkok doesn't have to travel to Bolivia to find the latest Bolivian writers. And, it should be added, it is the way around government censorship: today you can't publish a book by Bei Dao in China, but you can read him on the web, for the hackers will always be one step ahead of any bureaucracy.

In literature, we are already seeing the effect of this extraordinary mass migration and intercommunication. There are various models of the "post-national" writer, each with entirely different ramifications.

One model is the writer born in a former colony, who writes in the colonial language, and who now lives in the colonizing country or another first-world country where that language is spoken. Many, or most, of the liveliest books now being written in French or English are by African, South Asian, or Caribbean writers living in the UK, the US, Canada, and France. As they often write about their countries of origin, all of these writers face the dilemma of audience: For whom are they writing? And what should they do about local things and customs? Should a woman in a novel by an Indian writer have a "bindi" or a "red dot" on her forehead? If you write "bindi," the readers in your country of residence will be bewildered; if you write "red dot," the readers in your country of origin will accuse you of toadying to the West. Conversely, if you choose to write about white couples getting divorced in Fairfield, Connecticut, this will be considered either bizarre or a tour-de-force. (White writers who set their novels in Fez or Benares of course do not have this problem.)

What is not said often enough is that this new wave of writers is the best thing that could happen to a national literature. Contrary to the reactionary forces—particularly now in Europe—who are warning of imminent destruction, immigration revitalizes a national culture. Any given literature thrives in eras when there is a great deal of translation, and/or an influx of new people speaking and writing in the language: new ideas, new stories, new forms of expression. A literature stagnates when it's the same old people repeating the same old things.

The second "post-national" model is the writer who moves to another country and adopts the language of that country. This is hardly new. In English, the tradition goes back at least as far as Charles d'Orleans in the 15th century; much of the greatest German prose of the modern era was written by people who were neither German nor Austrian nor German Swiss; most of the major modern Rumanian writers did not write in Rumanian; and so on. But like everything else, the pace has accelerated. It is now only slightly unusual to find, as at this festival, a German novelist, Yoko Tawada, who is Japanese, or the French and American writers, Shan Sa and Ha Jin, who were born and raised in China.

The third model is the writer who lives abroad, often for political reasons, but continues to write in the mother language—Adam Zagajewski being our example here. These writers live a kind of double exile, both from the language of home and the language of their residence—and one that becomes even more complicated when, as is often the case, they are not allowed to publish in their countries of origin. Bei Dao, in his first years of exile in northern Europe, used to say that he spoke Chinese to the mirror.

A fourth model, and one that I think will become more common, is the Third World writer who lives in and writes about another non-Western country—exemplified at this festival by José Manuel Prieto and Pedro Rosa Mendes. This is a kind of horizontal dialogue—beyond the old hierarchies of colonialism—that is just beginning. An interesting recent example from another medium is the movie *Midaq Alley*, a funny melodrama about an extended family in one of the anonymous slums of Mexico City. It is a quintessentially Mexican movie, in hilarious Mexican slang, with all the familiar Mexican stock characters—the fierce patriarch, the good-for-nothing son, the trashy daughter trying to sleep her way out of the ghetto—except that it is based on a novel by Naguib Mahfouz, set in an anonymous slum of Cairo. Put that in the context of the so-called "clash of civilizations," and the next time you hear more drivel from television pundits about the "Arab street," think of it as populated by Mexicans.

A fifth model, perhaps more "neo-national" than "post-national," but equally subversive to the status quo, are the Western-educated Third World writers who are realizing that their regional languages are untapped treasure troves, ones that have been rarely or never utilized in such Western genres as the novel, the play, or the written poem. And that, furthermore, to write in an original, pre-colonial language is to rectify history, to restore what has been erased, to assert the intellectual capabilities of those who were once taken to be incapable. At the moment—to take two examples—in Mexico there are vibrant movements of poets in their twenties and thirties writing in such languages as Mazatec, Zapotec, and Nahuatl, complete with their own literary magazines and presses. And, in Africa, the Kenyan novelist Ngugi wa Thiongo may be the first writer of international reputation to abandon writing in a Western language in order to return to the regional, in his case, Kikuyu. I should also add that these writers are generally bilingual, or multilingual, and tend to translate themselves, and thus are working in an unprecedented triple role as regional writers, international writers, and the bridges between themselves.

Menwhile, back in the USA, the "dead white male" critique of Western Civ—that Bellow and so many others attacked—did not lead, as many of us had hoped, to a new internationalism, but rather to a new form of nationalism that emphasized hyphenated Americans. Chinese-Americans and Chicanos were now part of the intellectual universe, which was fine as far as it went, but Chinese and Mexicans were still excluded. Multiculturalism was, and is, not very multicultural at all.

Less than 20% of Americans have passports. The total number of literary books in translation published in the US each year—all genres, all languages—by presses with some sort of national distribution, is about 250. When the National Geographic Society tested American high school students a few years ago, 11% could not find the US on a world map; 29% could not find the Pacific Ocean (and of course many of them live next to the Pacific Ocean) and, almost needless to say, 85% could not find our current bombing targets, Iraq and Afghanistan. Americans may be the most insular people on earth, apart from a few nomadic tribes in the deserts and rain forests.

This was apparent a few years ago when the State Department commissioned fifteen famous American writers to write essays for a book on what it means to be an American. This was to be translated into many languages, beginning with Arabic, and distributed free around the world, as a publicity campaign to show that, despite all the evidence, we're really not such bad guys. Leaving aside the fact of their collaboration with the Bush administration, it was astonishing that none of these writers had any sense of writing for people who are not Americans. Nearly all of them evoked their childhoods, and all did so in terms of nostalgic referents that would be meaningless abroad. It never occurred to them that their presumed reader in Yemen or Burundi might well wonder, "Who is this Leave it to Beaver?"

The post-national writer, in all its manifestations, is the most interesting and fruitful thing to have happened to world literature since the birth of modernism. It's safe to say this will be the literary hallmark of the new century, with the internet its Gutenberg. And post-nationalism itself is a sign of hope. After centuries of barbarity, a Union in Europe only became possible when it was harder to define who was French or German or Italian or Dutch. We can imagine what the world would be like if only Americans would become post-American.

[PEN World Voices Festival, New York City, April 2005]

IV.

IN 2005 I heard that Coalition forces were camped in the ruins of Babylon. I heard that bulldozers had dug trenches through the site and cleared areas for helicopter landing pads and parking lots, that thousands of sandbags had been filled with dirt and archeological fragments, that a 2,600-year-old brick pavement had been crushed by tanks, and that the molded bricks of dragons had been gouged out from the Ishtar Gate by soldiers collecting souvenirs. I heard that the ruins of the Sumerian cities of Umma, Umm al-Akareb, Larsa, and Tello were completely destroyed and were now landscapes of craters.

I heard that the US was planning an embassy in Baghdad that would cost $1.5 billion, as expensive as the Freedom Tower at Ground Zero, the proposed tallest building in the world.

I saw a headline in the *Los Angeles Times* that read: AFTER LEVELING CITY, US TRIES TO BUILD TRUST.

I heard that military personnel were now carrying "talking point" cards with phrases such as "We are a values-based, people-focused team that strives to uphold the dignity and respect of all."

I heard that 47% of Americans believed that Saddam Hussein helped plan 9/11 and 44% believed that the hijackers were Iraqi. 61% thought that Saddam had been a serious threat to the US and 76% said the Iraqis were now better off.

I heard that Iraq was now ranked with Haiti and Senegal as one of the poorest nations on earth. I heard the United Nations Human Rights Commission report that acute malnutrition among Iraq children had doubled since the war began. I heard that only 5% of the money Congress had allocated for reconstruction had actually been spent. I heard that, in Fallujah, people were living in tents pitched on the ruins of their houses.

I heard that this year's budget included $105 billion for the war in Iraq, which would bring the total to nearly $300 billion. I heard that Halliburton was estimating that its bill for providing services to US troops in Iraq would exceed $10 billion. I heard that the families of American soldiers killed in Iraq receive $12,000.

I heard that the White House had entirely deleted the chapter on Iraq from the annual Economic Report of the President, on the grounds that it did not conform with an otherwise cheerful tone.

Within a week in January I heard Condoleezza Rice say there were 120,000 Iraqi troops trained to take over the security of the country. I heard Senator Joseph Biden, Democrat from Delaware, say that the number was closer to 4,000. I heard Donald Rumsfeld say: "The fact of the matter is that there are 130,200 who have been trained and equipped. That's a fact. The idea that that number's wrong is just not correct. The number is right."

I heard him explain the discrepancy: "Now are some getting killed every day? Sure. Are some retiring at various times or injured? Yes, they're gone." I remembered that a year before he had said the number was 210,000. I heard the Pentagon announce it would no longer release Iraqi troop figures.

I heard that 50,000 US soldiers in Iraq did not have body armor, because the Army's equipment manager had placed it at the same priority level as socks. I heard that soldiers were personally buying their own flak jackets with steel "trauma" plates, Camelbak water pouches, ballistic goggles, knee and elbow pads, drop pouches to hold ammunition magazines, and load-bearing vests. I heard they were rigging their vehicles with pieces of scrap metal as protection against roadside bombs, for the production of armored Humvees had fallen more than a year behind schedule and the few available armored vehicles were now mainly reserved for officers and visiting dignitaries.

I heard that the private security firm Custer Battles had been paid $15 million to provide security for civilian flights at the Baghdad airport at a time when there were no planes flying. I heard that US forces were still unable to secure the two-mile highway from the airport to the Green Zone.

I heard that the President's uncle, Bucky Bush, had made half a million dollars cashing in his stock options in Engineered Support Systems Inc., a defense contractor that had received $100 million for work in Iraq. Bucky Bush is on the Board of Directors, but I heard Dan Kreher, Vice President of Investor Relations for ESSI, say: "The fact his nephew is in the White House has absolutely nothing to do with Mr. Bush being on our board or with our stock having gone up 1,000 percent in the past five years."

I heard that a Pentagon audit of merely one part of the Halliburton contracts had found $100 million in "questionable costs." I heard them cite a purchase of $82,100 worth of liquefied gas and a bill of $27.5 million to transport it. I heard that eight other government audits of Halliburton were marked as "classified" and not released to the public.

I heard that African-Americans normally form 23% of the active-duty troops, but that recruitment of African-Americans had fallen by 41% since the war began. I heard that a "US Military Image Study" prepared for the Army had recommended that, "for the Army to achieve its mission goals with Future Force Soldiers, it must overhaul its image as well as its product offering."

I heard that the military was developing robot soldiers. I heard Gordon Johnson of the Joint Forces Command at the Pentagon say: "They don't get hungry. They're not afraid. They don't forget their orders. They don't care if the guy next to them has just been shot." I heard him say: "I have been asked what happens if the robot destroys a school bus rather than a tank parked nearby. The lawyers tell me there are no prohibitions against robots making life-or-death decisions. We will not entrust a robot with that decision until we are confident they can make it."

· · ·

In March, on the second anniversary of the invasion, I heard that 1,511 US soldiers had been killed and approximately 11,000 wounded. There was no way to know exactly how many Iraqis had died in the war.

I heard Donald Rumsfeld say: "Well, if you have a country of 25 million people and you have X thousands of criminals, terrorists, Baathists, former regime elements who want to blow up things and make bombs and kill people, they can still do that. That happens in most major cities in the world, most countries in the world, that people get killed and there's violence."

I heard that, along with banning photographs of the caskets of American soldiers, the Administration was actively preventing photographs of the wounded, who were flown in from Iraq late at night, transferred to military hospitals in unmarked vans, and unloaded at back entrances.

I heard about despair. I heard General John Abizaid, Commander of US Central Command say, of the insurgents: "I don't think they're growing. I think that they're desperate."

I heard about hope. I heard General Richard Myers, Chairman of the Joint Chiefs of Staff, say: "I came away more positive than I've ever been. I think we're getting some momentum built up."

I heard about happiness. I heard Lieutenant General James Mattis say that "it's a lot of fun to fight" in Iraq. I heard him say: "You know, it's a hell of a hoot. I like brawling."

I heard that Donald Rumsfeld had created his own intelligence agency, the Strategic Support Branch, "designed to operate without detection and under the Defense Secretary's direct control," without the oversight laws that apply to the CIA, and that it was employing "notorious figures" whose "links to the US government would be embarrassing if disclosed." I heard about the practice of "extraordinary rendition," where suspected terrorists are kidnapped and flown to countries known to torture prisoners or to secret US prisons in Thailand, Afghanistan, Poland, and Rumania.

I heard that there were 3,200 prisoners in Abu Ghraib, 700 more than its capacity. I heard Major General William Brandenburg, who oversees US military detention operations in Iraq, say: "We've got a normal capacity and a surge capacity. We're operating at surge capacity." A year before, I had heard the President promise "to demolish the Abu Ghraib prison, as a fitting symbol of Iraq's new beginning." I heard that outside the prison there is a sign that reads: "No Parking. Detainee Drop Off Zone."

I heard that some American soldiers had made a heavy metal music video called "Ramadi Madness," with sections titled "Those Crafty Little Bastards" and "Another Day, Another Mission, Another Scumbag." In one scene, a soldier kicks the face of an Iraqi who is bound and lying on the ground, dying. In another, a soldier moves the arm of a man who has just been shot dead, to make it appear that he is waving. I heard a Pentagon spokesman say, "Clearly, the soldiers probably exercised poor judgment."

I heard that the Army released a 1,200-page report detailing the torture of Iraqi prisoners at a single military intelligence base during a few months in 2003. In response to the report, I heard Lieutenant Colonel Jeremy Martin say, "The army's a learning organization. If we have some shortfalls, we try to correct them. We've learnt how to do that process now."

I heard a US soldier talk about his photographs of the twelve prisoners he had shot with a machine gun: "I shot this guy in the face. See, his head is split open. I shot this guy in the groin. He took three days to bleed to death." I heard him say he was a devout Christian: "Well, I knelt down. I said a prayer, stood up, and gunned them all down."

• • •

In April I heard General Richard Myers say: "I think we're winning. Okay? I think we're definitely winning. I think we've been winning for some time."

I heard Major General William Webster, Commander of the 3rd Infantry Division, say: "We think the insurgency is weakening over time. Some of these attacks appear to be very spectacular and well-coordinated, but, in fact, are not."

I heard Lieutenant General James Conroy of the Marines say that American troop withdrawal would soon begin, because "Iraqis are starting to take care of their own situation." I heard Rear Admiral William Sullivan report to Congress that there were 145,000 "combat-capable" Iraqi forces. I heard Sabah Hadhum, a spokesman for the Iraqi Ministry of the Interior, say: "We are paying about 135,000, but that does not necessarily mean that 135,000 are actually working." I heard that as many as 50,000 may be "ghost soldiers"— invented names whose paychecks are cashed by officers or bureaucrats.

I heard Army Staff Sergeant Craig Patrick, who was training the Iraqi troops, say: "It's all about perception, to convince the American public that everything is going as planned and we're right on schedule to be out of here. I mean, they can bullshit the American people, but they can't bullshit us."

As many countries pulled their small numbers of troops out of Iraq, I heard the State Department announce it would no longer use the phrase "Coalition of the Willing."

I heard that of the forty water and sewage systems in Iraq, "not one is being operated properly." I heard that of the nineteen power plants that had been rebuilt by the US, none works correctly. I heard a US official blame this on the "indifferent work ethic" of Iraqis. I heard that new Pentagon audits now showed that Halliburton had overcharged by $212 million.

I read, in a news article in the *New York Times*, that thanks to the "sustained momentum" of the "military operation," the "Administration's goal of turning Iraq over to a permanent, elected Iraqi government" was "within striking distance." I heard General Richard Myers say: "We're on track"; and I heard Major General Adnan Thabit say: "We are gaining more victories now because more people are cooperating with us."

I heard General John Abizaid predict that Iraqi security forces would be leading the fight against the insurgents in most of the country by the end of 2005. I heard General George Casey, Commander of the Multinational Forces in Iraq, say: "We should be able to take some fairly substantial reductions in the size of our forces."

I heard that the insurgents had been driven out of the cities and into the desert and that they were having trouble finding new recruits. I heard Lieutenant General Raymond Odierno say: "They're slowly losing."

I heard Donald Rumsfeld say: "We don't have an exit strategy, we have a victory strategy."

•   •   •

A few weeks later, I heard the Pentagon spokesman, Lawrence di Rita, admit that "there's been an uptick" in violence. I heard Pentagon officials dismiss this as "desperate attacks by desperate individuals," but I heard General Richard Myers now say about the insurgents: "I think their capacity stays about the same. And where they are right now is where they were almost a year ago."

I heard that a report by the CIA National Intelligence Council had stated that "Iraq has now replaced Afghanistan as the training ground for the next generation of 'professionalized' terrorists," providing "a recruitment ground and the opportunity for enhancing technical skills." I heard that it said that Iraq was a more effective training ground than Afghanistan, because "the urban nature of the war in Iraq was helping combatants learn how to carry out assassinations, kidnappings, car bombings and other kinds of attacks that were never a staple of the fighting in Afghanistan during the anti-Soviet campaigns of the 1980s."

I heard that the State Department refused to release its annual report on terrorism, which would show that the number of "significant" attacks outside of Iraq had grown from 175 in 2003 to 655 in 2004. I heard Karen Aguilar, the Acting Coordinator for Counterterrorism at the State Department, explain that "statistics are not relevant" to "trends in global terrorism."

I heard Donald Rumsfeld say: "Goodness knows, it doesn't take a genius to blow up a building."

I heard that in the month of April there were 67 suicide bombings. I heard Colonel Pat Lang, former Chief of Mideast Operations at the Defense Intelligence Agency, say: "It's just political rhetoric to say we are not in a civil war. We've been in a civil war for a long time."

I heard that 1,600 US soldiers were dead. I heard that every week over 200 Iraqis were dying in the suicide bombings.

I heard Condoleezza Rice, on a surprise visit to Iraq, say: "We are so grateful that there are Americans willing to sacrifice so the Middle East will be whole and free and democratic and at peace." On that same day, the bodies of 34 recently killed men were found in a mass grave; a high official in the Ministry of Industry was shot dead; a leading Shi'ite cleric was shot dead; and the Governor of Diyala province survived a suicide bombing, though four others in his entourage did not and 37 nearby were wounded.

I heard Donald Rumsfeld, asked whether we were winning or losing the war in Iraq, reply: "Winning or losing is not the issue for 'we,' in my view, in the traditional, conventional context of using the word 'winning' and 'losing' in a war."

I heard a truck driver named Muhammad say: "With my own eyes I've seen the Americans, when their patrol was hit by a roadside bomb, open fire on all the civilian cars around them," and another driver, from Fallujah, say: "If Bush is a real man, he should walk down the street alone!"

I heard that the Iraqi President Jalal Talabani has 3,000 Kurdish peshmerga soldiers stationed around his house.

I heard the President proclaim a "critical victory in the War on Terror," with the capture of Abu Farraj al-Libbi, whom the President said was a "top general" and the #3 man in al-Qaeda. I heard him say: "His arrest removes a dangerous enemy who was a direct threat to America and for those who love freedom." A few days later, I heard that the man had probably been confused with someone else with a vaguely similar name. I heard that a former associate of Osama bin Laden in London had laughed and said: "What I remember of him is that he used to make the coffee and do the photocopying." I never heard this reported in the American press.

At the dedication of the Abraham Lincoln Presidential Library and Museum, I heard the President compare his War on Terror with Lincoln's war against slavery.

I heard the President say that Iraqi forces now outnumber their American counterparts.

• • •

In May I heard that there were three suicide bombings every day.

I heard a journalist ask the President: "Do you think that the insurgence is getting harder now to defeat militarily?" And I heard the President reply: "No, I don't think so. I think they're being defeated. And that's why they continue to fight."

I heard a human rights worker say: "In Baghdad today, four clerics (three Sunni and one Shi'a) were assassinated. The bodies of two other Sunni clerics who had been abducted last week were found. A suicide car bomber detonated his vehicle in the Abu Cher market killing nine Iraqi National Guard troops and injuring twenty-eight civilians. Two engineering students were killed when a bomb (or rocket) struck their classroom at a local school. The dean of a high school in the Shaab neighborhood was assassinated. One judge, two officials from the Ministry of Defense, and one official investigating corruption in the previous Interim Government were assassinated. In all, thirty-one dead, forty-two injured, and seventeen abducted. Rumors abound in Baghdad about who is responsible for all the attacks but no one has claimed responsibility. And yet compared to some days in recent weeks here in Baghdad the number of dead and injured was fewer in number. So comparatively speaking it was a fairly quiet day here in Baghdad."

I heard Donald Rumsfeld say, "We don't do body counts," but then I heard the Pentagon releasing body counts. It said 1,600 insurgents had been killed last year in Fallujah, but then I heard that the Marines had discovered "few bodies" after the city was captured, and months later a "martyr's cemetery" was found to contain only 79 graves. I heard that the Army had completely destroyed a "guerrilla training camp" near Lake Tharthar, killing all 85 insurgents, and I heard the television news report that this was "the single biggest one-day death toll for militants in months, and the latest in a series of blows to the insurgency." But then I heard that some European journalists visited the camp the next day and the insurgents were still there. Then I heard US officials claim that the insurgents must have dragged away their own dead. But then I heard a reporter ask how all 85 dead insurgents could have dragged themselves away. And I heard Major Richard Goldenberg reply: "We could spend years going back and forth on body counts. The important thing is the effect this has on the organized insurgency."

I heard about despair. I heard Colonel Joseph DiSalvo, Commander of the 2nd Brigade Combat Team, say: "What we're seeing is the terrorists are in desperation." I heard him say: "By the end of the summer, the terrorists will be captured, dead, or, in the least, severely disrupted."

I heard Dick Cheney say: "The level of activity that we see today, from a military standpoint, I think, will clearly decline. I think they're in the last throes, if you will, of the insurgency."

I heard Porter J. Goss, Director of the CIA, say that the insurgents were "not quite in the last throes, but I think they are very close to it."

I heard Dick Cheney later explain: " If you look at what the dictionary says about throes, it can still be a violent period. When you look back at World War II, the toughest battle, at the most difficult battles, both in Europe and in the Pacific, occurred just a few months before the end. And I see this as a similar situation, where they're going to go all out."

I heard Donald Rumsfeld say: "Last throes could be a violent last throe, or a placid and calm last throe. Look it up in the dictionary."

· · ·

I heard Senator Chuck Hagel, Republican from Nebraska, say: "Things aren't getting better; they're getting worse. The White House is completely disconnected from reality. It's like they're just making it up as they go along. The reality is that we're losing in Iraq."

I heard Lieutenant Colonel Frederick Wellman say, about the insurgents: "We can't kill them all. When I kill one, I create three."

I heard that Congressman Walter Jones, Republican from North Carolina and the man who renamed french fries as "freedom fries," was now calling for the withdrawal of US troops. I heard him say: "The American people are getting to a point here: How much more can we take?" I heard Congressman Mike Pence, Republican from Indiana, explain why he is opposed to a timetable for withdrawal: "I never tell my kids when my patience is going to run out, because they'll usually try it."

I heard Condoleezza Rice speak about a "generational commitment" in Iraq.

I heard the President say: "We have put the enemy on the run, and now they spend their days avoiding capture, because they know America's Armed Services are on their trail."

I heard him tell the American people: "As we work to deliver opportunity at home, we're also keeping you safe from threats from abroad. We went to war because we were attacked, and we are at war today because there are still people out there who want to harm our country and hurt our citizens. Our troops are fighting these terrorists in Iraq so you will not have to face them here at home."

I heard the President say: "See, in my line of work you got to keep repeating things over and over and over again for the truth to sink in, to kind of catapult the propaganda."

• • •

I heard that US troops had killed the #2 man in al-Qaeda in Iraq. I heard that US troops had killed another man who was the #2 in al-Qaeda in Iraq. I heard that US troops had killed yet another man who was the #2 in al-Qaeda in Iraq.

I heard that, in Baghdad, 92% of the people did not have stable electricity, 39% did not have safe drinking water, and 25% of children under the age of five were suffering from malnutrition. I heard that there were two or three car bombings a day, on some days killing a hundred people and wounding many hundreds more.

I heard General William Webster say: "Certainly saying anything about 'breaking the back' or 'about to reach the end of the line' or those kinds of things do not apply to the insurgency at this point."

I heard a "high-ranking Army officer" say: "There's simply not enough forces here. There are not enough to do anything right; everybody's got their finger in the dike." I heard that the soldiers of Marine Company E had set up cardboard dummies of themselves to make it appear that they had more men in battle.

I heard the President say: "I'd say I'd spend most of my time worrying about right now people losing their life in Iraq. Both Americans and Iraqis. I worry about my girls. I used to worry about my wife, until she hit an 85% popularity figure. Now she's worried about me. You know, I don't worry all that much, other than what I just described to you. I attribute that to—I've got peace of mind. A lot of it has to do with my particular faith, and a lot of that has to do with the fact that a lot of people pray for me and Laura. I'm sleeping pretty good. Seriously. I get asked that. There's times when I hadn't been. I've got peace of mind."

•   •   •

In 2005 I heard about 2001. I heard that on September 21, 2001, the PDF (President's Daily Brief), prepared by the CIA, reported that there was no evidence that Saddam Hussein was connected to the September 11 attacks.

I heard Condoleezza Rice say: "The fact of the matter is that when we were attacked on September 11, we had a choice to make. We could decide that the proximate cause was al-Qaeda and the people who flew those planes into buildings and, therefore, we would go after al-Qaeda. or we could take a bolder approach."

I heard Karl Rove say: "Liberals saw the savagery of the 9/11 attacks and wanted to prepare indictments and offer therapy and understanding for our attackers. Conservatives saw the savagery of 9/11 and the attacks and prepared for war. Conservatives saw what happened to us on 9/11 and said we will defeat our enemies. Liberals saw what happened to us and said we must understand our enemies."

In 2005 I heard about 2002. I heard that on July 23, 2002, eight months before the invasion, Sir Richard Dearlove, chief of MI6, reported in a secret memo to Tony Blair that he was told in Washington that the US was going to "remove Saddam, through military action, justified by the conjunction of terrorism and WMD." However, because "the case was thin, Saddam was not threatening his neighbors, and his WMD capability was less than that of Libya, North Korea or Iran," "the intelligence and facts were being fixed around the policy."

I heard that this "Downing Street Memo" was a scandal in the British press, but I didn't hear it mentioned on American network television for two months. During those two months, ABC news had 121 stories on Michael Jackson and 42 stories on Natalee Holloway, a high school student who disappeared from a bar while vacationing in Aruba. CBS news had 235 stories about Michael Jackson and 70 about Miss Holloway.

I heard that in the second half of 2002, the US Air Force and the RAF dropped twice as many bombs on Iraq as they had done in all of 2001. I heard that the objective was to provoke Saddam into giving the allies an excuse for war.

I heard that the primary source of information about Saddam's mobile biological weapons labs and germ warfare capability, used by Colin Powell in his presentation at the United Nations and in the President's 2003 State of the Union address, was an Iraqi defector held by German intelligence. The Germans had repeatedly told the Americans that none of the information supplied by this defector, an advanced alcoholic, was reliable. He had been given the code name Curveball.

I heard that the primary source of information about the tons of biological, chemical, and nuclear weapons buried under Saddam's private villas and under Saddam Hussein Hospital in Baghdad and throughout Iraq, was a Kurdish exile named Adnan Ihsan Saeed al-Haideri. He was sponsored by the Rendon Group, a Washington public relations firm that had been paid hundreds of millions of dollars by the Pentagon to promote the war. (Rendon, among other things, had organized a group of Iraqi exiles in London, given them the name the Iraqi National Congress, and installed Ahmad Chalabi as their leader.) I heard that after Al-Haideri completely failed a lie detector test, administered by the CIA in Thailand, his stories were nevertheless leaked to journalists, most prominently Judith Miller of the *New York Times*, which published them on the front page.

I heard Donald Rumsfeld say: "Well, you never know what's going to happen. I presented the President a list of about 15 things that could go terribly, terribly wrong before the war started. And the fact that the oil fields could have been set aflame like they were in Kuwait, the fact that we could have had mass refugees and dislocations and it didn't happen. The bridges could have been blown up. There could have been a fortress Baghdad with the moat around it with oil in it and people fighting to the death. So a great many of the bad things that could have happened did not happen." I heard a journalist ask him: "Was a robust insurgency on your list that you gave the President?" and I heard Rumsfeld reply: "I don't remember whether that was on there."

In 2005 I heard about 2003. I heard a US Marine, who was a witness to the event, say that the capture of Saddam Hussein was a fiction. Saddam had been caught the day before in a small house, and then placed in an abandoned well, which was invented as the "spider hole" where he was hiding. I never heard about this Marine again.

In 2005 I heard about 2004. I heard that, during the attack on Fallujah, the President had suggested to Tony Blair that the headquarters of the Al Jazeera network in Qatar should be bombed. I heard that Blair persuaded him that it wasn't such a good idea.

· · ·

Because it was difficult for the military to attract new recruits, I heard that an Army directive recommended "alleviating the personnel crunch by retaining soldiers who are earmarked for early discharge during their first term of enlistment because of alcohol or drug abuse, unsatisfactory performance, or being overweight, among other reasons." I heard that the Pentagon had asked Congress to raise the maximum age for military recruits from 35 to 42.

I heard that the US military was actively recruiting in Latin America, offering citizenship in exchange for service. I heard that Hispanic-Americans make up 9.5% of the actively enlisted, but 17.5% of those given the most dangerous assignments.

I heard that the government had offered $15,000 cash bonuses to National Guard personnel who agreed to extend their enlistment. I heard that the government never paid, and cancelled the offer after many had signed up.

I heard that in veterans' hospitals, the only televison news that is permitted is the Pentagon Channel, a 24-hour news station that features programs like "Freedom Journal Iraq."

I heard Rory Mayberry, a former food manager for Halliburton in Iraq, say that they routinely served the troops food that had expired by as much as a year. I heard that they would salvage food from convoys that had been attacked. I heard him say: "We were told to go into the trucks and remove the food items and use them after removing the bullets and any shrapnel from the bad food that was hit."

I heard that, in a poll of American soldiers in Iraq, more than half rated their unit's morale as "low" or "very low."

I heard the Army Center for Health Promotion and Preventive Medicine state that one out of four veterans required medical treatment, and that it expected that as many as 240,000 would suffer from some form of Post-Traumatic Stress Disorder. I heard one soldier say: "My nightmares are so intense I woke up one night with my hands around my fiancee's throat."

I heard that members of the Westboro Baptist Church of Topeka, Kansas, were demonstrating at the funerals of soldiers who had died in Iraq, claiming that the war was divine retribution for American immorality. I heard that they held signs depicting "homosexual acts," with the words "God Hates Fags"; "God Hates America"; "Thank God for IED's [roadside bombs]"; "Fag Soldiers in Hell"; "God Blew Up the Troops"; and "Fags Doom Nations."

I heard that headstones in Arlington National Cemetery were now being inscribed with the slogans "Operation Enduring Freedom" and "Operation Iraqi Freedom," along with the traditional name, rank, and date of death of the deceased soldier. I heard Jeff Martell, who makes headstones for the cemetery, say: "It just seems a little brazen that that's put on stones. It seems like it might be connected to politics."

• • •

On the first anniversary of the "transfer of sovereignty," I heard that there had been 484 car bombs in the last year, killing at least 2,221 people and wounding at least 5,574. I heard 890 US soldiers had been killed in the last year and that there was now an average of 70 insurgent attacks a day. That same day I heard the President say: "We fight today because terrorists want to attack our country and kill our citizens, and Iraq is where they are making their stand. So we'll fight them there, we'll fight them across the world, and we will stay in the fight until the fight is won."

I heard him say: "Iraq is the latest battlefield in this war. Many terrorists who kill innocent men, women, and children on the streets of Baghdad are followers of the same murderous ideology that took the lives of our citizens in New York, in Washington, and Pennsylvania."

I heard him say: "Some may disagree with my decision to remove Saddam Hussein from power, but all of us can agree that the world's terrorists have now made Iraq a central front in the War on Terror."

And I remembered that, three years before, to justify the invasion, he had said: "Imagine a terrorist network with Iraq as an arsenal and as a training ground."

• • •

I heard Tom DeLay, then still House Majority Leader, say: "You know, if Houston, Texas, was held to the same standard as Iraq is held to, nobody'd go to Houston, because all this reporting coming out of the local press in Houston is violence, murders, robberies, deaths on the highways."

I heard Donald Rumsfeld say that the Shi'ites "are reaching out to the Sunnis and allowing them to come into the constitutional drafting process in a very constructive and healthy way. So there's an awful lot good that's happening in that country."

I heard Scott McClellan, the White House Press Secretary, say: "I think we have a clear strategy for success, and there is great progress being made on the ground. We are succeeding and we will succeed."

I heard the President say: "We have a clear path forward."

I heard that Halliburton had built a wall around the Green Zone, made of 12-foot-high, 5-ton concrete slabs, topped with concertina wire. I heard that mortars fired into the Green Zone often fell short and landed in the neighborhoods just outside the wall, and that frustrated suicide bombers, unable to get into the Green Zone, would blow themselves up outside the wall. I heard Saman Abdel Aziz Rahman, owner of the Serawan Kebab Restaurant, which is next door to a restaurant where a suicide bomber at lunchtime had killed 23 people, say: "We are the new Palestine." I heard Haider al-Shawaf, who lives on Al-Shawaf Street, now bisected by the wall, say twice, in English: "It was very nice street. It was very nice street."

I heard the President say: "America will not leave before the job is done." I heard Dick Cheney predict that the fighting would be over by the time the Administration ends in 2009.

• • •

After Amnesty International compared American treatment of Afghan and Iraqi prisoners to the Soviet Gulag, I heard the President say: "It's an absurd allegation. The United States is a country that promotes freedom around the world. It seemed like to me they based some of their decisions

on the word of—and the allegations—by people who were held in detention, people who hate America, people that had been trained in some in-
stances to disassemble—that means not tell the truth."

I heard that most of the insurgent violence in Iraq was personally directed by a Jordanian, Abu Musab al-Zarqawi. I heard that rumors of
his presence had led to the US bombings of Fallujah, Ramadi, Mosul,
Samarra, and a village in Kurdistan, but each time he had narrowly
escaped. I heard that he had been seen recently in Jordan, Syria, Iran,
and Pakistan. I heard that he was closely linked with Osama bin Laden,
Saddam Hussein, and the government of Syria. I heard that he was the
bitter enemy of bin Laden, the secularist Saddam, and the secularist
Syrian government. I heard that he had died in Afghanistan. I heard
that, after an injury in Afghanistan, his leg had been amputated in a
hospital in Iraq, which was proof of Saddam's connections to terrorism. I heard he was still walking on two legs. I heard he was one of the
hooded men in a video showing the decapitation of a young American, Nick Berg, although the men never removed their hoods. I heard
that he had died recently in Mosul when eight men blew themselves
up rather than surrender to the US forces who had surrounded their
house. I heard Sheikh Jawad al-Kaesi, an important Shi'ite cleric in
Baghdad, say that Zarqawi had been killed long ago, but the US was
using him as a "ploy." I heard the President compare him to Hitler,
Stalin, and Pol Pot. I heard that he had less than a hundred followers
in Iraq.

I heard that there could be as many as a hundred groups responsible for
the suicide bombings and I heard that many of them were connected to
Ansar al-Islam, which had many more followers in Iraq than Zarqawi and
had actual ties to Osama bin Laden before the war. Ansar al-Islam was almost never mentioned in Administration speeches or in the press, for it is a
Kurdish group, and all Kurds are presumed to be allies of the US.

I heard that unemployment for young men in Sunni areas was now 40%. I
heard that the per capita income was $77, half of what it was the year before;
that only 37% of families had homes connected to a sewage system, half of
what it was before the war.

I heard General George Casey say: "Iraq slowly gets better every day." I heard Lieutenant Colonel Vincent Quarles, Commander of the 4-3 Brigade Troops Battalion, say: "It's hard to see all the progress that has been made. But things are getting better."

I heard that the Pentagon was supposed to deliver a report to the Congress on the training and capability of the Iraqi security forces, but that it had missed the deadline and was reluctant to release the report. I heard Donald Rumsfeld say: "It's not for us to tell the other side, the enemy, the terrorists, that this Iraqi unit has this capability, and that Iraqi unit has this capability. The idea of discussing weaknesses, if you will, strengths and weaknesses of 'this unit has a poor chain of command,' or 'these forces are not as effective because their morale's down'—I mean, that would be mindless to put that kind of information out."

I heard General William Webster say that the insurgents' ability "to conduct sustained, high-intensity operations, as they did last year—we've mostly eliminated that." In the next few days, I heard that suicide bombings in Baghdad had increased, including one at a school that killed some two dozen children, and the explosion in the central square of a stolen truck of liquefied gas, killing at least 71 people and wounding 156 others. I heard that the highest-ranking diplomat from Algeria had been kidnapped. I heard that the highest-ranking diplomat from Egypt had been kidnapped and killed. I heard that no Arab country would send an ambassador.

I heard an unnamed "senior Army intelligence officer" say: "We are capturing or killing a lot of insurgents, but they're being replaced quicker than we can interdict their operations. There is always another insurgent ready to step up and take charge." I heard him say that the US military was having a hard time understanding the insurgency's unlikely coalitions of secular Baath Party members and Islamic militants.

I heard that, after a car bombing killed several children, the Task Force Baghdad 3rd Infantry Division released a statement quoting an "Iraqi man who preferred not to be identified": "They are enemies of humanity without religion or any sort of ethics. They have attacked my community today and I will now take the fight to the terrorists." A few weeks later, after a car bomb killed 25 people near the al-Rashad police station, I heard that the Task Force Baghdad 3rd Infantry Division released a statement quoting an "Iraqi man who preferred not to be identified": "They are enemies of humanity without religion or any sort of ethics. They have attacked my community today and I will now take the fight to the terrorists."

I heard that the Administration had decided it would no longer refer to a War on Terror. The new name was now Global Struggle Against Violent Extremism.

I heard General Richard Myers say: "I've objected to the use of the term 'War on Terrorism' before, because one—if you call it a war, then you think of people in uniform as being the solution. And it's more than terrorism. The long-term problem is as much diplomatic, as much economic—in fact, more diplomatic, more economic, more political than it is military."

I heard that the Administration had decided it would no longer refer to the Global Struggle Against Violent Extremism, which was too long. The new name was now the old War on Terror.

I heard the President say: "Make no mistake about it, we're at war. We're at war with an enemy that attacked us on September the 11th, 2001. We're at war against an enemy that, since that day, has continued to kill."

I heard Abdul Henderson, a former Marine corporal, say: "We were firing into small towns. You see people just running, cars going, guys falling off bikes. It was just sad. You just sit there and look through your binos and see things blowing up, and you think, man they have no water, living in the third world, and we're just bombing them to hell. Blowing up buildings, shrapnel tearing people to shreds."

· · ·

I heard a "former high-level intelligence official" say: "This is a war against terrorism, and Iraq is just one campaign. The Bush administration is looking at this as a huge war zone. Next we're going to have the Iranian campaign." I heard Condoleezza Rice say that an invasion of Iran "is not on the menu at this time."

I heard that John Bolton, the new US Ambassador to the United Nations, had said: "There is no such thing as the United Nations. There is an international community that occasionally can be led by the only real power in the world—and that is the United States—when it suits our interest and when we can get others to go along." I heard that he keeps a bronzed hand grenade on his desk.

I heard the President say: "This notion that the United States is getting ready to attack Iran is simply ridiculous. Having said that, all options are on the table." I heard the White House Press Secretary, Scott McClellan, say: "The President makes decisions based on what is right for the American people."

I heard about despair. I heard the President say: "As democracy in Iraq takes root, the enemies of freedom, the terrorists, will become more desperate." I heard about hope. I heard him say: "These terrorists and insurgents will fail. We have a strategy for success in Iraq. As Iraqis stand up, Americans and Coalition forces will stand down."

I heard an unnamed "top US commander" question how the current Iraqi Ministry of Defense, largely staffed by civilians appointed by the US, would be capable of maintaining an army: "What are lacking are the systems that pay people, that supply people, that recruit people, that replace the wounded and AWOL, and systems that promote people and provide spare parts." I heard that the Iraqi Bureau of Supreme Audit could not account for $500 million in the Ministry's budget, and had discovered that the Ministry had deposited $759 million in the personal bank account of a former money trader. I heard Iraqi Lieutenant General Abdul Aziz al-Yaseri say: "There's no rebuilding, no weapons, nothing. There are no real contracts, even. They just signed papers and took the money."

• • •

I heard a White House spokesman, Trent Duffy say: "The President knows one of his most important responsibilities is to comfort the families of the fallen." I heard Cindy Sheehan, whose son, Casey, had been killed in Iraq, describe her meeting with the President.

I heard her say: "He first got there, he walked in and said, 'So who are we honoring here?' He didn't even know Casey's name, he didn't, nobody could have whispered to him, 'Mr. President, this is the Sheehan family, their son Casey was killed in Iraq.' We thought that was pretty disrespectful to not even know Casey's name, and to walk in and say, 'So who are we honorin' here?' Like, 'Let's get on with it, let's get somebody honored here.' So anyway, he went up to my oldest daughter, I keep calling her my oldest daughter but she's actually my oldest child now, and he said, 'So who are you to the loved one?' And Carly goes, 'Casey was my brother.' And George Bush says, 'I wish I could bring your loved one back, to fill the hole in your heart.' And Carly said, 'Yeah, so do we.' And Bush said, 'I'm sure you do,' and he gave her a dirty look and turned away from her."

As the President moved to his ranch for a six-week summer vacation, Cindy Sheehan camped out at the entrance, demanding another meeting, which the President refused. I heard him say: "I think it's important for me to be thoughtful and sensitive to those who have got something to say. But I think it's also important for me to go on with my life, to keep a balanced life. I think the people want the President to be in a position to make good crisp decisions and to stay healthy. And part of my being is to be outside exercising."

I heard that privately he had said: "I'm not meeting again with that goddamned bitch. She can go to hell as far as I'm concerned."

·   ·   ·

I heard that 82% of Iraqis were "strongly opposed" to the presence of foreign troops and 45% supported armed attacks against them. Less than 1% believed that the foreign troops had made the country more secure.

I heard "top military commanders" say that we could expect "some fairly substantial reductions" in troops by next spring. I heard them add that the reduction would come after "a short-term bulge in troop levels."

I heard that 1,100 bodies were brought to the Baghdad morgue in one month, many with hands bound and a bullet in the head. I heard that 20%

were too disfigured to be identified. I heard that in the Saddam era the number was normally around 200. I heard that doctors were ordered not to perform post-mortems on bodies brought in by US troops.

On a single day, I heard that fighting had broken out between two Shi'ite militias in Najaf, leaving 19 dead; that the bodies of 37 Shi'ite soldiers, killed with a single bullet to the head, had been found in a river south of Baghdad; that the Iraqi President Jalal Talabani had escaped an assassination attempt in which eight of his bodyguards were killed and 15 injured. On that same day, I heard an "unnamed White House official" say that the Iraqis were "making substantial and real progress."

I heard Condoleezza Rice say: "It's a lot easier to see the violence and suicide bombing than to see the rather quiet political progress that's going on in parallel." I heard her say that the insurgency was "losing steam."

As riots broke out in Baghdad over the lack of electricity, I heard Nadeem Haki, a shop owner in Baghdad, say: "We thank God that the air we breathe is not in the hands of the government. Otherwise they would have cut it off for a few hours each day."

I heard General Barry McCaffrey say, after returning from an inspection of Iraq: "This thing, the wheels are coming off of it."

• • •

I heard that the President's approval rating had fallen to 36%, lower than Nixon during the summer of Watergate. I heard that 50% now believed that sending troops to Iraq was a mistake. I heard Trent Duffy, the White House spokesman, say that the President "believes that those who want the US to begin to change course in Iraq do not want America to win the overall War on Terror. He can understand that people don't share his view that we must win the War on Terror—but he just has a different view." I heard that the President, at a strategy meeting, had said: "Who gives a flying fuck what the polls say? I'm the President and I'll do whatever I goddamned please. They don't know shit."

I heard Donald Rumsfeld say: "It's been alleged that we're not winning. Throughout history there have always been those who predict America's failure just around every corner. At the height of World War II, many Western intellectuals praised Stalin. For a time, Communism was very much in vogue. Those being tossed about by the winds of concern should recall that Americans are a tough lot and will see their commitments through."

I heard General Douglas Lute, Director of Operations at US Central Command, say that the US would withdraw a significant number of troops within a year. I heard him say: "We believe at some point, in order to break this dependence on the Coalition, you simply have to back off and let the Iraqis step forward." The day before, I heard the President say that withdrawal would "only embolden the terrorists and create a staging ground to launch more attacks against America and free nations. So long as I'm the President, we will stay, we will fight, and we will win the War on Terror."

I heard the President, still on vacation at his ranch, say: "A time of war is a time of sacrifice." I heard a reporter ask him if he planned to do any fishing, and I heard the President reply: "I don't know yet. I haven't made up my mind yet. I'm kind of hanging loose, as they say."

I heard that the US was now spending $195 million a day on the war and that the cost had already exceeded, by $50 billion, US expenses in all of World War I. I heard that $195 million would provide 12 meals a day to every starving child on earth.

• • •

I heard the President, at North Island Naval Air Station in San Diego, compare the War on Terror to World War II. I heard him quote the words of Captain Randy Stone, a Marine in Iraq: "I know we will win because I see it in the eyes of the Marines every morning. In their eyes is the sparkle of victory." In a long speech, I heard him briefly mention Hurricane Katrina, which had struck a few days before and which, at the time, was believed to have killed tens of thousands. I heard him say: "I urge everyone in the affected areas to continue to follow instructions from state and local authorities."

I heard that emergency response to the hurricane had been hampered because 35% of the Louisiana National Guard and 40% of the Mississippi
National Guard, as well as much of their equipment and vehicles, were in
Iraq. Approximately 5,000 Guards and troops were eventually deployed; in
1992, following Hurricane Andrew in Florida, George Bush Sr. had sent in
36,000 troops. I heard that the Guardsmen in Iraq were denied emergency
two-week leaves to help or find their families. I heard they were told by their
commanders that there were too few US troops in Iraq to spare them.

A few weeks after the hurricane, I heard the President say: "You know,
something we—I've been thinking a lot about how America has responded,
and it's clear to me that Americans value human life, and value every person
as important. And that stands in stark contrast, by the way, to the terrorists
we have to deal with. You see, we look at the destruction caused by Katrina,
and our hearts break. They're the kind of people who look at Katrina and
wish they had caused it. We're in a war against these people. It's a War on
Terror."

. . .

On the day after an estimated 200,000 people demonstrated against the war
in Washington, a pro-war rally was held on the Mall. I heard Senator Jeff
Sessions, Republican from Alabama, address the crowd: "The group who
spoke here the other day did not represent the American ideals of freedom,
liberty and spreading that around the world. I frankly don't know what they
represent." The crowd was estimated at 400.

I heard the Special Inspector General for Iraq Reconstruction, Stuart
Bowen, tell Congress that the Administration had "no comprehensive policy or regulatory guidelines" for postwar Iraq. I heard him say that Iraq's
Bureau of Supreme Audit had reported up to $1.27 billion missing in the
period from June 2004 to February 2005 alone.

I heard that, along with the $30 billion appropriated by Congress, the US
Agency for International Development was also seeking private donations:
"Now you can donate high-impact development assistance that directly im-
proves the lives of thousands of Iraqis." I heard that USAID's "extraordi-

nary appeal" had raised $600, but I heard Heather Layman, spokeswoman for USAID, say that she was not disappointed: "Every little bit helps."

In 2003, Dick Cheney had said: "Since I left Halliburton to become George Bush's Vice President, I've severed all my ties with the company, gotten rid of all my financial interest. I have no financial interest in Halliburton of any kind and haven't had, now, for over three years." I heard that he was still receiving deferred compensation and owned more than 433,000 stock options. Those options were worth $241,498 in 2004. In 2005 they were worth more than $8 million. Along with its $10 billion no-bid contracts in Iraq, Halliburton was hired to expand the prison at Guantanamo and was among the first to receive a no-bid contract for Hurricane Katrina relief.

I heard the President say: "At this moment, more than a dozen Iraqi battalions have completed training and are conducting anti-terrorist operations in Ramadi and Fallujah. More than 20 battalions are operating in Baghdad. And some have taken the lead in operations in major sectors of the city. In total, more than 100 battalions are operating throughout Iraq. Our commanders report that the Iraqi forces are operating with increasing effectiveness."

An Iraqi battalion has about 700 soldiers. The next day I heard General George Casey tell Congress that the number of "combat ready" Iraqi battalions had dropped from three to one. I heard him say: "Iraqi armed forces will not have an independent capability for some time." When asked when the American people can expect troops to be withdrawn from Iraq, I heard him reply: "I don't want to get into a date. I wouldn't even want to go there, wouldn't even want to go there."

I heard Colonel Stephen Davis, Commander of Marine Regimental Combat Team 2, tell a group of Iraqis that the US was not leaving: "We're not going anywhere. Some of you are concerned about the attack helicopters and mortar fire from the base. I will tell you this: those are the sounds of peace."

I heard General George Casey say, nevertheless, that the insurgency "is failing. We are more relentless in our progress than those who seek to disrupt it."

I heard General John Abizaid say: "The insurgency doesn't have a chance for victory."

I heard Condoleezza Rice say: "We have made significant progress."

I heard Major General Rick Lynch, chief military spokesman in Iraq, say: "Zarqawi is on the ropes."

As the Administration celebrated the approval of the long-delayed Constitution, I heard Safia Taleb al-Suhail—the daughter of a man who was executed by Saddam Hussein and who, in a staged moment during the State of the Union address, embraced the mother of an American soldier killed in Iraq—say: "When we came back from exile, we thought we were going to improve rights and the position of women. But look what has happened—we have lost all the gains we made over the last 30 years. It's a big disappointment."

I heard an Iraqi Shi'ite sergeant say: "Just let us have our Constitution and elections in December and then we will do what Saddam did—start with five people from each neighborhood and kill them in the streets and then go from there."

• • •

I heard Melvin Laird, Secretary of Defense under Nixon during the Vietnam War, call for the withdrawal of troops. I heard him say about the President: "His West Texas cowboy approach—shoot first and answer questions later or do the job first and let the results speak for themselves—is not working. When troops are dying, the Commander in Chief cannot be coy, vague, or secretive."

I heard Brent Scowcroft, National Security Adviser and close friend to Bush Sr., say: "I thought we ought to make it our duty to help make the world friendlier for the growth of liberal regimes. You encourage democracy over time, with assistance and aid, the traditional way. Not how the neocons do it." They "believe in the export of democracy, by violence if that is required. How do the neocons bring democracy to Iraq? You invade, you threaten and pressure, you evangelize." I heard him say that America is now "suffering from the consequences of this brand of revolutionary utopianism."

I heard Colonel Lawrence Wilkerson, Colin Powell's Chief of Staff at the State Department, say that foreign policy had been "hijacked" by the "Cheney-Rumsfeld cabal." I heard him say that Rumsfeld was "given carte blanche to tell the State Department to go screw itself in a closet somewhere." I heard him say: "If something comes along that is truly serious, something like a nuclear weapon going off in a major American city, or something like a major pandemic, you are going to see the ineptitude of this government in a way that will take you back to the Declaration of Independence."

· · ·

I heard that 2,000 US soldiers had been killed in Iraq; 15,220 had been wounded in combat, including more than 7,100 who were "injured too badly to return to duty," and that thousands more had been "hurt in incidents unrelated to combat."

I heard that a spokesman for the US military in Iraq, Lieutenant Colonel Steve Boylan, had sent an e-mail to journalists asking them to downplay the marker of 2,000 dead: "When you report on the events, take a moment to think about the effects on the families and those serving in Iraq. The 2,000 service members killed in Iraq supporting Operation Iraqi Freedom is not a milestone. It is an artificial mark on the wall set by individuals or groups with specific agendas and ulterior motives."

I heard that 65% of Americans now believed that the Iraq war was based on falsified information; only 42% considered the President "honest and ethical" and only 29% considered Dick Cheney "honest and ethical."

I heard the President say: "Anti-war critics are now claiming we manipulated the intelligence and misled the American people about why we went to war. The stakes in the global War on Terror are too high, and the national interest is too important, for politicians to throw out false charges. These baseless attacks send the wrong signal to our troops and to an enemy that is questioning America's will."

I heard Dick Cheney say: "The suggestion that's been made by some US Senators that the President of the United States or any member of this Administration purposely misled the American people on pre-war intelligence is one of the most dishonest and reprehensible charges ever aired in this city."

A few days later, I heard Dick Cheney complain that the "liberal" media had distorted his remarks. As evidence, I heard him cite a headline that read "Cheney says war critics 'dishonest,' reprehensible.' " Then, in the same speech, I heard him say: "I will again say it is dishonest and reprehensible. This is revisionism of the most corrupt and shameless variety."

· · ·

I heard Congressman John Murtha, Democrat from Pennsylvania, a Marine colonel decorated in the Korean and Vietnam wars, and prominent military hawk, with tears in his eyes call for the withdrawal of US troops within six months. I heard Scott McClellan, the White House Press Secretary, say: "It is baffling that he is endorsing the policy positions of Michael Moore and the extreme liberal wing." I heard Congressman Geoff Davis, Republican from Kentucky, say: "Ayman Zawahiri, Osama bin Laden's deputy, as well as Abu Musab Zarqawi, have made it quite clear in their internal propaganda that they cannot win unless they can drive the Americans out. And they know that they can't do that there, so they've brought the battlefield to the halls of Congress." I heard Congresswoman Jean Schmidt, Republican from Ohio, say: "Cowards cut and run. Marines never do."

I heard the President say: "Some contend that we should set a deadline for withdrawing US forces. Let me explain why that would be a serious mistake. Setting an artificial timetable would send the wrong message to the Iraqis, who need to know that America will not leave before the job is done."

I heard that, at an extraordinary "meeting of reconciliation," one hundred Shi'ite, Sunni, and Kurdish leaders had signed a statement demanding "a withdrawal of foreign troops on a specified timetable."

I heard that their statement also said: "National resistance is a legitimate right of all nations."

I heard Congresswoman Jean Schmidt say: "The big picture is that these Islamic insurgents want to destroy us. They don't like us. They don't like us because we're black, we're white, we're Christian, we're Jew, we're educated, we're free, we're not Islamic. We can never be Islamic because we were not born Islamic. Now, this isn't the Islamic citizens. These are the insurgents. And it is their desire for us to leave so they can take over the whole Middle East and then take over the world. And I didn't learn this just in the last few weeks or the last few months. I learned this when I was at the University of Cincinnati in 1970, studying Middle Eastern history."

•   •   •

I heard that, in Fallujah and elsewhere, the US had employed white phosphorus munitions, an incendiary device, known among soldiers as "Willie Pete" or "Shake & Bake," which is banned as a weapon by the Convention on Conventional Weapons. Similar to napalm, it leaves the victim horribly burned, often burning through to the bones. I heard a State Department spokesman say: "US forces have used them very sparingly in Fallujah, for illumination purposes. They were fired into the air to illuminate enemy positions at night, not at enemy fighters." Then I heard them say that "US forces used white phosphorous rounds to flush out enemy fighters so that they could then be killed with high explosive rounds." Then I heard a Pentagon spokesman say that the previous statements were based on "poor information," and that "it was used as an incendiary weapon against enemy combatants." Then I heard the Pentagon say that white phosphorus was not an illegal weapon, because the US had never signed that provision of the Convention on Conventional Weapons.

I heard that US troops had accidentally come across an Interior Ministry bunker in Baghdad with more than 170 Sunni prisoners who had been captured by Shi'ite paramilitary groups and tortured, some with electric drills. I heard Hussein Kamal, Deputy Interior Minister, say: "One or two detainees were paralyzed and some had their skin peeled off various parts of their bodies." I heard State Department spokesman Adam Ereli say:

"We don't practice torture. And we don't believe that others should practice torture."

I heard that the Senate, after an hour of debate, voted to deny habeas corpus protection to prisoners in Guantanamo. The last time the US suspended the right to trial was during the Civil War.

I heard that a human rights organization, Christian Peacemaker Teams, was distributing a questionnaire to inmates released from American prisons in Iraq. Those surveyed were asked to check "yes" or "no" after each question:
Stripped of your clothing (nude)?
Beaten by hand (punches)?
Beaten by stick or rod?
Beaten by cables, wires or belts?
Held at gunpoint?
Hooded?
Had cold water poured on you?
Had a rope tied to your genitalia?
Called names, insults?
Threatened or touched by dogs?
Dragged by rope or belt?
Denied prayer or *wudhu* [ablution]?
Forced to perform sexual acts?
Were you raped or sodomized?
Did someone improperly touch your genitalia?
Did you witness any sexual acts while in detention?
Did you witness any rapes of men, women, or children?
Urinated on or made to touch feces, or had feces thrown at you?
Denied sleep?
Denied food?
Witnessed any deaths?
Did you witness any torture or mistreatment to others?
Forced to wear woman's clothes? [Question for men only]
Were you burned or exposed to extreme heat?
Exposed to severe cold?
Subjected to electric shock?
Forced to act like a dog?

Forced in uncomfortable positions for a lengthy period of time?
Forced to stand or sit in a painful manner for lengthy periods of time?
Lose consciousness?
Forced to hit others?
Hung by feet?
Hung by hands or arms?
Threatened to have family killed?
Family members detained?
Witnessed family members tortured?
Forced to sign anything?
Photographed?

I heard a man who had been in Abu Ghraib prison say: "The Americans brought electricity to my ass before they brought it to my house."

• • •

I heard that the Lincoln Group, a public-relations firm in Washington, had received $100 million from the Pentagon to promote the war. As well as bribing Iraqi journalists, often with monthly stipends, The Lincoln Group was writing its own articles and paying Iraqi newspapers to publish them. I heard the articles, intending to have local appeal, had titles such as "The Sands Are Blowing Toward a Democratic Iraq" and "Iraqi Forces Capture Al-Qaeda Fighters Crawling Like Dogs." I heard a Pentagon spokesman, Major General Rick Lynch, say: "We do empower our operational commanders with the ability to inform the Iraqi public, but everything we do is based on fact, not based on fiction." I heard him quote the al-Qaeda leader, Ayman al-Zawahiri: "Remember, half the battle is the battlefield of the media."

I heard that the average monthly war coverage on the ABC, NBC, and CBS evening newscasts, combined, had gone from 388 minutes in 2003, to 274 in 2004, to 166 in 2005.

I heard that 2,110 US troops had died in Iraq and over 15,881 had been wounded. 94% of those deaths had come after the "Mission Accomplished" speech, the first two sentences of which were: "Major combat operations in

Iraq have ended. In the Battle of Iraq, the United States and our allies have prevailed." I heard there were now an average of a hundred insurgent attacks a day and an average of three American soldiers dying, the highest violence and casualty rates since the war began.

I heard that the President, in response to the increasing criticism, was going to reveal a new strategy for Iraq. On November 30, 2005, the Administration issued a 35-page report: "National Strategy for Victory in Iraq." On a page titled "Our Strategy Is Working," I read that, on the "Economic Track," "Our Restore, Reform, Build, strategy is achieving results"; on the "Political Track," "Our Isolate, Engage, and Build strategy is working"; and on the "Security Track," "Our Clear, Hold, and Build strategy is working." General goals would be achieved in the "short," "medium," or "long" term. The report ended with "The Eight Strategic Pillars" ("Strategic Pillar One: Defeat the Terrorists and Neutralize the Insurgency; Strategic Pillar Two: Transition Iraq to Security Self-Reliance . . .") like the Five Pillars of Islam or *Seven Pillars of Wisdom*. I heard that the "Strategy" contained few specific details because it was the "public version of a classified document." Then I heard that there was no classified document. Then I heard that the military commanders in Iraq were unaware of its existence. Then I heard it was largely written by a pollster who specializes in public opinion during wartime.

On the same day that the "National Strategy" was released, I heard the President address the US Naval Academy in Annapolis. I heard him say: "We will never back down. We will never give in. And we will never accept anything less than complete victory." I heard him say: "To all who wear the uniform, I make you this pledge: America will not run in the face of car bombers and assassins so long as I am your Commander in Chief." In a front of a huge sign that read "PLAN FOR VICTORY," he stood at a podium bearing a huge sign that read "PLAN FOR VICTORY." I wondered whether "plan" was a verb.

That same day, I heard that members of the Christian Peacemaker Teams had been kidnapped by members of the Swords of Islam.

[December 4, 2005]

"THE ARTS AND THE WAR IN IRAQ"
(RESPONSE TO *October*)

I AM NEITHER an artist nor an academic; nor am I connected to any cultural institution. I am a literary writer, responding as such, and the first thing to notice is the absence of literary writers from your list of invited participants. This is only partially attributable to *October's* general purview or web of connections: there are hardly any "obvious" literary writers to ask. With few exceptions, writers have been as invisible politically throughout the outrages of the Cheney administration as they were during the Reagan-Bush I years.

Like your questionnaire, discussions of what's currently happening too often begin with the 1960s, and those of us who were young then have become as tedious as old soldiers. Yet it's worth recalling to the collective amnesia a few of the ways in which that era was quite different from the present. Above all, art was the alternative, often openly hostile, to middle-class America and all of its institutions, including universities. Art was largely the product of bohemians, and the few who made money tended to keep it a secret. Even the most commercial branches—say, rock music—existed with a minimum of marketing. (Woodstock may have represented the end—or more precisely, the suburbanization—of hippiedom, but it's interesting to note that no t-shirts or other memorabilia were sold there.) Publishing was mainly the domain of a group of independent family businesses that made a modest profit; serious writers and editors tended to stay with the same house for most of their careers; ambition was aesthetic ("the great American novel") rather than monetary. In the visual arts, reputations were made by critics and fellow artists, though Warhol was marking the beginning of that change. And almost everyone in the arts needed to have a day job—usually one unconnected to their art—which kept them in touch with, and aware of, the society at large. Art was by its nature oppositional; it was not part of the counterculture, it created it. The specific political activism around civil rights, the Vietnam War, and the draft was only one facet of the new "consciousness"—the counterculture was also thriving in countries where these were not issues—but was inextricable from it in a romance of political, social, and psychological revolution, whose strands could not be separated. It's almost impossible to imagine now how taking drugs or having sex were seen as political acts, the other side of demonstrating in the streets.

Now of course the market rules. The visual arts are driven by collectors, and successful artists have lifestyles identical to their patrons. Publishing is controlled by multinational corporations and is directed by agents and the sales forces. The bad boys and girls of popular music have zillion-dollar contracts and houses in Greenwich, Connecticut. Sensitive kids today are obsessed with the Beats who, for them, are the last authentic people in the arts: genuine outsiders, not the products of marketing strategies. The old "shock of the new," if it exists at all, has been reduced to advertising campaigns or "sensational" art publicity stunts (usually British). And the world is too expensive to have a bohemian life in most of the major cities in the West.

Two phenomena in the early 1970s: The creation by Johnson and implementation by Nixon of the National Endowment of the Arts, in a conscious effort to shut up the artists by buying them off. (It worked: it's forgotten that most of the antiwar activity in the arts ended long before the actual war ended.) This became the foundation of a vast public and private arts bureaucracy. Artists and writers, like politicians, suddenly were devoting a great deal of energy to fundraising for themselves, their art increasingly tailored to what would look attractive on a grant proposal. By the 1980s, this had become so normal that supposedly transgressive performance artists were dutifully filling out the multiple pages and copies of a NEA application, and crying "censorship" when their applications were rejected by a Republican administration. Small wonder, then, that during the Reagan-Bush I years, as the middle class became poor, the poor were devastated and three million became homeless, practically the only protest from artists and writers occurred when it was proposed to cut the NEA budget, their tiny slice of the pie.

Secondly, the transformation of the universities, which also became increasingly market-driven, catering to a consumer group formerly known as students. In response to the 1960s student demands for "relevancy,"contemporary art was introduced into the curriculum and arts practitioners were placed on the faculty. In literature, the proliferation of creative writing departments simultaneously created a comfortable middle-class career for poets and non-commercial novelists and decentralized them from a few urban areas into the diaspora of campuses, effectively neutral-izing the varied senses of literary communities. Meanwhile, politics as the world knows it was transformed into identity politics, and ideology became strictly theoretical, losing even its dream, however utopian, of practical ap-plication. A salutary reexamination of everything along gender/race/class lines was not matched by any interest at all in what was happening to women, minorities, and the poor in the very real Reagan America. It's easy to blame the current apathy of students on the absence of the draft, but this ignores what they're learning in the classroom. As Rome burns, they're being taught to root out "essentialism."

Although the Christian right still believes in the subversiveness of art, the arts in America are no longer the alternative to, let alone the enemy of, anything. They have become self-contained niche industries, newsworthy when large sums of money are spent. Its workers are as colorless as insur-ance agents; their reputations largely determined by publicists. As everyone knows, a tableful of painters is likely to be talking about real estate and vaca-tion spots; a tableful of writers, grants, prizes, and who's teaching where. Moreover, they live in the only country on earth that does not take nation-alistic pride in its cultural producers, and where what passes for public in-tellectuals are policy wonks, not people in the arts. The sense of living in a larger world has become so attenuated that, immediately after 9/11, when for the first time in decades American literary writers were asked by news-papers and mass-circulation magazines to comment on a public matter, they could only summon up some autobiographical anecdotes. (9/11, said one Pulitzer-prize novelist, reminded him of the day his father died.) As a judge for a poetry prize last year, I read through some 600 new books of American poetry; no more than four or five had even any allusions to the events of the 21st century; none had any significant engagement.

As far as I can tell, the Cheney-Bush II era has not produced a sin-gle poem, song, novel, or artwork that has caught the popular imagination as a condemnation or an epitome of the times. The only enduring image is a product of journalism: the hooded figure in the Abu Ghraib photographs. By and large, the artists and writers have been what used to be called "good Germans," making their little sausages while the world around them went insane. There are only a few who have used their skills—or their magazines!—to even attempt to change the way people think.

Fortunately, the silence of the artists is in contrast to the cacophony of ordinary citizens, all of them on the web. The mass media under Cheney-Bush II (until Katrina introduced a slight hint of skepticism) has been worthy of the Soviet Union in its mindless repetition of what the government wants them to say. (The untold story is the extraordinary extent to which policy was, in fact, directed by public relations people, paid hundreds of millions of dollars by the Pentagon and other agencies.) For the last seven years, the only source of reliable information and oppositional opinion has been the internet (including, of course, its ease of receiving and circulating articles from the foreign press). Furthermore, web archives and search engines have given the websites and bloggers the ability to expose and demolish the lies and contradictions of the politicians, the press, and the leading columnists and pundits. I don't know what we would have done without it. An authoritarian state only succeeds through absolute control of information. Cheney-Bush II—the most radical administration in American history—certainly tried hard enough, but in the end the web miraculously managed to elude its grasp.

The web gives the lie to the usual excuses made by individual artists and writers: "What can one person do?" "It's preaching to the converted." Etc. With the web every person is his or her own publisher, editor, journalist, columnist. Thanks entirely to the web and a few comedians, a majority of Americans (at this writing in August 2007) think Cheney should be impeached, and some 40% want Bush impeached along with him. A vast majority believes the Iraq war is a disaster and wants the US out of there immediately. Meanwhile, the arts in America—all of them—have become largely irrelevant to what is actually happening in the world. Crusading bloggers are the closest we get to a Zola, Brecht, or Ginsberg. They're valiant, but they're not art.

[August 2007]

THE UNITED STATES OF OBAMA

O N THE FINAL night of the relentless presidential primary campaign, Jesse Jackson compared Barack Obama's victory to the signing of the Declaration of Independence. Erica Jong compared Hillary Clinton's defeat to watching Joan of Arc burning at the stake. Obama was in St. Paul, Minnesota, pointedly in the very arena where the Republicans will hold their convention in September, at times barely audible in the nearly continual cheering of 17,000 fans (with another 15,000 listening outside). Clinton was off on what has come to be known as the remote island of Hillaryland—in this case several stories below ground at Baruch College in New York, inaccessible to cell phones or Blackberries—still insisting that, according to Hillarymath, she had won the popular vote, still declaring that she was ready to be Commander-in-Chief on "Day One," and still repeating the creepiest line of her stump speech, the one about the boy who had sold his bicycle to give money to her campaign. (She and Bill had made $109 million in the last seven years and she's taking toys from children? And gloating over it?) She threatened that the 17 million who had voted for her must be "respected"— as though she were a warlord and they her private army—while some in the crowd chanted "Den-ver! Den-ver!," meaning that she should take the fight all the way to the Democratic convention in August. And then there was John McCain, in what seemed to be a high school auditorium somewhere in Louisiana (even he wasn't sure: he thought he was in New Orleans, but he wasn't), addressing a few hundred sleepy geriatrics, struggling with the teleprompter and grinning weirdly at random moments. Standing in front of a hideous green backdrop, he looked, as one blogger wrote, like the cottage cheese on a lime jello salad. Apparently no longer an officer and a gentleman, he took the occasion of this extraordinary moment in American history not to congratulate the first African-American nominee, but rather to deride, with soporific sarcasm, Obama the young whippersnapper and his belief in "change." A bizarre line from McCain's speech has already become a six-second YouTube classic: "We should be able to deliver bottled hot water to dehydrated babies."

Watching Obama speak, it was hard to believe that this was the USA. I flashed back to a scene fifty-odd years ago: I was four years old, on a family trip to Florida, and caused a minor scene in a bus station when I wandered over and took a drink from the water fountain marked "Colored." (I could read the sign, but had no idea what it meant.) I'd grown up during the civil rights movement, had heard Martin Luther King speak. And here was an African-American who had risen higher than any non-white person in any Western country, and moreover had done so in a nation that has never, with the exception of the Irish John Kennedy, elected a president from even its white minorities—no Jews, no Poles, no Italians—and had nominated only two others, Al Smith in the 1920s and the hapless Michael Dukakis.

But this was the response of a baby boomer, when in fact one of the remarkable things about the Obama campaign was that it wasn't about race at all. Obama, though he studiously had copied his speaking style from King and other preachers, was not running as a black man. It has already been forgotten that until his victory in the first primary in Iowa, many blacks didn't know what to make of him. The veterans from the civil rights movement didn't much like him: he hadn't come out of their struggle, was an "African" African-American with no personal roots in slavery, and seemed to have a very different agenda: his sense of injustice was universal, and not specifically the indignities suffered by African-Americans. The majority of black women and half of black men supported Clinton. They began to rally behind him when it became clear he was appealing to whites, that he was a new kind of African-American politician and might actually succeed. And they deserted Hillary en masse after the first of what would be a series of shocking remarks from the Clintons, who had always been superstars in the black communities: Bill dismissing Obama as another Jesse Jackson (that is, a minor protest candidate appealing only to blacks) and Hillary, drawing an unspoken parallel, declaring that King may have been a great orator, but it was Lyndon Johnson who got the civil rights legislation passed.

Certainly there are those who voted and will vote for or against Obama because of his race, but a kind of horizontal racism has largely disappeared in the USA. These days, a white office worker generally has no problem with a black office worker—though poor blacks, of course, remain an alien Other, and an institutionalized racism has kept young black men out of college and in prison. There is a new generation that has grown up with King's birthday as a national holiday, and the kind of American Heroes I learned about in elementary school, Teddy Roosevelt and Daniel Boone, have been replaced by Rosa Parks and Sacajawea. Nor can one underestimate how pop culture has cleared the path for both Obama and Hillary. (As one comedian cracked, "If there's a black or woman president in the Oval Office, it means an asteroid is about to hit the Statue of Liberty.") Among Obama's precursors is certainly Oprah Winfrey, the only self-made woman billionaire in America, who has built her television and magazine by assuming the role of an upbeat friend, helping you to help yourself. Obama's slogan "Yes we can!" is Oprah's essential message; and it's worth noting that some 90% of her audience is white.

Moreover, virulent racism in the USA is now directed at the new arrivals, the Hispanics. Anti-immigrant sentiments were cleverly fused by the Cheney-Bush Administration with their War on Terror, and in the current, however waning, rhetoric—exemplified by the fanatical anchorman Lou Dobbs on CNN—"terrorist" and "illegal alien" have become interchangeable in the fear-mongering over "security" and "protecting our borders." A journalist who investigated white supremacist websites found that most of their anger was directed against McCain, considered "soft" on immigration, rather than Obama. (In Aryan Nation logic, Obama as a black man is incapable of thinking and is merely a tool of ZOG—the Zionist Occupational Government—which runs the country.) In the South, the white sheriffs of the civil rights days are now finding any pretext—even fishing without a licence—to arrest Hispanics and deport them if they are in the country illegally. For these guardians of justice, blacks may be black, but they're at least one of "us."

The Obama phenomenon is not, except among justifiably proud African-Americans, about race at all. It's about a new generation kicking out, at last, the baby boomers and getting past what Obama has called their "psycho-drama," which has continued to polarize and paralyze the government. Bill Clinton had once said that if you think what happened in the sixties was a good thing, you're a Democrat; and if you think it was bad, you're a Republican. Obama, before he ran for president, used to say that American politics was still stuck in the late-night dorm-room arguments of the time.

In both style and substance, this was a contest between the end of the 20th century and the beginning of the 21st. Clinton modeled her campaign on Bill's success in 1992: get the big donors, concentrate on winning the big states. (Bill hadn't won Iowa, the first state to vote, therefore it wasn't worth much of an effort.) Mark Penn, the pollster who had overseen Bill's 1996 re-election, was hired to run Hillary's equally poll-driven campaign. (Penn's specialty is dividing the electorate into minuscule special-interest groups and then devising messages for each.) Much of Clinton's early rhetoric was about restoring the good old days of Clinton I. ("It took a Clinton to clean up after the first Bush and it will take a Clinton to clean up after the second Bush.") She abandoned it as Bill became increasingly visible and strangely choleric, bringing back memories of the less happy moments of the Clinton years, and leading many to wonder whether she would be able to control him in a Hillary White House.

Obama took his experience as a grassroots organizer, and brought it into the age of the internet—a force first recognized by Howard Dean in his unsuccessful 2004 campaign. Combining the "50 state strategy" that Dean, as the head of the Democratic National Committee, had devised (to the absolute derision of the Clintonistas) with the decentralized nature of the web, Obama realized that a lot of small states would provide as many delegates as a few big states and that a lot of small donors would ultimately give more money than a few big ones (who under the campaign finance laws can only give so much). With a brilliant website modeled on "social networking hubs" like Facebook and MySpace, and full of things to do for a generation that lives on the internet, he assembled an e-mail list of eight or ten million names, and received donations—90% of them less than $200 each, and about half less than $100 each—from a million and a half people, giving them a sense of participation and encouraging them to engage in the actual campaigning. (He raised $55 million in February without holding a single fundraiser.) Meanwhile, he grasped the power of YouTube both for reproducing his ads and speeches and Clinton's worst lines; these were watched by millions. Most of all, he understood that the entire country was fed up with Bush, the most unpopular president in modern American history, and that the message of "change" was one that would appeal to vast numbers of voters, transcending the Clinton-Penn so-called "slicing and dicing" of the electorate, where, for example, soybean farmers are guaranteed continued subsidies. In a decentralized world that was a macrocosm of Obama's own personal history (a Kenyan-American growing up in Hawaii and Indonesia, with grandparents in Kansas), what would bring people together were universal aspirations, communicated through the new level playing field of the web.

The Clintons were utterly clueless about the political force of the internet— Bill doesn't even know how to use e-mail—and were accustomed to the era when money came from the rich, opinions were expressed by a manageable group of pundits on television and in the newspapers, and where one's message can be somewhat controlled in the media. The web is, of course, a whole new world, with many thousands of opinion-makers, fact-checkers, and amateur experts. Every statement by a politician is vetted by legions of volunteer investigative reporters of a kind that now rarely exists in the major media, and who somehow manage to instantly produce the quotes or video clips that demonstrate the candidate's hypocrisy—as Clinton discovered when she told the tales of braving sniper fire in Bosnia or how she brought peace to Northern Ireland. Throughout the campaign, the web was reporting news that, say, the *New York Times*, wasn't. And the most accurate predictions for each primary were not made by any of the polling organizations, but by an anonymous blogger named Poblano, who polled no one but had devised some sort of system based on demographics and previous voting records. At the end of the race, Poblano revealed himself as a professional baseball statistician.

But the web aside, one of the surprises was how generally inept Hillary's campaign was. She'd been planning her ascension to the throne for at least six years (and some say even before Bill became president). Believing that it was the only way a woman could be elected, she had built her image as a Thatcher-like Iron Lady, not only supporting the Iraq war, but also identifying with various military and defense issues. Assuming she would be running against the right, never imagining a challenge from the left, Clinton was not prominently identified with any progressive legislation in her six colorless years in the Senate, for fear that it would ultimately be used against her. On the contrary, she largely tried to burnish her credentials as a hardline patriot, even introducing a bill for a constitutional amendment against flag-burning, though there had been only one known incident since the Vietnam War—some drunken frat boys at a party.

She started out last year with universal name recognition and a 30-point lead in the polls, convinced of her own inevitability. In December she said: "I'm in it for the long run. It's not a very long run. It'll be over by February 5th." That day, Super Tuesday, caught her by surprise: 22 states voted and 13 of them went for Obama. Utterly unprepared for a setback, she made the fatal mistake of playing, not to her strengths, but by Karl Rove rules.

Hillary is the administrator whom no one particularly likes but everyone respects for her efficiency. She is an über-policy wonk, with an encyclopedic knowledge of legislation and position papers. Tremendously articulate— and a much better debater than Obama—one can throw any question at her ("What can be done about protecting the salmon fisheries of the Northwest?") and get a detailed response. In a country tired of the sheer ineptitude of the Cheney-Bush Administration—epitomized by the destruction of a major American city and its failure, still, to do anything about it (New Orleans today has half its population)—Clinton could have won simply by demonstrating her competence, as she had in her two Senate races, winning over the largely conservative upstate New York voters.

Instead, she couldn't stop talking about her competence, interminably reiterating her "ready on Day One" mantra, as though her experiences as a presidential wife somehow made her more presidential. Worse, she went on the attack, sarcastically deriding Obama's inspirational speeches:

> Now, I could stand up here and say, 'Let's just get everybody together. Let's get unified. The sky will open. The light will come down. Celestial choirs will be singing, and everyone will know we should do the right thing and the world will be perfect.'

(She was surely the first campaigning politician to tell voters that their dreams are delusions.) She ridiculously charged Obama with plagiarism ("change you can xerox") over a single line in one of his speeches and tirelessly repeated that Obama knew someone who had been a member of the Weather Underground (when Obama was a child). Democratic Party regulars were appalled when she began to praise McCain at Obama's expense: only she and McCain were ready to be Commander-in-Chief, or, in Bill's formulation, only she and McCain were "true patriots." Obama was a wimp—Bill called him "the kid"—who wanted to talk with Ahmadinejad; Clinton would nuke and "obliterate" Iran if they dared attack Israel.

Just when you thought she had hit bottom, she went even lower. She tried to cast Obama as a Scary Black Man who, as subliminally suggested in her infamous (and mercilessly parodied) "3 a.m." ad, would break into your house and murder your cute little sleeping blonde daughter. She cast doubt on whether Obama was really a Christian and not a Scary Muslim. And when that didn't work, she reinvented herself as a Woman of the People, waxing eloquent on her hunting days with grandpa and downing shots in working class bars, as she derided Obama—son of a single welfare mother—as an elitist, out of touch with the regular people she'd presumably been hanging out with all these years at Yale Law School, the Arkansas Governor's Mansion, the White House, and the Senate. Those regular people, she explained in one of many embarrassing moments, were "hard-working Americans, white Americans."

Every time she lost a state, her minions would go on television declaring that that state (and by extension its voters) didn't matter; bloggers began calling it the "insult 40-states strategy." A victory in backwater West Virginia was hailed as a major triumph. No one in the Clinton camp ever admitted that she had remained behind in the popular vote and in the pledged (elected) delegates from the beginning, and television, of course, promoted the illusion that this would be a photo finish to keep us all immobile before our sets.

The funniest moment came when Clinton joined McCain in proposing a summer holiday from the federal gas tax—a strictly vote-pandering gesture, especially as neither of them introduced a bill in the Senate to turn it into law. Asked about the fact that not a single economist supported the plan, Clinton, Supreme Commander of the Position Paper, replied: "I'm not going to put my lot in with economists. . . . We've got to get out of this mind-set where somehow elite opinion is always on the side of doing things that really disadvantage the vast majority of Americans."

In her last acts of desperation, she tried to change the Party rules, which she had supported, that discredited the primaries in Florida and Michigan. Now she was comparing the vote in Florida to the abolition of slavery and the elections in Zimbabwe—as though Florida had been ruled by Obama for 25 years and Clinton voters had been terrorized and murdered by Obama thugs. In Michigan, where Obama's name had not even appeared on the ballot, she insisted she was due all of the votes and Obama none.

And then she reached the lowest of the low, in a line that turned many superdelegates and much of the country against her. Asked in May why she hadn't dropped out from what was so clearly a losing campaign, she answered that we shouldn't forget that Robert Kennedy was assassinated in June on the night of the California primary, and one never knows what will happen. Quite apart from the obvious point that, in any political campaign, one does not suggest the murder of one's opponent, Obama is clearly the most inspirational figure in American politics since Robert Kennedy and Martin Luther King, and their fates have been very much on everyone's mind, however unspoken.

By the end, Clinton, the candidate who had been working on this for years and whose greatest attribute was dogged competence, ended up with $30 million in debt, much of it owed to small businesses, with $11 million owed to herself. (It is unclear how she will manage to pay this off, as lost causes don't attract donors.) Obama, who had rapidly come from nowhere, finished with a surplus of about $30 million. Her communications director was paid $266,000 a month; his $14,000. Her staff had been in a very public civil war, leading to the dismissals of top advisers and managers; his staff had no visible internal dissension. She was the one who was supposed to have the managerial skills, Obama was the dreamer. But even Republicans are calling Obama's the best organized campaign in memory. Some years from now, when the memoirs appear, we'll find out exactly how he did it.

The day after the final primary and Clinton's delusional speech, a group of her most ardent supporters from Congress staged an intervention to send her into symbolic rehab for her self-addiction. For the good of the Party, she had to admit that she had lost. Three days later, she gave a speech endorsing Obama. The pundits all called it "gracious," but one could see that she was not exactly warming to the task. It was strange that she didn't once mention McCain. Perhaps, in her mind, the race had been entirely Clinton vs. Obama; now that she had lost, the rest hardly mattered.

Hardcore Clinton supporters saw the race in terms of gender, and blamed her loss on the sexism of the media and of the general public. But, again, the lines of division were generational: Women over 65 voted overwhelmingly for Clinton; women 40-65 were or more less split evenly; and women under 40 voted for Obama. Younger women in urban America are now better educated and earn more than younger men. They're filling the executive positions and clearly do not believe that Clinton was their only hope of seeing a woman president.

Obama didn't win because Clinton lost. He was, in American terms, the better candidate. I knew he'd win when I first watched him on television in Iowa, for he has the quality Americans most prize in their presidential candidates: sincerity. They have voted for Republicans in seven of the last ten elections, even though they often disagreed with the Republicans on many of the specific issues and even though they were clearly voting against their own general self-interests, because the Republicans appear to mean what they say. With the exception of Bill Clinton—who had the knack of being all things to all people—the Democrats have repeatedly tried to out-Republican the Republicans and have ended up looking like hypocrites: Dukakis, a nerd riding in a tank with a helmet that was too large for him. Mr. Science Al Gore, refusing to condemn the Kansas Board of Education for ruling that creationism must be taught in biology courses. Kerry pathetically beginning his acceptance speech at the Democratic convention by saluting and intoning "Reporting for duty." And now Hillary, the lifelong antiracist playing to racism, opposed to the war she supported, the Ivy League policy wonk denouncing elitism.

Obama, by all accounts, has remained true to his vision of grassroots organization and politics through reconciliation; he has yet to be caught holding any contradictory positions. In a country that believes, above all, and largely to its great detriment, in individual self-reliance, he is a self-made man whose message emphasizes that progress must also begin at home. Clinton, for example, as an old-fashioned Democrat, talked of policy changes to improve education. Obama, as what has become the new-fashioned Democrat, said we must both change policy and sit down at the kitchen table and help our kids with their homework. It's a message with enormous appeal to conservatives, and though I personally don't meet many where I live in New York, I keep hearing stories of friends' parents and aunts and uncles out in the heartland, solid Republicans, who are enthusiastic for Obama. The other day, a leading publicist for Christian groups said that he expects 40% of evangelicals to vote for the Democrat—a startling erosion of the Republican base—for they, too, have a new generation, and one that is more tolerant on social issues.

Meanwhile, on the other side, it seems that, unless there is a cataclysmic event setting off a new round of fear, McCain doesn't have much of a chance. He became the nominee only because the others—Romney, Giu-

liani, Huckabee—were, each in different ways, hopeless. He has generated
little enthusiasm among Republicans: in the last two months of the primaries, after he had already won, 25% of them voted against him. As Ralph
Nader did to Gore in 2000, the Libertarians Bob Barr and Ron Paul will
chip away Republican votes. McCain's reputation as a "maverick" on the
Straight Talk Express is based on the McCain of 2000, when Bush defeated
him in a vicious campaign. Now the man who attacked evangelical preachers as "agents of intolerance" is begging for their support; the man who
denounced the Bush tax cuts for the rich believes they are the best hope
for the sinking economy; the man who had once called Bush "dumb as a
stump" is now seen, in photographs that have become iconic, awkwardly
hugging Bush's stomach or sharing a birthday cake with him on the very day
that Katrina struck the Gulf Coast. In his first national advertisement, the
ardent enthusiast for a 100-year occupation of Iraq declares, "I hate war."
His sincerity quotient, once high, will sink rapidly now that the Democratic
race is over, as the media picks up on the information already provided on
the blogosphere and begins to look at him more carefully. And, especially
alongside Obama, he is an old man who doesn't seem particularly wise, the
hell-raising good time boy who aged into a crank. If Clinton was the last
candidate of the 20th century and Obama the first of the 21st century, Mc-
Cain is a remnant of America in the Cold War. His hero is indeed Teddy
Roosevelt; he is older than Mount Rushmore; he has never used a computer;
some of his associates are already calling Obama a "Marxist."

Michelle Obama, in an unguarded moment early in the campaign, said,
"For the first time in my adult life, I am really proud of my country." It was
an intemperate remark for a candidate's wife, and one that will come back to
haunt the general election, but there are many of us who knew exactly what
she meant. I have yet to meet anyone under forty who is not an Obamama-
niac. They are filling stadiums to hear him, and turning out in huge numbers to campaign and to vote with an enthusiasm for electoral politics that
has not been seen in forty years. Hearing Obama's frequently repeated, New
Age-ish line, "We are the people we've been waiting for," it's hard not to
think that they are the people we've been waiting for.

[June 11, 2008]

A JOURNEY ON THE YANGTZE RIVER

June 27, 1177:
Joining River Pavilion.
Fragrant and Flowery Tower.
Patrol and Investigation Barracks for Managing the Border.

(Each year, the Patrol and Investigation Inspectorate sends a written report when the plum trees are about to blossom.)

June 28:
Attendant Esquire Causeway.

(The road was lined with people who had never seen a Regulation Marshal before.)

June 29:
Exalted Virtue Temple, overlooking the Assembled River.

(Each year, 50,000 sheep are sacrificed at a festival honoring Grand Protector Li. I wrote a poem against this practice and ordered it engraved in stone.)

June 30:
Jade Citadel Gate.
Floating Clouds Pavilion.
Cherishing Antiquity Pavilion.
Rope Bridge.

Nine-Chambered Grotto Heaven of the Precious Immortals Gate.
Realized Lord Hall.
Jade Splendor Tower.

July 1 (my birthday):
Exalted Virtue Temple.

(As the abbots performed the Pacing the Void ceremony, a strange red light appeared and then appeared again.)

(Elderly men and women from Old Folks Village came to see me.)

July 2:
Supreme Clarity Palace.
Snow Mountains.

(At night, thousands of strange lights appeared.)

July 3:
Long-Life Abbey.

July 4:
Sage Buddha Cloister.

> Su Tung-p'o wrote:
> "The clear wind—what is it?"

July 5:
Serene Spring Hall.

(I ordered the name changed to Ministerial Accomplishments Hall.)

July 6:
Skillful-in-Expressing-Praise Hall.

July 7:
(Detained by well-wishers.)

Su Tung-p'o wrote:
"Only in wine is man himself,
his mind a cave empty of doubt.
He can fall from a carriage and never get hurt—
Chuang Tzu told us no lies."

Chuang Tzu said:
"When a drunken man falls from a carriage, though the carriage may be going very fast, he won't be killed, because his spirit is whole. He didn't know he was riding, and he doesn't know he has fallen out."

(I can't remember who helped me get into bed.)

July 8:
(Heavy rain. I could not climb Cultivating Enlightenment Hill to visit Absolute Splendor Pavilion.)

Transparent Glass River.
Scenic Expanse Tower.

July 9:
Revitalizing Prose Hall.

(People here are fond of argument.)

July 10:
(Farewell banquet.)

The crabs are delicious, but I could only eat a few, thinking of the mother of Instructor Sha, the doctor in Hu Prefecture. She was too fond of crabs, and ate dozens of them every day. She died in the seventeenth year of the Period of Continued Ascendancy. The family gathered for a ceremony at the Heavenly Felicitation Temple. At the gate, her ten-year-old granddaughter saw the old lady, bleeding all over. She said, "I have been convicted of eating crabs." At her death she was taken to a tremendous mountain of crabs, which she was forced to climb, and keep climbing, as the crabs nipped and pinched her all over.

July 11:
Central Precipice.
Calling Fish Tarn.
Compassionate Dame Precipice.
Compassionate Dame Precipice Monastery.
Precious Jug Peak.

(Leaned on the railing and talked with friends long into the night.)

> Su Tung-p'o wrote:
> "Funny—I never could keep my mouth shut;
> it gets worse the older I grow."

July 12:
(I could not bear to leave Compassionate Dame Precipice Monastery.)

> Su Tung-p'o wrote:
> "How long before you've lost it—a scene like this?"

July 13:
Snow Hall.
Query-the-Moon Hall.

(I could not sleep, so I picked up my brush.)

> I wrote:
> Ten thousand cicadas start humming at sunset,
> frogs and toads croak all night.
> If only I had been born deaf,
> a sweet dream would have come to my wicker cot.

July 14:
Traversing-the-Clouds Hill.
Traversing-the-Clouds Monastery.
Heavenly Peace Gallery.

For some reason I thought about the story of a man named Chang from
Lin-an, which then was under siege. The Buddha appeared to him in a

dream and told him that the next day soldiers would come and kill him. In a previous life, Chang, as a soldier, had killed a man during the Huang Ch'ao Revolt. Now that man was known as Li Li.

The next day a soldier appeared at the gate, waving his sword. "Are you, by chance, Master Li Li?" "How do you know my name?" Chang explained. Li Li threw his sword on the ground. "If I kill you, then in the next life you will kill me again. And then I will kill you again. Today we must break the chain."

July 15:
Myriad Prospects Tower.
Black Prominence Peak.
Garden of Security and Happiness.
Extensive Prosperity Cloister.
Rectangular Chimes Grotto, formerly known as Clink-Clank Waters Grotto.

(Strange sounds were heard.)

July 16–20:
Big E Mountain.
Middle E Mountain.
Little E Mountain.

> Su Tung-p'o wrote:
> "Do you recall that day, steep winding slopes,
> road long, all of us tired, our lame donkeys braying?"

July 21:
(Groups of village women, their heads wrapped in cloth turbans, were watching me.)

> My old friend Lu Yu wrote:
> "Too bad I didn't spend my life
> tending a vegetable patch!"

July 22:
Benevolent Fortune Cloister.
Universal Security Cloister.

White Stream Manor.
Divine Dragon Hall.
Green Bamboo Bridge.
Plum Tree Bank.
Two Dragons Hall.
Central Peak Cloister.
White Cliff Peak.
Shout-and-Response Peak.
Camphor Tree Ridge.
Ox Heart Ridge.
Ox Heart Monastery.
Precious Manifestation Stream.

(A painting could not capture this scene.)

July 23:
White Stream Monastery.
Prosperity and Peace Hall.
Sutras Depository.
Three Thousand Iron Buddhas Hall.

> I wrote:
> I woke at dawn in a cold bed, terrified by a nightmare.
> One more night's sleep in this drifting life.

July 24:
Luminous Light Monastery.
Seven Treasures Cliff.

(Thirty mountain lads had to pull my sedan-chair up with heavy ropes.)

White Stream Monastery.
Brush-the-Heart Mountain.
Thatched Pavilion Point.
Small Stone Thunder.
Greater Deep Gully.
Lesser Deep Gully.
Camel Ridge.

(I bounce on the litter like a fish hooked on a long rod.)

Clustered Bamboo Way-Stop.
Peak Gate.
Illusory Joy and Delight.
Tree Bark Village.

(These mountain folk are born and die here. They cannot imagine what a flat road is.)

Monkey's Ladder.
Thunder Grotto Flat.

(A dragon lives in a deep pool here. If it has not rained, people throw dead pigs and women's shoes into the pool to irritate him, and provoke him to cause a storm.)

Luminous and Bright Cliff.
New Way-Stop.
Eighty-Four Switchbacks.

(The path twists and turns and doesn't seem to go anywhere, just like an inept official.)

Azalea Flat.
Longing-for-the-Buddha Pavilion.

(No birds here.)

Tender Grass Flat.
Foot-Washing Stream.
Luminous Light Monastery.

(I put on all the clothes and furs I had with me, and still was shivering.)

Heavenly Immortal Bridge.

(If you boil rice in the water from this spring it will never cook.)

Thunder Grotto Mountain.

(A great globe of light appeared.)

Strangely, I dreamt of a slave girl I had once seen, many years ago, who had the character "escapee" carved on both cheeks.

July 25:
Thunder Grotto Mountain.

(A dense fog called the Silvery World.)

(A heavy rain to cleanse the cliff before the Great Manifestation.)

(A globe of light called the Body-Absorbing Light. In its center I could see my reflection, but not that of the person standing next to me.)

(High winds scattering clouds. Another globe of light, called the Clear-Sky Manifestation.)

July 26:
White Stream Monastery.
Black Stream Monastery.
Moon Peak.

(I must remember that in the *Analects* it is said that the Master never spoke of extraordinary things.)

July 27:
White Cloud Gorge.
Ox-Heart Monastery.
Sifting Pearls Spring.
Amusing Elixir Rock.
Dragon Gate Gorge.
Dragon Gate Grotto.

(I am no longer in the human world.)

July 28–30:
(Uneventful.)

> Su Tung-p'o wrote:
> "Will I spend all my life on rivers and lakes?"

> My old friend Lu Yu wrote:
> "Success/failure—one turn of the palm."

July 31:
Looking-at-the-Moon Gazebo.
Murmuring Jade Grotto.

(All my life I've been obsessed with searching for that which is hidden.)

August 1:
(The riverbanks have boulders that resemble horses, and the villagers hitch
them with ropes. If they do not, they say, strange things happen.)

August 2:
Great Death Retreat.
Locked River Pavilion.
Horse Lake River.

(I changed the name of the local wine from Double Cyan to Spring Cyan.)

August 3:
(Did not bother to go ashore. The villages look poor and shoddy. The men
wear felt hats and watch the boats go by.)

For some reason I thought about my old friend Lu Yu, when he stopped in
No Tin District, next to Tin Mountain, a few years ago. He wrote:

"Toward the end of the Han Dynsasty there was a written prophecy that
declared: 'While there's tin, war in the world; no tin, the world at rest! While
there's tin, struggle in the world; no tin, the world at peace!' From that time

until now, whenever any tin comes to light the people here immediately
bury it and are afraid to use it."

August 4:
Southern Pacification Tower.
Arriving Breeze Pavilion.

August 5:
(Detained by a banquet.)

(For the guests, I spontaneously composed a poem, following the rhyme
scheme of Judge Ts'u Chi-shao's poem on a river banquet.)

> I wrote:
> South wind eases sorrow; rain provokes a poem.
> Peacetime: even hawks and ravens celebrate.
> I'd need a five-color brush to capture this scene.
> My poem as cool as the clouds and water.

(The singing girls sing "Bamboo Branch" three times in a row, and the
guests forget to go home.)

August 6:
Heaven-Ascendent King Temple.

(Fishermen make offerings of fish. If they have no fish, they offer fish
pickle.)

> Su Tung-p'o wrote:
> "Boatmen and water birds dream the same dream;
> a big fish splashes off like a frightened fox."

August 7:
Fisherman's Grotto.

> There is an old saying:
> "Water is not a chisel and yet it pierces stone."

Mud Mound Village.

August 8:
Repaying Kindness Monastery.

(Vapors from the water here are noxious. The women all have goiters.)

> I wrote:
> You may think these women are ugly,
> but their boyfriends buy them silver hairpins.

August 9:
(Storm. The boat could not be steered.)

August 10:
Flocking Pigs Rapids.

(People on the other boats were screaming.)

Spectacular Virtue Abbey, formerly known as Immortal Metropolis Abbey.
Bathe-in-Cinnabar Pool.

August 11:
The Four Worthies Gallery.
Lychee Tower.

> I wrote:
> A single tree, a hundred years old, stands on the riverbank.
> I'd like to hear his life story, but alas
> he speaks no human language.

August 12:
West Mountain.
Misty Rain Gallery.
Lower Cliff.
Auspicious Light Gallery.

(This scene is very unusual.)

August 13:
Fish Belly.
Recumbent Dragon Mountain.

(When birds see this cliff, they fly the other way.)

(The mountain folk say: "This is no place for humans to travel. What is
Your Honor doing here?" I smile and can't think of anything to say.)

August 14:
(Too dangerous to proceed.)

> My old friend Lu Yu, when he was here, wrote:
> "When I was young I used to dream of the joys of official
>   travel;
> older now, I know just how hard the going can be."

Three Gorges Hall.
Lofty Studio.

(Shaggy yaks who had lost their balance rot on the canyon floor.)

August 15:
(River still rising.)

(Whirlpools.)

(This is the most dangerous place in the world.)

(I entrusted everything to Nature and did not ask any questions.)

August 16:
Divine Woman Temple.
Twelve Peaks.

(In the gorges at noon it is as dark as sunset.)

Meng Chiao wrote:
"Unearthly voices rise from hidden dens."

He wrote:
"There is nothing human in the sound of gorges."

Sun-and-Clouds Terrace.
Approaching Crane Peak.

(Paintings of this scene cannot resemble this scene.)

Congealed Truth Abbey.

(Whirlpools.)

He wrote:
"A boat leaves earth entering earth here."

Li Tao-yuan wrote:
"This landscape has a soul."

August 17:
(Nothing but thatched-roof huts.)

Here the fishermen sing:
"A gibbon howls three times
and your clothes are drenched with tears."

August 18-25:
(Rainstorms, river rising. Could not proceed.)

I wrote:
Miserable at a miserable inn, lying in bed.
Water drips through the ceiling and extinguishes dreams.

I wrote:
Little mosquitoes, you and I have the same problem:
hunger keeps us flying around.

August 26:
White Dog Gorge.
Jade Void Grotto.
New Rapids.
Yellow Ox Gorge.
Yellow Ox Mountain.

(The river has so many twists, the view of the mountain doesn't change.)

> Here the fishermen sing:
> "In the morning, set out from Yellow Ox;
> in the evening, stay at Yellow Ox;
> three days and three nights,
> Yellow Ox will be the same."

Folding Fan Gorge.
Toad Rock.
Flat and Good Embankment.

(Everyone celebrates here.)

August 27:
Ultimate Joy Pavilion.

(Nobody knows how many mountains there are here. They disappear into the haze, and the fat clouds are endless. One can only long to go home.)

[2008]